FRAN
TARKENTON

WITH WES SMITH

WHAT LOSING TAUGHT ME ABOUT WINNING

THE ULTIMATE GUIDE FOR SUCCESS IN SMALL AND HOME-BASED BUSINESSES

A FIRESIDE BOOK
PUBLISHED BY SIMON & SCHUSTER

FIRESIDE
Rockefeller Center
1230 Avenue of the Americas
New York, NY 10020

First Fireside Edition 1999

FIRESIDE and colophon are registered trademarks
of Simon & Schuster Inc.

Designed by Karolina Harris

Manufactured in the United States of America

10 9 8 7 6 5 4 3 2 1

Library of Congress Cataloging-in-Publication Data is available.

ISBN 0-684-83413-8
ISBN 0-684-83879-6 (Pbk)

To my wife, Linda,
who is my best friend and biggest supporter.

CONTENTS

ACKNOWLEDGMENTS

I would like to thank my agent, Jan Miller, who is more tenacious, but much better-looking, than any lineman who has ever protected me.

Thanks also to Dominick Anfuso, my editor at Simon & Schuster, and his assistant, Ana DeBevoise, who kept the clock from running out on this book.

Many thanks to my collaborator on this project, Wes Smith, a guy who knows nearly as much about scrambling as I do.

And, finally, my thanks go out to two of my favorite entrepreneurs: Ruth Brooks and Charlie Poole of the North Georgia Mountains.

WHAT LOSING TAUGHT ME ABOUT WINNING

RUTH BROOKS' TEN RULES FOR SMALL BUSINESS

1. You got to be really honest, 'specially with yourself.
2. You got to work real hard and stay as late as the customers do.
3. You got to kinda learn to read peoples' faces to know if they's good or bad.
4. You cain't be no quitter.
5. Don't let nobody have what you already bought without paying for it.
6. Make some profit on whatever you sell.
7. Separate each one who comes in from some of his money before he gets out the door.
8. You have to be nice to folks if you want them to come back.
9. It ain't what you make, it's what you still got.
10. The main thing is to be happy in whatever you do.

ALL OF MY HEROES ARE ENTREPRENEURS

THE ORIGINS of this book and the sources of many of my greatest childhood memories lie in the foothills of the Appalachian Mountains in North Georgia, a beautiful and unique part of the world where I spent many boyhood summers at camp.

Aside from its mountains, lakes, rivers and forests, North Georgia has many great characters—one of them is Ruth Brooks, who just may be the most savvy small-business entrepreneur I have ever known. Ruth and her entrepreneurial spirit inspired me to do this book.

Though she has never been within 50 miles of a business school, Ruth's entrepreneurial instincts and her common sense approach to business and life have resulted in considerable success for this self-educated country woman. Along with her Brooks's Lil' General Store And Cafe, she and her husband Bobby also own a 315-acre farm and chicken ranch, a mobile-home park, rental properties, and real estate up and down the hills and hollers behind her store.

I love going down to Ruth's place to talk about business because she cuts through the jargon and fads and gets straight to the heart of it. Running a small business is hard work, but it is not all that complicated, though sometimes we try to make it seem that way. When I find myself doing that I come and crawl up on the counter next to Ruth's cash register and I talk to her while she rings up the sales. She sets me straight.

"When we first bought this place, I talked to this ol' feller from Monroe, Georgia, who had a place for years and years, and he told me the key to stayin' in business is to always make sure that you separate a feller from some of his money before he gets out the door, no matter what it takes," Ruth told me recently. "I always keep that in my head and even if someone comes in here and is ugly to me, I'm nice to them and I take their money and when they leave, I wave goodbye because you have to be nice to folks or they won't come back."

Simple? Without a doubt. Why is it then, that so many businesses, even major corporations, forget? How many businesses have faltered or even failed because they got away from serving the customer or client and instead became focused on serving only their own interests?

Whenever I leave Ruth's store after talking business with her, I find myself charged up to get back to what I most enjoy doing—starting and running businesses the way they should be run, with the focus on bringing value to my customers and clients.

In this book, I have set out to do for you what Ruth always does for me. My goal is to bring value to you as a small-business entrepreneur by cutting through the jargon and fads, setting you straight and charging you up to get out there and do business the way it *has* to be done, with enthusiasm and energy. In these pages, I offer you advice and encouragement on small-business entrepreneurship and all that it encompasses including:

- Looking at what it takes to be a successful entrepreneur in today's dynamic small business market
- Learning to spot and move on business opportunities
- Identifying the business best suited to your interests and talents
- Starting a business and dealing with all of the challenges that will confront you
- Finding sources of financing best suited to your business and to your own financial health
- Marketing your business by pouring ingenuity and thoughtfulness into it rather than money
- Building your employee team and developing a healthy and responsive culture within your business
- Training yourself to read the signs for potential problems that may arise in your business
- Learning to view setbacks and difficult times in business as opportunities to increase your understanding and knowledge rather than being defeated by them
- Sustaining your small business over the long term by focusing on bringing value to your customers and clients

THE SCRAMBLING ENTREPRENEUR
· · · · · · · · · · · · · · · · · ·

Where do I get off as an authority on small-business entrepreneurship? To paraphrase an old television commercial, "I'm Fran Tarkenton and I am no longer a football player, although I used to play one on TV." You probably are aware that I was a professional quarterback for the Minnesota Vikings and the New York Giants, but you may not know that I have been a business entrepreneur for much longer than I ever played football. A great deal of the advice and examples in this book will come out of my own experiences over more than 30 years of starting and running diverse enterprises ranging from health insurance and employee-benefits companies, to management consulting, fast-food restaurants, software sales, infomercial-making, and other businesses. In these pages, you will find scores of examples and tips from other small-business entrepreneurs across the country—many of them friends of mine.

I may be best known as a former professional athlete, but I have been an entrepreneur nearly all of my life. In my early childhood, my father was a preacher in a poor neighborhood of Washington, D.C., and later, in Athens, Georgia. I worked as a child to help my family survive, and I have never stopped working. In fact, even when I was the starting quarterback for the University of Georgia Bulldogs in my hometown of Athens, I paid my living expenses by selling policies for the Franklin Life Insurance Company. You won't find it in any of the NCAA record books, but as I led the Georgia Bulldogs to a 10-and-1 season and victory in the Orange Bowl, I was also leading all other Franklin Life salesmen across the state of Georgia in the sale of policies.

Yes, I have thrown a lot of football passes in my life. But I have also made hundreds of business presentations. I played in three Super Bowls but, as I noted earlier, I also launched nine of my own businesses.

As I write this, I am sitting in my office 11 stories above Atlanta's Buckhead retail, commercial, and residential neighborhood. I am wearing blue jeans, an old Polo shirt, and no shoes. This is my standard work outfit and my normal working posture when I am not talking on the speaker phone while wandering around my office swinging a baseball bat, tossing a football in the air, or enjoying a Coca-Cola. (After all, I am on the board of directors of Coca-Cola Enterprises.)

If you see me in a suit and tie, I am either on my way to a funeral, a wedding, or a business meeting. I don't dress up if I don't have to. And most of the time, I *don't* have to because I work for myself. As the owner of my own business, nobody tells me what to do—other than my wife, my kids, my grandkids, and sometimes my administrative assistant, Jill, of course.

I imagine that you are pretty much the same way. You may not have your own business yet, but you would like to. You may not even know for sure what kind of business you want to have, but you like the idea of being your own boss, setting your own hours, vacationing when the urge strikes you, and reaping the full rewards of your own hard work.

Welcome to the club—it is growing bigger and bigger every day. One third of all households have been or are involved in small business, according to the *Wall Street Journal.* There is a huge new wave of small business entrepreneurship sweeping the country and the world right now, and I have written this book to help you join that movement and provide you with information that will help you to thrive.

I don't know if I understand the small-business entrepreneur any better than anyone else, but I do know that I have spent many fruitful hours with all sorts of them over the years, sitting in their offices and shops, talking about the issues and challenges they face day in and day out. I do it in airports at shoe-shine stands. I do it in towns all over the country when I am speaking to business groups.

If I am asked to give a speech or take part in a seminar, I don't do my bit and go home, I make it a point to hang around if I can, to sit in hotel lobbies or restaurants and talk with people about their businesses. I believe that the best way to learn about entrepreneurship is to talk to those who have walked the walk.

LEARNING FROM THOSE WHO HAVE DONE IT

Most successful entrepreneurs I know love to talk and share information with other entrepreneurs. Nearly all of them are information junkies. They gather and share information rabidly because they realize it is a wellspring of fresh ideas and opportunities. I don't think there is a better source of information about small business than small-business owners.

I majored in business in college, and I can honestly tell you that I don't think my college education has a thing to do with my business success. (I won't blame it for my failures either.) College business classes are too often taught by people who have never had to meet a payroll or fight the competition for customers. The subject matter in classes is largely theoretical and philosophical rather than practical, which may be why a high percentage of business-school graduates from Harvard and Wharton go into consulting or corporate jobs rather than starting their own businesses.

Business schools can give you a foundation of knowledge, and although more and more schools have courses or programs in entrepreneurship, even those programs tend to put grad students in charge. The problem with the highly structured colleges and universities is that entrepreneurship cuts across disciplines, which makes it difficult to fit it into the tenure track that is entrenched in conservative higher education.

No one should pass up the opportunity for an education, but if you ask most entrepreneurs how much of their success is a direct result of their formal schooling, I'd wager most would give it minimal credit. Entrepreneurs need practical advice from people who have gotten their hands dirty in the stockroom and faced a bank loan officer across the table.

I've always believe in going to the best source for information. When I started playing professional football, I was 20 years old. Although most quarterbacks watch game films to study opposing defenses, I also went to school on all the other quarterbacks in the league. After our regular team meetings were over, I would go to the film library and pull out tapes of opposing offenses, so I could see how other, more experienced quarterbacks were dealing with the challenges I was going to face. It worked for me in football, and it has worked for me in business, to study those who have played the same game.

That is what I want to share with you in this book: real life experiences related by successful small-business entrepreneurs. They can't survive by hiding in a bureaucracy or letting subordinates do all of the work. They are on the battle line every day. They learn quickly what works and they stick with it, or they simply don't last. If Ruth Brooks doesn't stock fresh bread on her store shelves or cold soda pop in the coolers, the customers will go down the road in a heartbeat.

Small businesses cannot afford to make the same mistakes that many larger and more established businesses get away with, and in this book, I want to help you learn to avoid mistakes and develop your entrepreneurial instincts.

SIMPLE TRUTHS, DIFFICULT LESSONS

IBM could have used Ruth Brooks a few years ago when it became so arrogant that it lost sight of its own market and was very nearly destroyed. IBM grew complacent because it controlled the computer market from top to bottom. When you had one of their mainframes, you had to buy their software because they refused to integrate with other computer companies. They controlled 60 percent of the computing market and had 75 percent of the profits in the industry. They were dictating to their customers what they could and could not buy.

In its greed and arrogance, IBM focused on serving its own needs first, and put its customers' needs way down the list. They tried to shut out the competition, but their neglect of customer service left a wide hole for the competition to step into. It was not long before young entrepreneurs capitalized on that attitude. Steve Jobs at Apple Computers and Bill Gates at Microsoft undermined the giant mainframe computer maker by creating personal computers and software that better served consumers' needs. Jobs himself later fell victim to the same problem when he decided that Apple could dictate what people should want, rather than responding to their needs, and his business took a plunge. Some say Gates could eventually fall prey to the same problem, but I doubt it. He seems more willing to form alliances in order to expand his product base.

Gates seems to be able to stay rooted in the basic truth of business, which is at the heart of Ruth Brooks's entrepreneurial success too: You have to remain focused on serving your customers. That simple philosophy seems to be lost by many entrepreneurs as their businesses grow, and that is why I will stress it in this book. That is the lesson, also, that I always am reminded of when I visit Ruth's place, which is business at its most basic level.

I met Ruth about 10 years ago when I walked into her general store in Habersham County on the edge of Lake Burton, where I have a family vacation home. I had stopped to get gasoline and after I pumped it, I went inside the simple little country store and began looking around for a few groceries. Ruth, a slow-talking woman with a wealth of common sense and a great deal of grit, was behind the counter eyeballing me suspiciously as I browsed the two aisles of food in her little store.

Finally, she said, "Ya'll have to pay for your gas first," and pointed to a sign with the same message.

You see, Ruth had been burned a few times by shifty tourists and travelers who would put gas in their cars, come in and buy a few food items or drinks, and then pay only for the groceries and not the fuel. So she had a policy. Pay for the gas, then shop for groceries.

I quickly discovered that Ruth had a lot of policies, and a lot of signs announcing them. *We don't take no checks. We don't take no credit cards. No pets.* "Every time somebody finds a new way to aggravate me, I write a sign, so I have a lot of signs," Ruth explained.

She grew up in the North Georgia mountains. Her dad was a dirt farmer and the local "cow doctor," a sort of folk veterinarian. Neither of Ruth's parents made it past the fifth grade. She got no further than high school herself, "but my Daddy and Mommy were really smart about telling us stuff."

Today, if you walked into Ruth's store, and judged her solely on her speech pattern, you might make the mistake of assuming that she is not a particularly astute business person. You would be most sorely wrong. "This is what is funny. 'Cause I don't talk proper and stuff, people thinks I am dumb, and sometimes they try to take advantage of me," she said.

Ruth is amused by this because, as you have probably figured out by now, Ruth is dumb as a fox. She is also probably one of the wealthiest women in North Georgia. Ruth Brooks may be country, but she is not simple. She is a very successful and resourceful small-business entrepreneur. She is smart, quick-witted, and tenacious. Just ask the escaped convicts who came into her store one day and thought they might take advantage of this slow-talking country gal behind the counter. Just recently, she caught a fuel-delivery man shorting her on her gasoline. "I told them they'd better fire him before I killed him," she said. "And they did too."

But that Ruth Brooks detective story pales compared to The Case of the Fugitive Shoppers. "These fellas broke jail in Florida and they come up here getting away and stopped to get 22 gallons of gas and while they were pumping out there, the mountain patrol called and asked if I had seen such-and-such a van because it was stolen by these escaped fellas. I said it was parked at my store right now getting filled with gas. The mountain patrol told me 'Detain them' and I said 'How?' and they said 'Ruth, we are sure you can think of somethin'.'"

"Well, these fellas had picked up an ol' girl in south Georgia somewhere, and her and one of them came in and packed up half the store and when they got it all, they said they was goin' to give me a check. I told them I wouldn't take no check because I had me a good job and they was hard to find and I can't take a check because I would get fired by my boss. They didn't know I was the owner and I didn't tell them because if they ever knowed I owned this store they probably would have shot me," she said.

Ruth stalled them for a while by pretending that she was having difficulty adding up all the items they had put in their grocery cart. Then she told the bad guys that she had to call her boss to see if she could take their check. As they watched, she dialed the sheriff's office and as they listened, she pretended to be talking to her boss but was really letting the lawmen know that the escaped cons were still at her store.

Finally, the police arrived and arrested the cons without any difficulty, although they later found a shotgun under the hood of the van. Ruth kept her groceries and when the sheriff asked if she wanted to press theft charges for the gasoline that they had not paid for, Ruth said no, she would just help herself to some of the goods in their van. "So I took me a Skil saw," she said proudly.

THE ENTREPRENEURIAL WAVE
• • • • • • • • • • • • • • •

Now do you understand why Ruth Brooks is one of my heroes? To me, Ruth represents the millions of small-business entrepreneurs out there fighting the good fight every day. Living by their wits and their hard work, they keep this country's economic heart beating. Today more than ever, the small-business entrepreneur is a driving force in our economy and a major stabilizing influence in our society overall. Keep in mind, every big business in this country was started by an entrepreneur who had little more than an idea and did extraordinary things with it.

In this decade alone, business owners with less than 20 employees have created 6.3 million jobs, even as the celebrated giants like IBM and AT&T have cut nearly 4 million. It is estimated that the number of small businesses in this country is now between 22 million and 25 million, and that could easily increase to nearly 35 million over the next 10 years as more and more Americans move out of the corporate environment and into their own businesses, allowing them to earn a living while doing what they really enjoy.

Although they are notoriously hard to track down, there are undoubtedly more entrepreneurs starting businesses today than ever before in our nation's history. Just how many are out there in their garages, basements, or cubicles is really anybody's guess. The U.S. Department of Labor has estimated that only about 770,000 are formed annually, although that does not include the roughly 140,000 new ventures started by existing companies each year, which would make nearly 900,000 startups.

What they don't track is the whole new phenomenon of the home-office entrepreneur; the millions of people starting businesses out of their homes as a secondary job or a daytime job. Dun & Bradstreet reports that the home-based business is one of the fastest-growing trends of the 1990s. D&B estimates that there are already 14 million home-based businesses that are full-time and another 13.1 million that are part-time. A new home-based business is launched every 11 seconds—that is 8,000 each day— and 95 percent of those are successful in the first year, according to D&B's study. Twenty percent of the home-based entrepreneurs in this country reported gross revenues between $100,000 and $500,000 last year. Interestingly, women are starting small businesses and home-based businesses at *twice* the rate that men are. If those figures don't convince you that small-business entrepreneurship is the hottest thing going, here is testimony from Steve Alesio, president of American Express Small Business Services: "Small business is the third-largest economy in the world, after the U.S. and Japan," he told *Business Week*. The number of companies with fewer than 100 employees has increased nearly 50 percent since the early 1980s. Most of the 20 million new jobs created during the past 15 years came not from the major corporations and manufacturers but from small businesses created by independent entrepreneurs, according to the Small Business Administration. Those enterprises now account for about half the nation's employment and more than a third of gross domestic product.

After steady growth from the 1950s through the 1970s, the nation's 500 biggest manufacturers began cutting their payrolls. From 16.2 million on the payroll in 1979, they cut employees to 11.5 million in 1993. The 500 biggest service companies did increase their employees in that period, but only slightly.

Small business, then, is the most dynamic sector of the American economy. Seventy-five percent of all job growth comes out of entrepreneurial small business and most of the job creation in the last decade has been by companies with fewer than five employees, according to the Small Business Administration. Jere Glover of the SBA feels that an environment that allows entrepreneurs to start businesses, and sometimes even fail, keeps the U.S. economy vibrant.

"In Europe, there is a stigma to trying and failing in business. . . . Many successful U.S. small business owners have failed at least once. In America, you can bounce back, start another business and be very successful," Glover said in an interview.

The tremendous growth in small-business entrepreneurship has not gone unnoticed by colleges and universities, which if nothing else are always tuned to market opportunities. In recent years courses in entrepreneurship have been established on campuses across the country, rising from a mere handful 15 years ago to more than 500 formal academic programs. You know small-business entrepreneurship is a hot field when conservative business schools, which traditionally have focused only on corporate training and big business management, begin to offer it as a course of study.

OFF-CAMPUS ENTREPRENEURS

Maybe the academics are finally getting the message. After all, some of the leading entrepreneurs today are people who grew impatient with school and either started businesses while still enrolled or left campus altogether to get their hands dirty in the real world of entrepreneurship. Here are examples:

- Jerry Yang, 27, and David Filo, 30, originally developed their computerized list of favorite Internet destinations just for their own use, but after they shared their list with friends and fellow students at Stanford, it became a hot commodity on campus. The two graduate students found a venture capitalist who sensed there was commercial value in an online service that was already luring a million visitors weekly. Yang and Filo dropped out of school, turned down takeover bids from America Online and Netscape Communications, and have not looked back since.

  Their Yahoo! Internet directory is now a publicly held company and their shares are valued at more than $130 million.
- Bill Gates was the sort of guy who read *Popular Electronics* for the articles, not just the pictures, even while attending Harvard University. A story by the magazine for techno-wizards inspired Gates and his boyhood friend Paul Allen to drop out of school so they could work together to build a programming language for computer hobbyists. They moved to Albuquerque and opened a small business developing computer soft-

ware. Their first product, called "Traf-o-Data," went over like a lead diskette, but subsequent efforts, such as MS-DOS, Microsoft Word, and Windows have done fairly well. These two small business entrepreneurs now employ about 20,000 people worldwide and in recent years the net revenue for their business has approached $6 billion.

• Paul Orfalea leveraged a $5,000 bank loan to open his first small business in a former hamburger joint in Isla Vista, California, while he was still a student at USC. The little print shop was so tiny that when a customer wanted to make copies on his copy machine, Orfalea had to push the machine out onto the sidewalk. He named the business after his own nickname, which sprang from his abundant mop of curly hair —Kinko's.

Paul is a good friend of mine and I consider him an entrepreneur's entrepreneur. Last summer I visited him and talked about getting Kinko's involved in the Fran Tarkenton Small Business NETwork (FTSBN) because he believes in bringing value to his customers. He and I started with dinner and were up well beyond midnight in a Santa Barbara restaurant just talking about business. Then, at 5 A.M., he was knocking on my door to take me to one of his stores because he wanted me to see what Kinko's is doing with the Internet.

Even though he has made millions, Paul still has his entrepreneurial motor running at full speed. He still gets excited about bringing greater value to his customers. He is not sitting on the beach somewhere counting his money; he is still in the game because he enjoys it. The same holds true of all of the great entrepreneurs I know. For them and for me, it is more fun than playing golf or sitting on the beach. Doing business is what entrepreneurs love to do.

BIG BUSINESS GOES SMALL

I enjoy stories about small-business entrepreneurs who became big business legends, but the big guys don't need my help and, besides, small business is the hottest thing going—so hot that companies like American Express and other corporate giants are falling all over themselves trying to tap into this dynamic market.

Just recently, Randy Rosler, the owner of a tiny greeting-card company in New York City, was wined and dined, flown to Boston, and treated to a Red Sox game by the top executives of AT&T eager to learn more about the needs of his business and others like it. AT&T created small regional councils of small-business owners like Rosler to help it develop products and services for them.

"A few years ago, you never saw anything targeted to small business. Now, it's like everybody woke up all at once and said, 'Hey. There's a big market here. Let's go get it,' " said Roger Jask, a vice president of the U.S. Chamber of Commerce in a *Business Week* report.

American Express has issued special small-business credit cards to serve this market. Pitney Bowes, Inc., has developed smaller, cheaper postage meters. Ernst & Young is offering online consulting services for them. IBM executives report that their fastest growing market is companies with fewer than 50 employees, with sales increasing at 14 percent a year.

THE NEW BREED

Today's small-business entrepreneurs are often generation x-ers who may have invented a better ski board, designed a cutting-edge software program, or taken street fashions to the retail market. They are fresh college graduates who, upon finding a poor job market among existing businesses, decide to start their own. They are downsized corporate employees who have decided to try and make it on their own doing something they have always wanted to do. They are women and minorities who have hit the glass ceiling elsewhere or simply decided to strike out on their own. They are retired business executives who decided that starting a business was more fun than going fishing. They are merchants and gas-station owners, franchise holders, and men and women who have tapped a market for old car parts, decorative baskets, or beauty-care products. They are solo operators working out of their homes and multilevel marketers selling Amway and Mary Kay during their lunch hours and on weekends. They do it to make money, to provide a service, and for the experiences it brings.

In a sense, the new breed of American entrepreneur is a throwback to the old breed of individualistic, enterprising businessmen and women. Like the merchants and factory owners of the past, today's entrepreneurs don't want anything handed to them. They only want the opportunity to chase their dreams. They are people like Ruth Brooks, regular folks, shrewd business people and hardworking entrepreneurs making a living, struggling occasionally, but at least doing what they enjoy.

LEVERAGING SMALL BUSINESS CLOUT

The one thing that this country's small-business entrepreneurs do not have is a unified voice. Too often, small-business entrepreneurs have been left to struggle on their own while banks and politicians and other potential allies focus on big business development.

"Unfortunately, for many people (in government), small business is their second priority," Glover conceded. "A lot of Democrats support small business—unless it's in conflict with labor. A lot of Republicans support small business—unless it's in conflict with big business. As a result, we're nobody's first priority."

Well, they are *my* priority. That is why I recently launched the Fran Tarkenton Small Business NETwork and introduced the WebTitan CD-ROM for small-business entrepreneurs. With these two new businesses, we are providing small-business entrepreneurs across the country and around the world with access to capital, information, partnerships, and buying power. We are also providing incredible value for them and their businesses through our more than 25 affinity partners, ranging from Federal Express to Sir Speedy, Frontier Airlines, and Dun & Bradstreet. The Small

Business NETwork will provide entrepreneurs everything from access to the highest-return money-market funds available, to the best long-distance phone rates in the business to high-quality, low-cost health and life insurance.

My latest entrepreneurial endeavor was, in part, also inspired by Ruth Brooks and her difficulty as a small-business owner in getting the same benefits that larger businesses offer their employees and owners.

Although she is as tough as any linebacker I ever faced, Ruth had a nagging medical problem and needed to see a doctor. The problem was that as a small-business owner the only medical insurance she could afford was an HMO that she had purchased from a salesman. It cost her $400 a month and she had to drive 60 miles to Gainesville, for the nearest doctor in the group. You don't drive 75 miles per hour on the mountain roads of North Georgia, so the driving time alone from Gainesville and back shot an entire work day for Ruth. If you are a small-business owner, you know how costly that can be, even before you add in the medical bills.

When Ruth told me about the high price in both money and time she had to pay for medical benefits as a small-business owner in an isolated location, my entrepreneurial curiosity was triggered. How many more small-business owners and entrepreneurs have the same problem? What other common problems and needs do they share? How could these be addressed by leveraging their collective economic clout?

Those questions sent me on a mission to become this country's leading advocate for the millions of entrepreneurs and small-business owners out there. Individually, they may not be in a position to negotiate good rates and good service for health care, life insurance, long-distance phone service, office products, travel services, and other necessities and perks enjoyed by those who operate and work in large corporate businesses. But if they could be brought together in a way that would enable small-business owners to leverage their collective economic power and marketing potential, then perhaps Ruth Brooks and those like her would be spared some of the extraordinarily high costs they sometimes must pay for products and services.

From that thought inspired by Ruth's plight, I began the journey that led to the launch of the Fran Tarkenton Small Business NETwork, which in its first year will sign up more than one million members.

I created the Small Business NETwork to give small-business entrepreneurs across the country a unified voice as well as economic opportunities and value. In the past, small-business entrepreneurs have not had the political clout wielded by large corporations. The network will utilize the latest technology, including the Internet, and the collective strength of millions and millions of small-business entrepreneurs across the country to level the playing field.

My goal is to sign up millions of small-business entrepreneurs nationwide and then help them make more money and expand their businesses by providing them with information and resources that were not readily available to them in the past because they were scattered and isolated from each other. By bringing them together in the network, we can bring them the best deals in accounting and legal services, health and life insurance, not to mention rental cars, hotel rooms, airline tickets, office furniture and equipment, and software packages.

The idea is to give the small-business entrepreneur—the general-practice physician, the decorative-basket dealer, the rental-equipment shop owner, the party planner, and the home day-care provider—all the buying power of General Motors and IBM. It is an idea whose time has come, given the incredible surge in small-business entrepreneurship in this country.

Through the affinity partners, the Small Business NETwork will provide a full complement of services and products unavailable from a single source anywhere else. The network will provide hands-on, helpful information to assist small-business owners in building their businesses and thriving. I am going to market it through a sponsor-driven business TV program, through multilevel marketing organizations, mass seminars, retail outlets, business journals, direct mail, and public relations. The network's television program will air on a weekly scheduled basis and contain advertising for sponsors. Each episode will be seen several times per week on major cable networks in the U.S. and Canada and on direct TV options. I designed the Small Business NETwork to be so rich with benefits that small-business owners will find it to be an invaluable resource.

I am telling you about the Small Business NETwork because my experience in putting it together over the last three years has provided examples and anecdotes for the book, but don't worry, I won't be trying to sell it to you here. The network is the latest and probably greatest project to spring out of what has become a mission for me, to help small-business entrepreneurs by providing them with useful information and services. I've had a great deal of success and the usual accompaniment of failures and mistakes in my own business career (okay, and in my football career, too), and now my challenge is to help others benefit from those experiences.

LIVING THE DREAM
. . . .

As a kid, my idea of fun was putting myself up against some obstacle and trying to overcome it, or setting a goal and going after it. Whether it was trying to get past my big brother, or trying to hit a baseball out of the yard, I was always testing myself. That's human nature, I think. By testing and pushing ourselves, we grow. Unfortunately, as adults, we too often lose some of that competitive edge; we are content to dream rather than to act on our dreams. Too many would-be entrepreneurs lack the self-motivation to break out and jump into the marketplace. I fear that is why you find so many people at so-called "success seminars" these days. Now, I have participated in some of these and I have observed others, and while there is certainly some value in listening to these speakers—and no serious harm that I can detect —the truth is that far too many of these seminars are conducted by people who have never actually walked the walk by starting, owning, and operating an actual business. Many of them are, in fact, seminar professionals who tell you that all you have to do to succeed is listen to them, even though their only business is talking to you. There is also a whole class of seminar entrepreneurs who spend so much time going to these sideshows that they never actually accomplish anything either. Take my word for it, folks, you will never become a successful businessperson if all you do is go to seminars. Don't dream it, do it.

Maybe it springs from my background as the son of a preacher, but I am positively evangelical about business entrepreneurship. My old high-school buddy "Snooks" Saye from Madison, Georgia, is one of my greatest converts. Not that Snook wasn't doing all right before I began preaching entrepreneurship to him. Snook, who was a pretty fair high-school and college football player, even if he did go to Georgia Tech instead of the University of Georgia, was a successful obstetrician and gynecologist in Atlanta with enough patients to keep him busy around the clock.

A few years back, he and I were talking about his practice and how well it was going, and I gave him my sermon on entrepreneurship just to stir him up a bit. Well, he got religion in a big way. Snooks decided that there were mountains he still wanted to climb. He had been fascinated with the use of miniature cameras or laparoscopy in abdominal surgery as a way to perform less invasive operations, lessening the risk of complications and speeding recovery time for the patients. I encouraged him to pursue that interest and he did it with a passion. He traveled around the country to learn from experts and pioneers in laparoscopic or *keyhole* surgery. The tiny cameras are mounted on a long handle and inserted through a small incision in the abdomen. The surgical instruments such as lasers and electrosurgical units are inserted through other small incisions. The cameras project the image of the internal anatomy on a screen in the operating room that magnifies the image to 15 times its true size. The surgeon watches that magnified image as he operates. Hysterectomies, appendectomies, hernia repairs, and other operations can be performed in this manner with minimal trauma to the body, allowing less scarring, less risk of infection, and quicker recovery times.

Snooks founded the Advanced Laparoscopy Training Center in Marietta, Georgia, in June of 1990. Already more than 14,000 physicians from around the world have gone through his program and learned to do everything from appendix removal to heart bypass surgery with lasers. "The only thing that limits laparoscopy is the imagination and judgment of the surgeon," says my friend, whose own success proves that the same holds true for entrepreneurs.

I want to inspire and motivate you just as I did Dr. Snooks. I want you to be charged up about getting out and living the life of an entrepreneur. Stop thinking and hoping and wishing and get out there and get *started*. I am certainly not going to tell you it will be easy. I've tried to start dozens of businesses that have never gotten out of the block. I've started others, built them up, and been knocked down. But I have always dusted myself off and gotten back up to try again. I have learned the hard way. My hope is that this book will spare you some of the mistakes I made.

I have taken my lumps in business, just as I did in my athletic career. I led the Minnesota Vikings to three Super Bowls, but we lost them all. During my entire football career, the standard report on me was "small but slow." I wasn't big enough or fast enough, and had a mediocre throwing arm, according to the experts. You can read their authoritative scouting reports in my file at the NFL Hall of Fame. I am in the Hall of Fame because I overcame my physical limitations and became a pretty fair player through determination, hard work, and a hard-earned understanding of how to play the game. I think my instincts for business are even sharper than they were for football.

I have experienced victory and loss in both arenas, and certainly there were times when I felt lost, but I have never allowed a loss on the playing field or in business to defeat me personally. Whether in sports or business, I've always tried to learn from my failures and then move ahead to the next challenge. I hope to convey some of that spirit to you.

Entrepreneurship can be every bit as bruising and challenging as football, but I love everything about having my own businesses. To me, entrepreneurship is a way of life. When you grow up having to earn your own way, and you see how you can change the direction and quality of your life through your own enterprise, you learn to appreciate business as a vital aspect of our economy and this country.

Most small-business owners that I know are in business to improve their own lives, of course, but even more, I've found that they are in it because of the satisfaction and fulfillment it gives them to generate a product or service from nothing and to build a business that contributes to the overall benefit of the world around them. I think their entrepreneurial energy is what drives this country and preserves its greatness in the world.

Big business has gone sour in many ways because of rabid downsizing, runaway executive greed, and merger mania, but I think small-business entrepreneurs are the heart and soul of this country. They build wealth and a sense of community. They build essential products. They provide vital services. They create jobs. Their spirit energizes the economy of the United States and the world. I am proud to be one of those who builds and contributes, and I am delighted to be in a position to help and encourage others to do it at this time of unprecedented opportunity.

ENJOYING ENTREPRENEURSHIP
· · · · · · · · · · · · · · · ·

If you get nothing else out of this book, I want you to learn how to *think* like an entrepreneur, always on full alert for signs of opportunity and for methods to achieve your goals. As an opportunity seeker, the entrepreneur has to be hypersensitive to the business and economic climate, emerging technologies, trends, and unnoticed or untapped sources. I want to help you develop your entrepreneurial senses in this book, but even more than that, I want you to learn to enjoy doing business as much as I do.

Please understand, reading this book will not make you instantly wealthy. There are no get rich quick schemes here. I am not going to give you seven habits, six maids a-milking, or anything else guaranteed to make you a huge success in business.

What I do have is a great understanding of not only how much hard work and preparation it takes to make it in business, but also how much self-motivation and creativity is required. I can help you sharpen your vision, your instincts, and your enjoyment of small-business entrepreneurship.

It's Not the Money

· · · · · · · · · · · ·

Money is a good way of keeping score in business, and it is certainly one of the primary motivations for going into business, but I don't think it is the real reason most people decide to do it. If money was the only motivation for being in business, we would all be concentrated in the highest-profit, lowest-risk enterprises, but, instead, people find themselves opening restaurants, leading group tours, running small airlines, operating health clubs, doing landscaping or organic farming.

Why do people go into businesses that involve substantial risk and sometimes meager profits? Because they want to enjoy what they do to make a living. Most of us yearn to do that. We want to have control of our own destinies while doing what we like to do. That is why we naturally try to get involved in businesses that are a blend of work and pleasure.

I have learned a lot from both my mistakes and my successes in business, and I hope that in sharing them here, you will be spared some of the trials and tribulations, and perhaps have even greater success than I have had. I can't guarantee, however, that you will have more fun than I have had. But you are surely welcome to try.

One day, these two girls come in and watched me work for a while and then asked me "Ruth, how come you never complain or get tired? How come you always are in such a good mood?" I told them, "The sunrise makes me high." When you've got a business, one thing you got to have is lots of energy.

— RUTH BROOKS

THE SKILLS IT TAKES

IN 1991, Gay Balfour was a small-business entrepreneur who had experienced a run of rotten luck. He had done well with his machine-shop business in Cortez, Colorado, but another start-up venture, a marina, had been brought down by delays and cost overruns. When the marina sank before it was even launched, it bankrupted Balfour, taking his machine shop down with it.

Then in his late forties, he found work repairing farm-irrigation systems on the Colorado plains, but, as a natural-born entrepreneur, Balfour was not about to stick his head in the ground and give up—which is not to say that he wasn't going to stick his head in the ground for other reasons.

One night, after much tossing and turning and trying to think of a way to make his comeback, Balfour had a dream. He swears this is true. He says he dreamed of an enormous yellow truck with a green hose sticking out of it. The hose, he says, was sucking prairie dogs out of the ground. (And you thought my football stories sounded farfetched.)

Whether you believe Balfour, it is true that the entrepreneurial brain never rests. Just ask my wife about all of the times I've awakened her with some sure-fire business concept that has come to me in the middle of the night. The entrepreneurial mind is always churning, burning, and, well, even sucking prairie dogs from the ground as we sleep.

The day after his strange, but he swears *true* dream, ol' Gay went to work on an irrigation system at the Ute Mountain Indian reservation near his home and, lo and behold, the farm fields were swarming with prairie-dog varmints digging up the freshly planted corn seed and creating holes that would play havoc with farm equipment. Tribe members had been pouring poison down the holes to try and kill the prairie dogs but they were losing that battle to sheer numbers.

I have a dream, thought Gay.

As a resourceful entrepreneur, he saw the opportunity down the prairie dog hole, and he acted on that dream. First stop was the local sewer district, where he found the sucking truck of his dreams—a truck rigged to clean out sewer lines. It was for sale. He bought it.

He then headed for the hardware store, where he found the hoses of his dreams—four-inch green hoses. He then modified the truck into a lean, mean, prairie-dog sucking machine. Gay Balfour was back in business. His effective, but relatively gentle Dog-Gone prairie-dog removal service is the hit of the high plains. It sucks the critters out of their underground domiciles at a speed of 300 miles per hour, but the furry cannonballs slam into thick foam padding in the back of his truck and usually are ready to scramble when he transports them to new locations far from the farm fields.

Being an entrepreneur, of course, he has also launched a side business selling prairie-dog pups as pets. The Japanese pay him $25 per pup, and sell them back home for $350. He has also sold the prairie dogs to breeders of black-footed ferrets, who love a good prairie dog casserole.

THE ENTREPRENEURIAL SPIRIT
· · · · · · · · · · · · · · · · ·

Gay Balfour is my kind of entrepreneur. He should be yours, too. Today, it seems that there is a self-proclaimed entrepreneur on every street corner, whether it is the guy selling fake gold watches or the CEO of a multi-national corporation who spins corporate divisions into new companies. They may consider themselves entrepreneurs, but I don't.

To me, an entrepreneur is someone like Gay Balfour who starts with little more than an idea or a flash of inspiration and builds a successful and long-term business out of it through hard work, imagination, savvy, commitment, perseverance, alertness, and no little luck.

To fit my description of an entrepreneur, you almost have to have started out as a small-business owner, because there is no other way to start when you have only an idea and a commitment. Very often, the true entrepreneur has been knocked down more than once in previous business endeavors, but it's hard to keep a good entrepreneur down. As you have probably realized by now, the small-business entrepreneur is my favorite sort of person. I generally find them to be quiet heroes, fighting to do something they enjoy, while providing for themselves and their families and creating wealth for their communities.

WHAT IT TAKES
· · · · · · · · ·

What does it take to be an entrepreneur? What sort of person do you have to be to operate your own business? What characteristics are most important? How can you tell if you have what it takes to make it in business?

I've thought about those questions a lot over the years because I've met a great many entrepreneurs and business owners from all walks of life, in every business imaginable. I've given speeches to them and their employees. I've been hired to consult with them on running their businesses. I've had partnerships with them. I've talked with them on airplanes, in hotel lobbies, or at business seminars.

I have done all these things—particularly in the last few years as I've traveled the country and met with other entrepreneurs while developing the Small Business NETwork. Here then is my scouting report on what drives the men and women who, I believe, drive the economy of this country.

1. Whether their businesses are big or small, entrepreneurs thrive on challenges.

I have never met an entrepreneur who was afraid of hard work or challenges. Most entrepreneurs thrive in times of adversity. I would even dare to say that a good many of them get bored when things go too smoothly; they then go out and look for new challenges. Of course, when you own your own business, there are always fresh problems to resolve. It is the nature of this game, which is why we take so much pleasure in it.

I love challenging myself in business, just as I once loved the challenges that football offered me, particularly when the "experts" always had it figured that physically, I was no great specimen. (By the way, they said the same things about Dan Marino and Joe Montana, a couple of pretty decent quarterbacks who came along later. The so-called experts are wrong more than they are right. I was a third-round draft choice. Joe Montana was a third-round draft choice. Marino was the fifth quarterback taken in his year; therefore, just because some *expert* has an opinion don't let it limit you.)

The football scouts were right, of course. I did not have great physical attributes, but what they had not figured into the equation with me, Marino, or Montana, was our natural competitiveness and our willingness to do whatever work was necessary to be a winner. Most small business entrepreneurs have the same attributes.

You have to be self-driven in order to go after whatever it is you want in life. I recognize it in myself, and in most of the other successful business people I know. One of my early business mentors was Mr. Sam Walton, the country boy from Bentonville, Arkansas who late in life developed the concept for a new sort of retail store that served the customers' needs rather than the suppliers'.

I called him "Mister Sam, because he wouldn't let me call him "Mr. Walton," and I couldn't bring myself to call him "Sam" because I had so much respect for his business sense. He also had a great deal of inner drive instilled in him by his mother, who started a milk business to help the family survive the Depression. The Depression motivated a lot of great entrepreneurs over the last fifty years. There is nothing like being poor and hungry to instill in a person the importance of hard work and continuous striving.

If you are to be a successful entrepreneur, you have to be self-motivated. I have found it extremely helpful to understand the source of that inner drive so that in really difficult times, you can reach inside and tap into that source to keep you going, growing, and thriving.

Like a good many entrepreneurs, Mister Sam started working as a young boy, selling magazine subscriptions and delivering newspapers at the age of eight. He also sold rabbits and pigeons and anything else he could get the neighbors to hand over a few pennies for. Even after founding Wal-Mart, which changed the face of American retailing and made him a multibillionaire, he never lost the inner drive created in those Depression years.

He had worked most of his adult life as a franchisee with Ben Franklin Stores but when he was in his late forties he suggested that Ben Franklin open a chain of discount stores in small towns across the country to test his idea of customer-driven merchandising. When his idea was rejected, he decided to do it himself. He was making good money, paying his mortgage, and doing fine, but he thought he could run the business better. He started his own place just to prove that he could do it. He wasn't driven by money, really, as much as by that inner need to challenge himself and his innovative ideas about discount retailing. I rode around with him in his old pickup truck many times. On one visit, I had just read a newspaper article reporting that he was worth $23 billion. That seemed like such an astronomical, overwhelming amount of money that I had to ask him, "Mister Sam, how much is enough?"

"It's never enough," he said. "It's not the money, it's the game."

For Sam Walton, and for most successful entrepreneurs, the real motivation comes from within. Money should not be your motivation. The journey is the thing. Climbing the mountain, not reaching the summit, is what you remember and enjoy. It should be the challenge, the competition, the sense of accomplishment. If you have that inner drive and use it wisely, the money will come on its own. You won't have to worry about that if you simply go about serving others with the best possible product or service.

I never started a company that, at some point, didn't cause me to have doubts. "This must be a stupid idea because no one else is doing it. Why don't people get it? Maybe there is nothing there." We all have self-doubts, but as entrepreneurs we don't let these thoughts stop us. It is only a sanity check, and is a normal thing. I bet even Bill Gates sometimes wonders if he is smart enough. There are always times when I wonder why I don't just go play golf or sit by the lake instead of pushing myself. But, in the end, I know that this what I was born to do.

All entrepreneurs go through periods of doubt, but then their competitive instincts generally kick in. In my days as an athlete, there were times when I thought the critics were right in saying that I couldn't run fast enough or throw far enough, or I wasn't tough enough. But that sort of thinking doesn't impact negatively on the best athletes and entrepreneurs; instead, they use it as motivation to strive for even greater accomplishments. I think Michael Jordan has proven what can be accomplished with mental tenacity. He is a great athlete even now in his later years, but time and time again you hear his opponents say that his greatest strength is his mental toughness. Michael, they say, can beat you with his mental game.

That competitive drive is a part of me, it is part of every entrepreneur I have ever known. I've found it helpful to trace the sources of mine in order to better understand it, and you might too. What stirs your competitive fires? What inner source can you tap into to help drive you and push you into doing what you have always wanted to do? What stokes your fires? Find it and use it, whatever it might be. Maybe you have to manufacture a motivation, maybe somebody called you incompetent or dumb or untalented; use that to motivate yourself in the way that coaches put negative press coverage on the team bulletin boards. Look for those things that get you going.

I've taken time to reflect on what it was that drove me to be such an overachiever athletically, and I guess I would have to attribute my drive as both an athlete and as a businessman to my early competitiveness with my older brother, Dallas, who was smarter and bigger and more of a natural athlete than I was. He also used to beat me up fairly regularly, which only made me more determined to whup him in every way I could. I never did manage to physically overpower him. Though we were only two years apart in age, he was a much bigger kid. With big shoulders and a powerful chest, he was a star fullback in high school, a basketball center, track star, and left fielder on the baseball team.

When my turn came, I wanted to be the quarterback. Dallas's success motivated me because he was older and competitive, gifted and tough and strong. He was the standard against which I measured myself. He would tease and taunt me, and it made me tougher, better, and more competitive. I didn't recognize it at the time but I see now that he made me into a better athlete than I might ever have been. My inner drive came from competing with him and also, to tell the truth, it came from wanting to rise above our family's economic situation.

Early in my childhood, we were not flat-out poor, but we were not in the country-club set, nor did we live in the fanciest neighborhood in town. We had the essentials of life but not the luxuries. As a minister, my father never had a job that paid much, but he had an entrepreneurial spirit and he provided for us, in part, by buying old houses, fixing them up, and selling them for a profit. I am probably most impressed and grateful for the way he provided for my mother, who died recently at the age of 84—decades after his death—and was able to live comfortably for the rest of her life on the money he left for her.

My father was a sweet, wonderful man who had been forced to make his own way in the world from early childhood. His father, a policeman, died when he was five years old. His older brother died when he was 12, and his mother died when he was 17, so he had to bootstrap himself. He lived with an aunt and uncle in the slums of Norfolk, and was taken in by a Pentacostal Holiness Church minister who then sent him to Holmes Bible College, a school that was "funded by faith." He continued to educate himself throughout his life. He got his master's and doctorate at the University of Georgia while pastoring churches.

In my younger years, he was a minister at the Pentecostal Holiness Church in Richmond, Virginia. We lived in a poor part of Washington, just a few blocks from the capitol. I grew up on the wrong side of the tracks, first in Washington and, later in Athens, Georgia, where I went to high school and college.

Driven by my desire to follow in the footsteps of my athletic brother, I did well in high-school football. I led the Athens team to the state championship and, as a result, I was recruited by most of the top schools in the South. The one school that didn't come knocking was the one just down the street, the University of Georgia. They had already recruited two of the top quarterback prospects in the country the year before. Charlie Britt and Tom Lewis were tremendous athletes. Both were high-school All-American. Like my brother, they were bigger, stronger, and faster than me. They could throw the ball farther. Georgia simply didn't need me. Georgia Tech and Auburn, however, both recruited me heavily and I was set to go to Tech, which is in Atlanta, just 30 miles away from home. Tech had a better program than Georgia at the time, so it looked like a good decision. At the very last minute, though, I changed my mind and enrolled at Georgia. Why? It was the greater challenge. I wanted to prove to them that I could play with the best of them.

Nearly everybody in Athens thought I was crazy, even though Georgia gave me a full scholarship. Most thought I would never get a chance to play with two All-World quarterbacks ahead of me. I wanted to prove them wrong. People have been underestimating me all my life and I have always used it as motivation. There were some who felt that the University of Georgia didn't want to recruit me at all but since I was the hometown boy, they felt they had to. Other schools may have wanted me more, but at Georgia, I knew I had more to prove.

Freshmen weren't allowed to play on the varsity back then, so I spent a year on the freshman team and played well. We won all three games. The second week in school, our freshman team had a full-game scrimmage against the Georgia varsity and beat them 13 to 7, which was unheard of. In my sophomore year, during spring practice, I was third-string, and their intention was to redshirt me since there were two strong junior quarterbacks ahead of me. It drove me crazy because I couldn't stand being on the sidelines.

Georgia football was in the doldrums; we were having a terrible season and I couldn't bear to simply watch it. We went to Texas to play the Longhorns in a Saturday night game that year, when I wasn't supposed to play. In the first two-and-a-half quarters of that game, I don't think we made a first down. We were behind seven to nothing and I kept tugging at the shirt of Coach Wally Butts, trying to get him to let me play. Finally, late in the third quarter, Texas punted the ball dead on our five-yard line. It didn't look good.

It was more than I could take. When our offense ran out on the field, I found myself running out there with them. To my surprise, no one stopped me. I think the starting quarterback saw me and just figured Wally had sent me out. I don't know what Coach Butts must have thought when he saw me sprinting out to the huddle, but I do know that when I got there nobody told me to go back to the sidelines. I was pumped up and my teammates were ready to try anything.

On that first 95-yard drive, we scored. After the touchdown, the coaches sent in a field-goal kicker to tie the game, but I waved him off and went for two points to take the lead. Some might say that was arrogant, but I knew we could go for two points and win the game. We made it, and my career was launched. They couldn't redshirt me after I had played, and after what I had pulled off they might have tarred and feathered any coach who tried to yank me out of the starting lineup.

Sometimes, you have to take action. What I did was pretty bold. I am not suggesting that everybody should be that bold, but I felt I had to prove I could play. I believed I could. If I hadn't jumped on that field and made something happen, I might never have had a football career at all.

If this is a business book, why am I telling football stories? Because this story illustrates my point about desire and drive. If being an entrepreneur is really what you want to do, then you can't stand on the sidelines waiting for someone else to put you in the game. If you sit around waiting for just the right time or just the right opportunity, you may be sitting through all of your prime years. Believe me, there is no better time than right now to get into business for yourself.

2. Entrepreneurs have a sense of urgency about their businesses.

You don't have to motivate the small-business entrepreneur. The vast majority of them are born with a fire in the belly and they are masters of self-motivation. If they don't have a deadline, they create one. If they have more than enough time, they pack more tasks into it. Have you ever known a small-business entrepreneur who didn't have enough to do? I have always created a sense of urgency in order to motivate myself. I have done it all my life without really realizing it, and I've noticed that other entrepreneurs do the same thing. A sense of urgency helps me focus; it is a way of using stress positively.

While stress can be harmful, in some cases you can train yourself to use it as a tool for self-motivation and peak performance. Psychologist Jim Loehr of Orlando, Florida, teaches athletes and business executives to become what he calls "stress seekers," in order to achieve "an ideal performance state."

He describes this as a relaxed, confident, and highly energetic state that allows you to perform at maximum levels under stress. Loehr studied top athletes to determine what mental and physical states they were in during periods of peak performance. They told him that they prepare for stress by flooding their minds with positive images in order to keep negative images out. They found that during stressful periods, the athletes had greater focus and energy because of those positive images.

I don't want to overwhelm you with football metaphors, at least not in the first chapter, but how many times have you watched a quarterback who has been struggling during the whole game put it all together in the final two minutes and make a drive that wins the game? I'll bet you've thought, "Well, why didn't he do that before?" The answer is that the focus wasn't there until the clock starting ticking down. The two-minute drill was my specialty, particularly later in my career, and I know exactly why it works— urgency. It forces you to focus on doing the things vital to winning.

Entrepreneurs are masters at creating a sense of urgency even where it may not exist. They are the people who quit their secure jobs in order to start their own businesses, because they fear if they don't make the leap they won't ever accomplish their goals. They create urgency by yanking out the safety net of the secure job. Developing a sense of urgency about pursuing your dreams of starting a business is vital.

I use this tactic in all aspects of my life. I even used it to make myself stop chewing tobacco. I chewed for nearly 25 years. I know it was a nasty habit, but it was something I picked up in football and could not kick. It is more addictive than smoking because the nicotine goes right into the bloodstream through the gums. It got so bad that I was spitting in porcelain cups during big business meetings. I would start chewing after my first cup of coffee in the morning, and I'd still be chewing when I went to bed at night. Awful habit, nasty habit, but it had me. I was addicted. My brain said it was going to kill me, but my body wanted to keep it up.

I knew I had to quit, if not for myself, then for my children and for my wife. Finally, I did it by creating a sense of urgency. When all else fails, common sense, the doctor's warning, the pleas of friends and family, a sense of urgency can get me motivated. I created that sense of urgency easily enough, by focusing on the harmful effects of chewing tobacco rather than on the soothing effects of the nicotine. I knew people who had gotten mouth cancer from chewing tobacco. I knew at least one who had to have the side of his face removed because of it. I started visualizing that every time I reached for the pouch of chew. It was still hard for the first few weeks, but it got a little easier week after week. I used the pain of withdrawal to create even more urgency because I didn't want to give in and face that pain again down the road. I haven't chewed in seven years now, and whenever the urge comes over me, I flash to an image of that friend with the face cancer. There is no greater sense of urgency than choosing life over death, health over painful illness.

My fight with tobacco chewing illustrates the effectiveness of creating a sense of urgency as a tool. That same tool can be used to help you in your drive to create a business. If you are having a hard time doing it while working for someone else, create the urgency by quitting that job. Don't risk your family's security or do anything foolish, make sure that you can meet your obligations and responsibilities, but create an urgency so that you can open up greater opportunities. Create urgency by thinking about the frustrations and limitations of working for someone else. Tell yourself, "If I don't make the leap now, I may never break free and then I'll always wonder what might have been."

3. Entrepreneurs are information junkies.

Several years ago, when my software business was booming, I took the plunge and bought a corporate jet. It was the sort of prestige, big-shot thing I don't normally do, as anyone who has ever seen me walking around my office in jeans, t-shirt, and bare feet would attest. I was traveling so much at the time, I thought it was a smart move, but I nearly went crazy, and I nearly drove a few pilots nuts by talking to them through entire flights. I was lonely!

I missed people. I missed talking to them in airports and on airplanes. I missed hearing their business ideas and dilemmas. I missed sharing mine with them. I got cranky and anxious and uptight and it took me a while to realize that it was because I was not getting information in regular doses.

Entrepreneurs need information; they thrive on it. It drives their minds and feeds their imaginations. They want to make their business decisions based on all of the available data. This need for information is based on the fact that most entrepreneurs are generalists; if they weren't they would be accountants or salespeople who focus on just one aspect of a business. I have seen this in salespeople I have worked with. They care about one thing, making a sale, and often that is fine, but in the formative period of a business, the owner has to think about the bigger picture. While the sales person is zeroing in on a sale, the owner might be more concerned with the question of whether the salesperson is going after the market with the greatest long-term potential, whether the product is ready for the marketplace, or whether it has been priced correctly.

That is why information is an entrepreneur's elixir: The small business entrepreneur needs to know not just one name or one place or one product. He or she needs to understand the entire environment. If you are going to be a small-business entrepreneur, or even if you are already in that position, don't become so focused on your business that you shut out the outside world. What happens all around you determines what happens to your business. Read the newspapers and a variety of magazines, particularly those that relate to and impact on your business. Stay involved in your community, so that you are aware of what is going on around you. Information is the lifeblood of the entrepreneurial business, particular the small business fighting for its niche. You never know where important information is going to come from. Talk to everybody, not just those who you think might help you or people who are considered to have status.

This is another lesson that I first learned in football. When I was traded to the Giants, they were a team with a small offensive line, which meant trouble for yours truly. The guys were good players but they just couldn't hold off the defensive charge for very long. We were fretting about this during training camp, me in particular, when we got a visit from a craggy old guy named Yelberton Abraham Tittle. Some might remember him as Y. A. Tittle, one of the toughest and greatest quarterbacks in pro football history. Y. A. stopped by to visit the Giants, whom he played for from 1961 to 1964, after having visited the San Francisco 49ers, whom he had played for earlier in his Hall of Fame career.

When we talked to this wise old veteran, who still loved football so much that he couldn't stay away, we told him of our concerns about the Giants' small offensive line. He told me and our offensive coordinator, Joe Walton, who later became head coach of the New York Jets, about some things the 49ers were doing with short passes and varied formations. The 49ers, he said, had picked up and refined this nifty offense from some things being done by the Dallas Cowboys.

We took the offensive scheme, refined and custom fit it for our special needs and a few years later, when I was traded back to Minnesota, I helped the coaches there refine it even further. I'm not suggesting that Bill Walsh ever looked at our films but he probably did. The 49ers offense, which became known as the *West Coast offense,* was essentially a refinement of the offense put together by Y. A. Tittle, Joe Walton, and me. Y. A. served as the Johnny Appleseed of that particular offense, spreading it all over the country, where it grew and flourished from the exposure to so many minds and talents.

4. Entrepreneurs have a warrior mentality that focuses on solutions, not problems.

To me, and to most entrepreneurs, the only unsolvable problem is death, and some of them are working pretty hard on that. More often than not, when people come to me with their heads down and say, "Fran, we have a problem," I can find a solution within a short time. It is not that I am any smarter or wiser or cleverer, it's just that I don't waste time saying *If only . . . ,* or *Why did this have to happen to us?*

No problems are bigger than life; they are all a part of life, and as long as we are living and breathing, we can find a way to overcome any challenge. If you don't believe me, look around you at the people in your life, in your office, or down the street who have been hit with incredible challenges, lived through them, and emerged stronger.

These days, business gurus and even some coaches, particularly Phil Jackson of the Chicago Bulls, refer to that love of challenges and winning spirit as a *warrior's mentality.* That's a catchy and not inappropriate term when you consider that most athletes today are big and powerful. But you don't have to be a male, an extraordinary physical specimen, or even an athlete, to have that mentality. The true warrior is one who remains focused on the task at hand even in the midst of chaos, which is a basic tenet of the business entrepreneur. It is a common misperception that successful entrepreneurs have to be control freaks. In truth, to be successful an entrepreneur has to understand that business is as sloppy, messy, and unpredictable as a toddler tackling a plate of spaghetti. The entrepreneur, like any parent, learns to be adaptable, and to appreciate that chaos is often a sign of growth and progress.

If you are going to successfully start and operate a business, your mind, not your emotions, must rule and dictate actions. The small-business entrepreneur has to focus on winning and attaining goals, so that when problems arise they are viewed as challenges to be savored and met rather than insurmountable obstacles. The warrior, as originally described in Eastern philosophy, channels anger and initial confusion into positive and productive action, not reaction or vengeance.

It may sound at first like macho mumbo jumbo to you, but if you look to the original sources of the warrior mentality, you will find that it is really not about violence or physical dominance. In ancient times, the way of the warrior was taught as a method of mastering *wisdom*. It was about acquiring a sense of personal freedom and power through courage and self-knowledge. The basic tenet of the warrior mentality is that we can find a good and meaningful life in serving others. That is essentially what business entrepreneurs do with their products or services, isn't it?

There are a lot of books, motivational tapes, and seminars out there that claim they can turn you into a successful businessperson simply by inspiring you or giving you 10 easy steps or five helpful habits, but the truth is nobody can do that for you, especially someone who has never gone through all the trials and tribulations of operating a business.

If you know exactly what you want to accomplish, then you naturally look for solutions rather than feeling overwhelmed by the problems that present themselves. When I think of this type of focus, I think of my remarkable friend Billy Payne, the Dunwoody, Georgia, real-estate lawyer who got it in his head one day in 1987 that it would be good for his native state to host the 1996 summer Olympics.

Billy had been a pretty fair football player at my alma mater, but he had never even been to an Olympics. Hell, Billy had never even traveled outside the United States. He wasn't a big shot in state or local politics. He wasn't a particularly well-known name around Atlanta's business circles. His only real management experience was as the volunteer chairman of a $2.5 million fund-raising drive for his church.

On top of all that, Billy was 43 years old and had already had heart bypass surgery. But Billy Payne focused on his goal and on finding solutions to problems that would have overwhelmed someone who was less focused.

You know the rest of the story. Billy Payne brought the centennial Olympic games to Atlanta and, as CEO of the Atlanta committee for the games, he put on the biggest Olympics in history. You don't pull something like that off if you turn tail and run at the first sign of resistance. Billy certainly didn't. In the beginning, nobody thought Billy Payne had a lick of a chance. He had no political, business, financial, or social clout. All he had was his dream, and a warrior's mentality about attaining his goal.

When Andrew Young, the former mayor of Atlanta, first met Billy, he thought he was way out of his league, and was suspicious of Billy's motives. But at that first meeting, Billy sold Andrew Young on both the idea and his commitment to it. Andrew Young then sold the rest of the world on Billy Payne's vision. But Young's mayoral successor, Maynard Jackson, refused to commit any city funds to the Olympic effort. In fact, the city of Atlanta charged Payne's Olympic committee $9.5 million for extra police and sanitation. Billy raised the money through corporate sponsorships, and this unknown, inexperienced guy somehow rounded up 42,500 volunteers to run the Games for him.

That is the power of someone who focuses on his dream rather than on his doubts and fears. That is the power of a warrior entrepreneur.

5. *Entrepreneurs are adaptable to change, and more inclined to find opportunity in it than frustration.*

Mike Staats likes to say that he was born wearing a tool belt. Mike's father opened a family appliance store in the all-American city of Peoria, Illinois, in 1944, and Mike grew up working in the store, moving inventory, selling to customers, and accompanying repairmen on calls. Staats Appliance Store thrived for more than 40 years in Peoria, but in the mid-1980's, the local economy took a blow that took down scores of businesses in the region, both big and small. Workers at the heavy-equipment manufacturer, Caterpillar Tractor Co., which is based in Peoria, went on strike for more than two years. Caterpillar, which at one time employed more than 20,000 people in the area, had long been the major employer and economic lifeblood of the region. When its employees stopped collecting paychecks, the local economy simply shut down. Staats Appliances went down with it.

"It was a very, very wicked period, a dismal time, particularly for our family-owned business," recalled Mike, who had taken over for his father in the early 1970's, after obtaining bachelor's and master's degrees in marketing.

Like many others in the area, the Staats family was forced to enter bankruptcy, a devastating thing for them. Mike Staats was emotionally drained by the experience, but his entrepreneurial spirit was not depleted. Change had come, and he changed with it. People in Peoria could no longer afford to buy new appliances because of the strike, but they still needed to keep their refrigerators, stoves, washers, dryers, and garbage disposals running. And, so, Mike Staats became their repairman. He started working out of his home, with his mother and his wife taking telephone calls and dispatching him in his truck. When the appliance superstores moved in, they too needed a repair service and Staats became their repairman.

The Staats name was already well-known in the community, and soon word spread of his reliable repair service. Within 10 years, there were Staats repairmen working in 13 surrounding counties for his new business called Staats Service Today! By the mid-1990's, Mike Staats was not only back in business but he was also spreading the gospel of reliable repair service on his own local radio show as "Captain Toolhead," an entertaining and informative call-in radio talk show that just recently began to spread nationally on the Equity Radio Network. As I write this, Mike Staats is chalking up nearly 10,000 repair calls a year, and more than a half-million dollars in business. When change hit, this small-business entrepreneur refused to lay down and die.

The entrepreneur has to be like the hunter in the woods. He must sleep lightly with one eye open and with his ear to the ground and his nose to the wind. The only guarantee you have in business is that circumstances will change and you will have to make adjustments. In all of my business ventures, I don't think I have ever ended up doing exactly what I had envisioned starting out.

With the Small Business NETwork, I originally had planned not an organization, but a television show aimed at the small-business entrepreneur. Sort of like *This Old House*, but for the builders of businesses rather than home renovators. When I shopped that idea around to potential advertisers, however, I kept getting feedback that led me to think that greater opportunities existed in the market represented by this nation's incredible explosion in small-business entrepreneurs. At first, my idea was to serve them with a magazine, but that notion grew into a national network of men and women involved in small business.

Entrepreneurs adapt to their surroundings even in times of rapid change. They often see changes coming before others do, and they are quick to capitalize on shifting markets and trends. Avid entrepreneurs are focused, but it is not at all tunnel vision. It is a wide-angle, big-screen, satellite view. In football (sorry, but here goes the old quarterback again), we called it "seeing the whole field." Players with that instinctive sense of the entire playing area rarely miss a play or get caught out of position. It works the same way for entrepreneurs who can see shifting trends or new technologies coming in order to capitalize on change and profit from it.

6. Entrepreneurs can't get enough business.

Thomas Yuen is 42 years old, allegedly retired, on dialysis treatment three days a week for renal disease, and working on *six* new high-tech startups. "I just couldn't hold back my enthusiasm. I'm an engineer by training and always have a yearning for leading edge technologies," this irrepressible entrepreneur told *Inc.* magazine.

By the way, Yuen isn't it for the money. He is retired as the cofounder of AST Research. He is a multimillionaire. But he is still doing business when ever and where ever he finds the opportunity.

I can't think of a single established entrepreneur I know who doesn't have at least one business going, another just starting up, and a third in mind. I am the same way. I am always juggling a whole bunch of balls, and I wouldn't have it any other way.

I've got too much energy for one business. I am like a 10-year-old kid, who does his homework while watching cartoons and listening to his boom box. I have to have a lot going on at all times, otherwise I'd find some sort of trouble to get myself into. As I am writing this, we are building a new house in Atlanta. I am in the final stages of launching the Small Business NETwork and the WebTitan. I am making infomercials, I am giving speeches all over the country, and I am discussing at least a half-dozen other projects. And I can't figure out what to do in my spare time.

Former Redskins quarterback turned television commentator Joe Theismann once went to my old Minnesota Vikings Coach Jerry Burns and asked him: "What kind of football coach would Fran Tarkenton have been?"

Burns replied, "Tarkenton never could have coached a football team. He would have had to coach all 28 teams in the league. One wouldn't have satisfied him.

"When he played for Minnesota, he had to be in on everything going on with the team from the scouts to the ticket sales to the laundry. When he came in on Monday mornings, he had already studied the box scores of every game in the league and he could tell you the stats for every team."

I have to admit, Jerry was right. Most entrepreneurs are like that. They simply have too much energy to settle into just one thing at a time. No matter how successful they become, they are always looking for the next deal, simply because they enjoy the game so much. For the entrepreneur, every day is a new adventure. Just this morning, I was up at an hour before dawn, thinking of more ways to develop the Small Business NETwork. I was on the phone almost immediately, talking to people, finding out what they were up to, how they were doing in their designated areas. Not surprisingly, a lot of people ask me if I ever sleep. I do, but my brain doesn't.

As you might guess, my friend Ruth Brooks is the same way. Recently we were talking about how we are both always trying to dream up new businesses, and she told me this story.

"When Bobby got cut with a power saw a while back I took him to the hospital and the doctor was sewing and sewing on him and finally, the doctor said to me, 'I know you must be getting bored because it is taking me so long.' But I told him I never get bored. Even when I am idle, I am thinking. When you have idle time you should think about things you can do."

7. Entrepreneurs get excited about fresh ideas and innovations.

Greg Maanum, 35, and Randy Zanatta, 39, both started with Best Buy when it was just one store selling records and tapes and struggling against heavy competition. Together, they rose through the ranks to become top executives as Best Buy itself grew into the nation's leading electronics superstore chain.

Zanatta, who was executive vice president of marketing, and Maanum, his vice president for merchandising, had long thought that they would never leave Best Buy, which had been very good to them. But then, the young retailers came up with a concept that neither one of them could resist taking to the marketplace.

They are both avid golfers and in their travels around the country for Best Buy, it had not escaped their attention that golf equipment had yet to be introduced into the superstore cosmos that had grown to include not only electronic equipment but also books, baby products, toys, shoes, general sporting goods, hardware, and pet supplies.

"We traveled a lot visiting our stores and we were always on the lookout for a killer golf store but most of them were mom and pop stores," said Zanatta. "It was the same with electronics stores in the early 1980's, so we thought we might have something if we could create *the* place for golf equipment," he added.

"Initially, most of our talks about it ended with 'Well, maybe someday . . .' But then, one day, we decided the time had come to make the leap," he said.

As Best Buy grew bigger and their jobs became more corporate than entrepreneurial in nature, the two young executives decided that the time had come to cash in on their stock and putt out. They put together a business plan, but, like male golfers everywhere, they didn't take off until they first consulted higher authority: "We had to sell our wives on it first," Zanatta said. "I have an eight year old and an 11 year old and my partner has 18-month-old twins, so it wasn't an easy decision to leave the security of Best Buy."

They also had to find investors willing to back what was then little more than a dream, they said. "We were just a couple of guys with a slide projector and an idea, but people bought into it," Zanatta said. "It's a great country when you can do something like that."

On the day in April 1997 when Tiger Woods recharged the world of golf with his electrifying performance at the Masters, Zanatta and Maanum opened the doors on their flagship 15,800-square-foot Golf Central superstore in Bloomington, Minnesota. Even with most of the area's golfers glued to their television sets, the two entrepreneurs sold nearly twice as much merchandise as they had projected. Their entrepreneurial instincts were right on target, and they are already planning two more stores.

The true entrepreneur learns to trust those instincts and to follow them and use them as motivation. I know, because I still get jacked up when I come upon an innovation or a new technology that opens up whole new frontiers for entrepreneurs. The Internet is probably the greatest example of that right now. At first, only the real high-tech wizards saw any use for it, and most business types scoffed that there wasn't any real way to make money on the Internet. While they were busy wagging their tongues, a whole generation of Internet entrepreneurs, or *netre-preneurs*, snuck in and created millions and millions of dollars of new wealth on the Internet.

Look at some of the most successful businesses on the Internet, things like book stores and record stores and computer equipment wholesalers and what do you see? Those are businesses dominated by giant corporations in the traditional retail market; but those same giants were slow to see and act on the potential for selling their products on the Internet, so the young, agile and visionary entrepreneurs moved in ahead of them. Now it is up to the big guys to play catch-up.

8. Entrepreneurs are highly charged take-charge people.

Like Ted Turner, who was a pretty fair sailor, most entrepreneurs love being the captain of the ship. I know I always enjoyed football the most when there were only two minutes left, the score was tied, and we had the ball. Entrepreneurs are take-charge people. They are instigators. They are catalysts. They are the ones who go boldly into the night and come home with a new business in their portfolios. Entrepreneurs generally think there is nothing they can't do, and they love it when someone challenges them by saying something can't be done. In fact, the best way to motivate an entrepreneur is to say he or she can't do something.

People sometimes make the mistake of thinking business is easier for me because my name is well-known. Admittedly, I can sometimes get a foot in the door because of the name recognition, but if I am there to talk business, I had better have more than an autographed football to put on the table, or it will be a quick conversation.

Believe me, I have to establish my business credentials over my athletic credentials every time I walk into a business meeting. The question is always hanging in the air: "Is he just a dumb jock or has he really got something on the ball?" That's okay; I am willing to prove myself because I have faith in myself. Most entrepreneurs do, otherwise, they wouldn't have the courage or the commitment to sell their dreams to the rest of the world.

When I was trying to get the Small Business NETwork going, I got bounced around AT&T and MCI and a bunch of other communications companies just like any other person with an idea to pitch. I spent months trying to convince them that this was not some half-baked idea. Once they caught onto it, a little late, I might add, they were banging on my door wanting back in. It takes a highly charged, take-charge person to keep plugging away. When I am working on a new business, I think I draw power from the sun, and probably the moon, and 100-watt light bulbs too. I take on a high charge. The only times I can remember being lethargic are those times when I was bored with whatever I was doing. My last two years of playing football in the NFL were that way. I was starting and playing well, but I knew it was time to do something else. I had lost interest and so my energy level was down. But as soon as I left football and got involved in business, my energy level picked right back up again.

9. Entrepreneurs are not gamblers, they are calculated-risk takers.

I have known some gamblers in my day, and I am not a gambler. I am, however, a *calculated*-risk taker. There is a difference between a gambler and a risk taker. A gambler is someone looking to get rich quick. They want to hitch on to a shooting star. Gamblers go to Las Vegas because their mentality says, "To score big, you have to gamble big."

Entrepreneurs are risk takers who believe that in order to score big, you have to work hard and constantly be alert to opportunity. The risks they take are the commitment of their time and energy and money to an idea that they believe in, sometimes without much support from anyone else. Their risks are not gambles because they normally test their idea, test their markets, and test every aspect of their business before they go all the way with it.

From the beginning, one of my key marketing strategies for the Small Business NETwork and WebTitan was to introduce it with an infomercial on stations all over the country. Now, infomercials are often considered a high-risk endeavor by many people because of the substantial cost involved and the fact that a high percentage of infomercials don't do what they are intended to do

—sell massive quantities of the goods being marketed. Production costs alone generally run more than $150,000, and you can spend hundreds of thousands more on television air time. The appeal, however, is that infomercials are really a form of direct marketing, because you provide an 800 number that the viewer can call immediately, so there is a direct response. It is, more often than not, an impulse buy, and if it hits the payoff can be extraordinary. I have sold more than $600 million in products via infomercials over the last nine years. The infomercials I did for the Power-Rider resulted in sales of $100 million in the first 12 months, and we are continuing to do well with it. I made more money with that infomercial alone than I made in 18 years as a professional football player. Although a high percentage of infomercials fail, like nine out of ten, I have been successful with most of the infomercials I have done. I know how to cut the gambling out of infomercial making, and to lower the risk to acceptable levels.

In the early days of infomercials, the major part of their appeal was that you could buy commercial air time in bulk by purchasing off-prime hours—late nights, weekends, and other time slots that most advertisers don't want—at bargain rates, but growing demand for that time by infomercial makers has driven up the price of even that air time, though it is still a much better price than prime time.

Gamblers lay it all on the line with their bets. Risk-taking entrepreneurs cover their bets by forming corporations so that they are not personally liable for loss or damage or lawsuits. They spread the risk out. Any entrepreneur who gambles his family's future on an unproven business concept is just flat-out nuts. You do not have to be a gambler in business. There are scores of ways to cover your business bets. There are no get-rich-quick schemes in business. Do some people get rich quickly? Yes! But generally the entrepreneurs who experience this are as surprised as anyone. Sometimes an idea just hits at the perfect time, the result of serendipity and good fortune. Sometimes, a business catches the public's imagination. At other times, the entrepreneur may struggle for years and then suddenly *Bam!* His enterprise takes off.

Ninety-nine percent of the time, there was no scheme or plan. It just happened! Although the entrepreneur doesn't set out to strike it rich quick, he or she does plan and prepare for success. Why are so few successful entrepreneurs gamblers? People who gamble set themselves up for failure because the odds are always against them. That is tremendous pressure, knowing that failure is inevitable. Entrepreneurs can handle failure because they know in the long run, if they plan carefully, take well-calculated risks, work hard, and follow a thoughtful plan, the odds favor their success. Entrepreneurs don't rush in. They are patient. They don't give away the store if the customers aren't buying, in the way a gambler will bet it all to try and recoup losses. The entrepreneur goes back to the chalkboard and rethinks strategy, seeks advice, changes marketing, and tries something new.

By the time a savvy entrepreneur opens a business, he or she has been living that business for months, if not years. Dreaming it. Studying it from all angles. Talking to people who own similar businesses. Drafting and re-drafting a business plan. Talking about that business to consultants, suppliers and distributors, bankers, lawyers, accountants, friends, family. Is there risk involved? Certainly. Should it be a gamble? Not in any way.

10. Entrepreneurs are not afraid of freedom.

Who is afraid of freedom, you ask? Take a drive by any corporate headquarters at the end of a working day. Now, there is nothing wrong with working in a corporation. There can be some great rewards. But freedom is not one of them. Security, perhaps. A sense of belonging and camaraderie, maybe. But there is very little freedom in most corporations. In those environments, most people are role players and they are rewarded for how well they fill their assigned roles. Again, there is nothing wrong with that. A great deal of this nation's wealth is created by people filling their corporate roles.

It's just not for me, and probably not for you, if you find all or most of the entrepreneurial characteristics I have described in this chapter apply to you. My bet is that you, too, are a freedom seeker.

Now, does that mean that the entrepreneur is free of financial worries, business worries, or responsibility? Absolutely not. Much of the time, the entrepreneur has more responsibilities and challenges than any insulated corporate employee. The freedom I am referring to is the freedom to control your own destiny, to make your own mistakes, to enjoy the full rewards of your labors, your talents, your creativity, drive, and initiative. The most happy fulfilled people see a direct correlation between what they do and what they get. They reap the rewards of their actions.

I never want to be in a position where I can be fired from my job. That is a freedom I covet, and one that few corporate employees have. There is no such thing as the secure corporate job anymore. So, that advantage is gone. If that is the case, then why not put yourself in a position to profit the most from your own hard work? Why not put your name on the front door so that you are the master of your own time, so that you can take vacations when you want, so that after years of hard work, you have a very exact measure of all that you have strived for?

As an entrepreneur, you can say, *I've got enough money, now I am going to have some fun.* But I bet that you won't say that, not if you are a true entrepreneur. Why not? Because the true entrepreneur has fun while making money. The dollars in the bank are a good measure of *how much* fun the entrepreneur is having, not of how much fun he or she expects to have *some* day.

I've done pretty well. I've created some wealth. I've lost some wealth. But I am well ahead of the day when I was a poor preacher's son, or a quarterback risking my neck for the enrichment of a team owner. I would be considered wealthy by most standards and, believe me, I have scrapped and scrambled for every bit of that wealth.

Believe this too, as a devoted entrepreneur, I will be scrapping and scrambling in business until I hit the wall going 100 miles an hour. I want to be where Oprah, Bill Gates, and Sam Walton have been. It's not the money, though, it's the freedom, and it's the game.

There is just a lot of opportunity out there if you think about it. If you just keep an eye out, behind you and everywhere, you can make a mint.

— RUTH BROOKS

DEVELOPING OSP

A FEW years ago, I was returning to my home in Atlanta from a vacation in Hawaii rested and ready with all of my entrepreneurial instincts fully charged. There in the airport, I picked up on an everyday item that turned out to be worth a few million dollars.

My eyesight is about like that of any person my age. I've even got those little magnifying glasses that sit on the end of my nose so I can read the newspaper without inhaling printer's ink, but over the years I have developed exceptional peripheral vision. You don't survive 18 years as a professional quarterback without being able to know exactly where each of those 300-pound defensive linemen are at all times. I may not see any better than most people, but believe me, I am in tune with my peripheral vision. It has saved my bones from being sacked many times over the years, not only in football, but also in life in general.

In addition to well-developed peripheral vision, I have trained myself also to see and sense *opportunities* that others might have missed. If you can sense things that most people can't sense, they call that gift *extrasensory perception* or ESP. If you can sense opportunities where other people do not, I call that *opportunity sensory perception*, or OSP. Most great entrepreneurs have a strong sense for spotting opportunities.

You may be familiar with Ted Turner, the creator of Turner Broadcasting and CNN, but few people realize that this Atlanta entrepreneur got his start by buying a washed-up, falling-apart old public-access cable station in Atlanta. He was in the billboard business, which he had inherited from his father, and Turner really knew very little about cable television or broadcasting, other than the fact that he kept hearing about the potential of cable television and was curious about it.

What he learned in following his curiosity inspired his imagination and sent him into action. He bought that little Atlanta station and in 1976, at the age of 37, when a lot of people thought of him as little more than a rich playboy, Turner founded television station WTBS, which he leveraged into the Turner Broadcasting System, the Cable News Network (CNN), and, just recently, a $7.5 billion merger with Time Warner.

Turner didn't have to fight off a crowd to buy that feeble little cable station in Atlanta for a bargain price. He was the only one to see the potential business opportunities in the station. He is a gifted entrepreneur.

TICKETS TO OPPORTUNITY
. . . .

Now, I'm not comparing myself to mighty Ted, but I've got pretty fair OSP myself. As I stood in line at the airline ticket counter that day, I noticed something that most people have seen hundreds of times without giving much thought to it. Everyone in line at the boarding gate, and for that matter, nearly everyone sitting, walking, and standing in that airport had one thing in common; an airline ticket tucked inside an airline-issued ticket jacket.

Pretty mundane observation, right? So what, Fran? Big deal. Yes, *big deal*, particularly to an avid entrepreneur coming off a two-week vacation. I was rested. I was tanned. I was ready to do some business.

My OSP antennae are particularly tuned to pick up opportunities with mass-market potential. My success with infomercials has made me alert to the fact that even if you have a product with very low profit margins, if it is something that *everyone* has to have, or everyone wants, then you stand to make a pretty penny.

When I spied those everyday airline ticket jackets in everyone's hands, I began to think about all of those ticket jackets being carried around by all those air travelers who generally rank among the most affluent of consumers. Did you ever notice the ads in airline magazines? They are usually for high-end, big-ticket items because air travelers are considered to have a lot of expendable income.

The more I thought about the millions and millions of ticket jackets being carried around airports and onto airplanes and then home, the wider my vision got. I went to bed that night with visions of little ticket jackets wrapped around greenbacks dancing in my head.

As a true believer in the gospel of mass marketing, it occurred to me that those airline ticket jackets were an underdeveloped resource. Sure, they were good for holding plane tickets, but what about advertising messages? I wasn't in the airline business, or in the ticket-jacket printing business or the advertising business, but I saw untapped marketing potential in those ticket jackets.

As soon as I got back to my office in Atlanta, I called a friend of mine at the corporate headquarters of Delta Airlines. I asked him how many ticket jackets they print and hand out monthly and annually. When he gave me the numbers, I thought *great gawd-almighty!* With the numbers whirling in my mind, I immediately began devising a game plan for my next business.

Like most small-business entrepreneurs, I didn't have millions of dollars to invest in this raw idea, but I did have a telephone, and so I called around Atlanta to find out if any printing companies had the capacity to print the number of ticket jackets I figured we would need. None of them could handle it, but I got the name of one of the largest printing companies in the country, a Chicago firm, called their president and asked for a meeting. At this point, you are probably thinking "Sure, it's easy for someone with a well-known name as a former professional athlete to get a meeting with the top guy," but that is not necessarily the case. Believe me, I may get phone calls returned—though there is no guarantee of that either—but in these competitive times, serious business people are not inclined to waste their work hours glad-handing with celebrity jocks. Like every other entrepreneur, I have to bring something to the table. Sometimes we get so enamored of our ideas we think if we can get somebody to help us we can make a lot of money, but what I have found is that people like your ideas only if they think *they* can make money. If I go to Federal Express or any other big company, I have to show them that my idea will make *them* money. If I can't do that, they tune me out. Many entrepreneurs make the mistake. They only think of how a partnership can make them money. That may excite you, but it won't excite your partners.

In this case, I carried with me something that no business-person can resist—a potentially lucrative deal for both of us. "If you can print 14 million ticket jackets a month for me and the airlines, I will give you half of the business," I told the printer. Simple as that. I didn't have a printing press, all I had was an idea. He bought in, without putting up a dime, because this was a great add-on business. He had a capital investment in his presses and this was another way he could make more money with that investment.

Next, I set up meetings with representatives of each airline. At this point, i had more than an idea, I had a partner with one of the biggest printing capacities in the world. Oh, I also had a very attractive enticement for the airlines: I was going to save them a whole lot of money.

My pitch to them was equally straightforward. "You will never have to pay to print another airline ticket jacket. If you will agree to use the jackets that my Chicago partner and I print for you, we will provide them at no charge to your airline." They liked the concept. Every one of them signed on because it added value to their companies. It made money for them.

At my next stop, I had not only an idea, a printing partner, and the key to a very, very big consumer market, I also had an advertising vehicle that would be seen, held and carried around by millions and millions of high-end consumers every day of the year. It was a no-brainer to sell advertising space on the ticket jackets to IBM, AT&T, Sprint, and other Fortune 500 companies. Unfortunately, my printing partner hadn't been able to get his sales staff keyed up about the idea, which was small potatoes to them, so I called up an old friend of mine, Marvin Bluestein, and asked him to go to New York with me and sell a few ads. Now Marv is not an advertising guy by trade. He has a small business in St. Simons, but he had taken a leave to chase his dream of becoming an actor, sort of a Jewish Danny DeVito. There didn't seem to be a big demand for his type; however, he was a gifted businessman. I needed his help because at the same time I also had a consulting business, an insurance business, and a software company. I was also co-hosting both *Monday Night Football* and *That's Incredible!* If anyone had firsthand knowledge of airline ticket jackets, it was me. Marv and I checked into the Waldorf-Astoria Hotel in Manhattan and, within a month, we had sold out the 12 advertising pages on the airline ticket jackets for $100,000 a month per page for one-year contracts. AT&T, Exxon, General Motors, Eastman Kodak, MasterCard, and others signed on. It was an amazing success story that was written up by the *New York Times*.

I don't want to leave you with the impression that it was a stroll into the end zone. No business is. There really are no easy sales when it comes to advertising. Frank Borman, the former astronaut who became head of Eastern Airlines, turned me down. (Bad mistake, Frank. If you had been more open to opportunities like that, you and your airline might still be in business). Another airline guy kept ducking me, so I finally offered to pick him up at the airport as he returned from a business trip and then pitch him the deal as we drove to his house. I sold him on the concept in the back seat, parked in his driveway. Then he died a couple weeks later.

There are no guarantees in life, or in business. It took a lot of work, but my original notion about the value of airline ticket jackets eventually proved out. Within a couple months, our new company, Ticket Marketing Inc., was producing 14 million ticket jackets a month. Each of those ticket jackets contained an insert with 12 pages of advertising. Each page sold for $100,000 a month. You can do the math.

OPPORTUNITY SENSING PERCEPTION

Just as my well-developed peripheral vision was key to my success, and my longevity, in my football career, my OSP has been invaluable in my business career. OSP is the ability to sense opportunities for new businesses or new and greater opportunities for your existing business, even while you go about the daily tasks of your workday. OSP is what distinguishes truly great and dynamic entrepreneurs from the person who is just making a living, getting by, or working from paycheck to paycheck.

Shiraz Balolia, a native of Kenya, made the *Inc.* 500 list in 1996, thanks to his keen OSP. "I see opportunities out there that are so easy, I can't help myself," he told the magazine. Balolia has 11 companies. He wholesales woodworking tools, sells cutlery, jewelry, and sculpture, and has a real-estate development company, among other things. "I have a bad case of capitalism," he claimed.

No, he has great OSP, and he has developed the ability to capitalize on opportunities that are all around him. By almost all accounts, there are more opportunities out there today than ever before. George Kozmetsky, 78, the founder of IC2 Institute, a research center in entrepreneurship at the University of Texas, said that global economic warfare has created "an economy that is wide open."

"No markets are safe or secure anymore. Everything is up for grabs. No matter what field you are talking about—electronics, education, entertainment, or anything else—it opens up more opportunities than I've seen in my entire lifetime. Very few generations in history, perhaps not since the Renaissance, have been accorded the opportunities this period provides. It's a profoundly different world."

How do you take advantage of this wide-open situation? By being prepared and open to opportunity, by having a wide range of vision with your OSP on full alert. Having finely tuned OSP is not an inherited trait, as far as I've been able to tell. In fact, my son Matthew, 26, has a degree from Princeton and works for a venture capital company, but recently he said he wants to go back to school for a master's degree because he hasn't found anything yet that interests him. I'm proud to say he has been accepted to the Harvard Business School. I think being sensitive to entrepreneurial opportunities is born of many factors. To help you develop your OSP, here are methods for improving your ability to spot opportunities where others may not see them.

1. Develop a hunger, whether you are hungry or not.

Many of the greatest businessmen in our nation's history were entrepreneurs who grew up in poverty and were eager to break the cycle by using the capitalist system to their advantage. Everyone has some source of inner motivation to tap into. Certainly much of my entrepreneurial drive stems from the fact that I grew up in a family where everyone had to pitch in to help pay the bills, so I was always on the lookout for ways to make money. Even later, when I was making serious money, I was programmed to stay on the alert for opportunities. I am also naturally competitive, and probably my strongest motivation in business comes from a desire to prove myself outside the athletic arena. It is always in the back of my mind that unless I keep pushing, I could end up poor again. You don't easily shake that sense of insecurity and, if you are lucky, you learn to use it as a tool rather than allowing it to weigh you down. What inner source can you tap into to drive yourself and sharpen your OSP?

While it is true that real hunger and poverty has inspired many of the great entrepreneurs in this country to strive for success, I believe you can develop a hunger for business success without having come from a background of poverty. Donald Trump certainly has, and so has Ted Turner. Sam Walton was a successful businessman when he broke off from another chain to start his own store. They all wanted to prove themselves and their ideas for one reason or another, and so they were hungry for opportunities and developed those opportunities.

Hunger can also exist within the most successful corporations. Just as we were completing this book, I received the 1996 annual report from The Coca-Cola Company. The bright-red cover of the report had only one word on it, followed by a question mark, but it said volumes about what makes this perhaps the best-run, most successful company in America.

The message on Coke's annual report was this: "Thirsty?"

That question was intended to convey the fact that the CEO of Coca-Cola, Roberto C. Goizueta is not about to rest on his laurels, nor are those under his supervision. "Even after another rewarding year The Coca-Cola Company is still unquenchably thirsty—thirsty for more ways to reach more consumers in more places with more products, creating more value for you," Goizueta wrote in his message to shareholders.

Even though some may think that Coca-Cola has saturated its market, Goizueta takes the position, as he once told me, that the average human being consumes 62 ounces of liquids each day but the average human consumption of Coca-Cola is only two ounces per day. *That* leaves plenty of room for expansion, he noted.

And *that* is the sort of hunger every entrepreneur needs to develop to get on top and stay there, as Coca-Cola has done.

2. Get out and about to open your field of vision.

One of the first businesses I launched on my own was a management-consulting firm serving the textile mills of the southeastern United States. I grew up around those mills in North Georgia and I knew both the workers and the executives. I was familiar with the difficulties and challenges of that life. I was in the seventh year of my pro-football career, and had just been traded from Minnesota to the New York Giants (who would later trade me back), when I came upon an opportunity to do something worthwhile for the people in those mills.

In the late 1960's, the federal government had created a program to try and help the people of Appalachia find employment, and one of the areas of concern was the high rate of turnover in the textile mills. Every year, the textile companies had to spend thousands of dollars while losing production because of turnover rates that ran from 65 percent to 100 percent. It was hard work, but what contributed most to the turnover was poor management. Mill workers were generally treated poorly, almost like slaves in some instances. There was simply no effort to give them positive reinforcement, or to make them feel valued. I learned about the government's program and, after talking to friends in the industry, I applied for a $1 million federal grant to train both management and employees in the mills.

I had studied psychology in college, and I'd always had an interest in the value of positive reinforcement in both sports and in the business world. I was not an expert, of course, so I brought in some real behavioral scientists and asked them to help me develop a program to train mill management and textile workers in order to reduce turnover.

In the past, plant managers had made feeble attempts to improve morale in the workplace by bringing in preachers and sitting the workers down around campfires. They'd get all warmed up by the preachers around the fire, but once they got back in the plant, they'd cool off in a hurry. We wanted to do something that would have a greater impact. We put together a system of positive reinforcement and feedback, and measurable response. Within a short time, we had contracts not only in the textile mills but in other industries as well. Behavioral Systems, Inc. became a highly successful business, and also gave rise to several other entrepreneurial moves simply because it put me in a position to see opportunities unfold.

Just as I learned to scramble out of the protective pocket when I couldn't see an open receiver in a football game, I have long made it a point to get out and open up my range of vision as a business entrepreneur. At one time I had as many as 100 consultants working for me in Behavioral Systems, and even though I was still playing football, I remained deeply involved with our clients. Whenever I wasn't on the road playing for the Giants or tied up in practices, I was back in the mills, talking to my employees and those in the plants. I wanted, first of all, to make sure we were providing the service we had sold to the plants and, second, I wanted to learn what the needs of these clients were so that I might find a way to serve this customer base in another way.

To stay in touch with our customers in the mills, I bought a Winnebago van and hired a driver named Robert, whom I called "Robert Winnebago." Robert and I would leave Atlanta at 4 A.M. many times to be in Greenville, South Carolina, or one of our other sites by the start of the first shift in the textile mills. I wanted our clients to see that I was there on the first shift as well as the third shift, so I would spend the day, take a break and a nap, and be there for the final shift of the day, too. It was a good marketing move, certainly, to let the customer know that I was personally on site and paying attention to what our people were doing, but more important, it put me in the position to see opportunities; whether they were opportunities to better serve the client, opportunities to expand our consulting business, or opportunities for new business.

I was there with the textile workers, breathing lint, hearing the sounds of the machinery and their voices, and my OSP was on full power. It was among those factory workers in the carpet mills that I came upon one of the more lucrative opportunities of my entrepreneurial career, one that also provided an even greater service to the employees of the mills.

By spending time with them in the factories, I got to know a lot of the textile workers through this business, and from them and the plant managers I learned that most of the employees had no insurance and no retirement plans, so that when their days in the mills were over, they retired with only a handshake and maybe a gold pin for all their years of service and toil. The only insurance they had was very expensive weekly debit insurance that gave high-cost, poor-quality life insurance. I had some experience in the insurance business from my college days as a salesman for Franklin Life, and it seemed sad to me that these good, hardworking folks had no backup plans for medical problems or for their retirement. The owners of the mills couldn't afford to add to their present benefits plan, but I saw an opportunity to provide this needed coverage for them, while also launching another entrepreneurial business. I formed a partnership with the National Life and Accident Insurance Company in Nashville, and we developed a payroll deduction system that provided quality health insurance and guaranteed life insurance and other benefits to the workers. It was a high-quality, low-cost plan that greatly benefitted the people in those mills. It was a very popular program for the employees and it made them more loyal to the company because they felt the company was looking out for them, even though it didn't cost the company any money. It also became a very good business for me and my partners. I sold out to them several years ago for more than a million dollars.

I never would have known that entrepreneurial opportunity existed if I did not have finely tuned antennae, strong OSP, and also if I had not taken the effort to go out into the field. You can be a one-person shop in your business, but you cannot afford to isolate yourself from the world if you want to constantly grow your business and seek greater entrepreneurial opportunities.

3. Think CIA: Use your curiosity to fire your imagination and propel you into action.

Simple curiosity won't get you anywhere. Your imagination may do you more harm than good if you do nothing but daydream. But if you put both curiosity and imagination into action, you have the ingredients and the catalyst for entrepreneurship.

In the early days of launching my latest enterprise, the Small Business NETwork, I was meeting with Rod Dahl who oversees technical support for the WebTitan software when I spotted a copy of *Internet World* magazine on his desk. I'd never seen the magazine before, so I picked it up and thumbed through it. It was packed with useful information and articles about the Internet. It was also packed with ads, a sure sign of a successful magazine.

"What is this?" I asked Rod.

"It's my favorite magazine," he said.

"No," I told him, "*This* is an asset and an opportunity for us."

Rod didn't get it, but I can't blame him. As a technician, he sees things inside computers that I will never grasp. What he is not trained to see are entrepreneurial opportunities. From his narrow perspective, he recognized *Internet World* as an important resource for technical information, but as an entrepreneur, I saw it as a potential partner in our Small Business NETwork. I borrowed Rod's copy of the magazine and took it back to my office. After carefully going through it, I found the name of the publisher, called him, and struck up a relationship that will likely bear fruit for both of our businesses. This probably never would have happened if I hadn't been nosing around Rod's desk. My curiosity, and my OSP, led to a relationship with *Internet World* that may one day add to the value of the Small Business NETwork and to the magazine's audience.

There are scores of opportunities like this right under our noses every day, every place we go; it is just a matter of training yourself to be curious about what lies around you, and then learning to see opportunities where other people do not. Every day, I remind myself of that, and nearly every day I come upon something that, in one way or another, contributes to my business enterprises.

Many small-business opportunities are the product of curious minds seeking how something works, or wondering how a need can be met or a demand supplied. No one has cornered the market on ideas or innovation, but entrepreneurs with a high level of curiosity generally lead the pack. Curiosity may have killed a lot of cats, but it has made a lot of entrepreneurs rich—but *only* if it fires the imagination and results in action.

How many people do you know who claim to have a great idea for a business, but have never acted on it? I could probably name you a couple dozen just off the top of my head. Having an idea for a business doesn't count for much, and it certainly doesn't qualify anyone as an entrepreneur. You have to take that idea and run with it into action.

What might have happened if, in the late 1940's, a Swiss engineer who came home from a hike with his pants legs covered in burrs hadn't taken action after wondering what might be done by creating a synthetic imitation of those tightly gripping burrs? For one thing, we wouldn't have Velcro. Another enduring product and business was created when a torsion spring was knocked off a workbench and kept tumbling along seemingly under its own power. The tool worker who saw it was curious about its slinky action, and he imagined that it would make a fun, slinky toy. The creators of the Slinky tested their toy by making 400 of them for Gimble's department store in Philadelphia, which sold out of them in less than an hour. At that point, they knew they were in business.

Another of my favorite down-home, natural-born entrepreneurs is Clark Stafford, who has OSP to the tenth degree. Clark lives in Seneca, Illinois, near the Illinois River, and he works for a quarry, hauling rock and sand. He also owns a used heavy-equipment business, a trailer park, a tavern and restaurant, and Concrete Elvis.

As a natural-born entrepreneur, Clark is always looking for opportunities. One day several years ago, he and his wife were on vacation in Florida and while driving to a flea market—which is the kind of thing Clark does on vacations—they drove past a shut-down used-car lot when something caught Clark's entrepreneurial eye and fired his curiosity. It was faded and weathered, but it was still recognizable as The King of Rock 'n' Roll. It was a trailer-mounted concrete statue of Elvis in full Las Vegas ensemble with a guitar in hand. It stood about 15 feet high and weighed a couple of tons, and it triggered Clark's imagination. He spent two months haggling in person and on the phone with the widow of the guy who had owned the used-car lot. When he finally made the deal, Clark drove back to Florida, hitched up Concrete Elvis and trailer, and hauled him back to Illinois.

After having him repainted and refurbished, complete with new speakers mounted inside his guitar, Clark began renting out Concrete Elvis to parades, grand openings, sales promotions, birthday parties, bar mitzvahs, and any other occasion fit for the King. He made a few dollars here and there, even got featured on television and in the media, but mostly, Clark and Concrete Elvis had a real good time together—all because Clark was ready and willing to act when he came upon an opportunity.

4. Be willing to cast a wide net.

After selling my software company and deciding that I was going to start another business, I began casting about for opportunities. I don't know any entrepreneurs who are couch potatoes.

Most are constantly on the go, always with the antennae up and finely tuned. If they don't have something cooking, they go fishing for ideas and opportunities.

One of my greatest sources for ideas and inspiration are the people I meet while traveling and giving speeches. These engagements take me all over the country. I get to meet with executives and salespeople involved in every kind of business imaginable. I know a lot of speakers who fly in, give a pat speech, and fly out as soon as they've palmed the check. I try to get in at least the night before so that I can have dinner with some of the folks I'll be talking to. I grill them for information about their business, their industry, their problems, new developments, the competition, management and employee concerns—everything I can get out of them. Then, either that night or in the early morning, I tailor my speech to the audience. Once I have given the speech, I stick around to talk to people, not just to sign autographs, although as the audience gets younger (not that the speaker is getting any older), those requests are diminishing.

When I am searching for a fresh enterprise, I may stick around for months, as I did a while back at Midas Mufflers Inc. I had been invited to speak at a number of Midas venues, and I became interested in their operation, so like a cousin who comes to visit for a few days and stays a month, I invited myself to settle in for a while. I wasn't billing anyone for my time, even though I did a lot of informal consulting. I was simply interested in learning how the large automotive-related franchise worked.

I ended up staying for months as a sort of troubleshooting consultant. Not that I camped out in a garage bay, but for several months, I tried to learn as much as I could about the company. I met with executives and franchise owners to learn what their problems were, what worked for them, and what didn't. I gathered all sorts of information. I can't say that any of it specifically sparked an idea for an entrepreneurial business right away, although a lot of it helped me formulate the concept of my small Business NETwork because I got to know the concerns and needs of the franchise holders.

I would not be surprised either if, somewhere down the road, something I learned from the folks at Midas will trigger an idea or open up an opportunity. It certainly was a good experience and a profitable use of time. By casting a wide net, I made contacts and gathered information that sooner or later will come into play.

5. *Learn to visualize your opportunities as actualities.*

I read an interview with a psychic—not one of those 1-900-U-L-B-RICH psychics—but a respected one who does a lot of work with police departments around the country. In the article, the psychic said that a great many people have at least some level of psychic powers, but very few learn to "tune in" to the psychic thoughts that come to them. The same can be said of entrepreneurs and OSP.

Many people have fleeting flashes of opportunity. They see something on television, or notice something on the job or in the world around them and it flashes through their minds that "I'll bet there is an opportunity for a business in that." But most of the time, they don't hold that thought. They don't tune into it by *visualizing* how the opportunity might be developed. They don't play it out in their minds enough to see how it might actually impact their lives.

Early in my playing career, I read a book called *Psycho-Cybernetics* by Dr. Matthew Maltz. It was a popular book of the time, selling more than 3 million copies, because it was one of the first to explain how people could use their imaginations as tools for bettering their lives. At the time, a lot of establishment scientists scoffed but today, of course, a great deal of research has been done showing that most of Maltz's theories are grounded in fact. We know today, for example, that *emotional intelligence*—self-control, self-motivation, and persistence—is every bit as important to your success in life as intellect.

Maltz, whose book is really a guide to building emotional intelligence, wrote about an experiment that he did with a group of basketball players. He had five of them practice shooting foul shots in the gym for five days while five other team members practiced shooting *mentally* by visualizing themselves shooting free throws and making each shot. Then, he staged a contest between the two teams and the guys who had spent five days just visualizing themselves making free throws blew away those who had done it physically.

Maltz's account of that experiment really intrigued me. As a relative midget in the NFL's land of the giants, I was looking for any advantage I could find, so I became a rabid practitioner of visualization. Every night before a game, I sat down for several hours in a quiet place and played the game out in my mind. I put myself in game situations with third down and two yards to go for the first on the left hash mark. I visualized the pass rushers and defensive backs knocking my receivers down. I visualized myself completing passes and running each of the plays in my game plan, so that when situations arose on the field and other guys might be panicking or upset, I could handle it because I'd already been there in my mind's eye.

After a while, visualization became almost instinctive for me. I would do it while riding from practice to my home, while watching television at night, and while getting dressed for the games. It became a natural part of my preparation for football and, later, for business.

Now, I visualize meetings before I go into them, and when I spot an opportunity, even if it is just a fleeting thought, I tune into it and visualize it all the way through to implementation and completion. Sometimes this only takes a few seconds if, in my mental runthrough, I run into some huge obstacle, or some aspect of it immediately seems unappealing. If the idea seems appealing, however, I might spend days turning it over in my mind, examining it from all angles and for all ramifications so that by the time I decide to go with it, I've already done it in my mind. Visualization is an extraordinary tool in developing OSP, because it focuses your mind and helps you explore all opportunities and avenues without taking risks.

Nearly three decades ago, freelance writers Milton and Larry Gralla envisioned creating a magazine devoted to kitchen design and remodeling. The entrepreneurial brothers sensed that the baby boom would cause that industry to explode, too. They kicked the idea around and even tried to raise some money from publishers but no one else shared their vision. They each went back to their freelance work until one day they began talking about the magazine again and realized that they would never forgive themselves if they didn't give it a try.

They raised $20,000 from savings and family members and put out their first issue of *Kitchen Business*. It did so well that in the years that followed, the brothers created 20 more specialty magazines and a trade-show division. Several years ago, they sold Gralla Publications and the magazine that no other publisher could envision, for $73 million, and today they are still active as consultants and entrepreneurs.

The abilities to sense opportunity, to act on creative and imaginative ideas, and to visualize products are all critical to your entrepreneurial success, but it is equally important, as you will learn in the next chapter, to decide which opportunities are most suited to your individual talents, interests, values, and personal goals.

I know I could work for somebody else but I'd always feel like I wasn't gettin' paid what I was worth, which probably ain't much of nothin'.

— RUTH BROOKS

WHAT SUITS YOU?

NEXT TO Ruth Brooks, my favorite small-business entrepreneur in the North Georgia mountains would have to be Charlie Poole, owner and operator of the Anchorage Marina on Lake Burton. When I am up at our lake place, I take my boat all the way across the lake, going flat out for 20 minutes and passing several other marinas, because I enjoy talking with Charlie so much. Like Ruth, Charlie is a small-business entrepreneur with an uncommon amount of common sense. His wife Suzanne makes awfully good coffee, too. They always have a newspaper for me to read. My kids and grandkids often come along because they love to play with the Pooles' cats and dogs. Their marina is a very comfortable, family type of place where people feel welcome. It is also a highly successful business developed by a savvy entrepreneur who is doing what he loves to do and making a good living at it.

Charlie, who holds a number of patents even though he never obtained a college degree, is a self-made, self-taught man. He

worked for 33 years as a mechanical engineer in the textile industry, but quit at the age of 50 to start his own business. "I got tired
of sitting in meetings rather than running a job," he said. "We
would have five-hour meetings three or four times a week and it
didn't help us at all."

After quitting his secure job, Charlie moved to the North Georgia mountains, where he loved to trout fish and had owned a cabin
for many years. He sold his cabin to raise the money needed to
buy a marina on Lake Burton. Back then, the marina was little
more than a filling station with a couple of boat docks, but Charlie
had plans for it.

Over the years, Charlie has built the little marina into a full-
service operation with a repair shop, year-round storage for 150
boats, a grocery store, bait shop, and boat dealership. Charlie, who
looks like Paul Newman modeling for one of those fashionably
rustic Ralph Lauren ads, is well into his seventies now, but he has
no plans to retire. He loves his work. It is his life. It suits him.

"When I sit down to breakfast each morning to have a sausage
biscuit and a cup of coffee, I look at the mountains and the lake
and the trees and think what a great place this is to live," he said.
"It's great to know too that our business is supporting the family
and that we are secure for as long as we want to run it, and that
we can run it the way we want to do it."

I think Charlie has built the sort of business and created the
sort of life that a great many people would like to have. He is
doing what he enjoys, living where he wants to live, and providing
for his family. That is probably the goal of a great many people
today. There is no reason why they shouldn't be able to achieve it
as Charlie has.

FINDING THE RIGHT FIT
. . . .

At the beginning of the previous chapter, I told you how I spotted
an opportunity for a very lucrative business while waiting in line at
the airport ticket counter. What I did not tell you is that as soon as I
got the ticket-jacket business up and running strong, I bailed out.

Why, Fran, why did you jump? you ask.

Because once I took this particular opportunity and turned it into reality, I realized it was not the sort of business I would enjoy being involved in over a long period of time. It was a very good business as far as making money, but for me there was no great challenge to it. It was, essentially, a printing business, so I sold it to the printer who had been my partner from the start.

The lesson in this story is that developing the ability to find opportunities is an important skill for the entrepreneur, but you must also be able to determine which opportunities are best suited to your talents and interests. Entrepreneurship is a lifestyle, and if you are going to live with your business, you had better make sure that it is compatible with the way you want to live your life. Charlie Poole may well be the perfect example of someone who has built a business perfectly suited to his preferred style of living. It shows. I think that is why I enjoy visiting his marina so much. It is such a comfortable place because Charlie is so comfortable with his life. I think that comfort level is something every small-business entrepreneur should strive to build. That's why I sold off the ticket-printing business. It just did not suit me.

One of the founders of our country, Thomas Jefferson, envisioned a nation of independent merchants and farmers and, less than 100 years ago, most Americans worked for themselves. Today, more and more are looking to go back to the future, to practice a craft, to do what they do best, to enjoy life while building wealth.

Quick, make a list of the 10 happiest people you know. What do they all have in common? I'll bet that the great majority, say eight out of the 10, are doing something that they love to do and making a good living at it. Such a simple concept, but it can be so difficult to achieve.

Jody Severson of Rapid City, South Dakota, had a successful small advertising agency, but he found that being the boss took him away from actually doing what he enjoyed the most— working as a political consultant. He unshackled himself from 15 employees, paperwork, and managing others to do what more than 20 million Americans are now doing, flying solo in their own one-person companies.

"I decided one day . . . I was going to do only what I really liked to do, which was not managing a bunch of people," Severson told *Inc.* magazine. "I told myself I'm not going to take on work I don't want to do and I'm not going to have anyone else's salary to worry about. I want no bosses, no employees hanging like an anchor around my neck."

Whether you fly solo in a *virtual business*, as some lone eagles call their one-man bands, or whether you start out with 100 employees, more and more people today want their work to bring quality and enjoyment to their lives, as well as more control and greater financial security. In many cases, too, they are looking for greater challenges and more stimulating work. Shortly after I left football, I received offers to coach probably once a week for several years. I still get them occasionally. Many people think it would be a great opportunity to get back into a game that I once loved. My feeling is been there, done that. I feel the same about offers to be a sports commentator or to get back in the booth for *Monday Night Football*. I had a lot of fun doing that years ago, but I am more interested now in the challenges of business entrepreneurship.

Why do people go into business for themselves? It isn't to be bored or unchallenged. You can get that working for someone else while letting the owner handle all the headaches. If you are going to go to all the trouble and take all of the risk involved in running your own business, at the very least you should be doing something that you love, something that makes it a pleasure to go to work.

The greatest advantage we have as small-business entrepreneurs is that we get to do something that interests us in a working environment and culture that we create to suit our tastes and temperaments. Why get into business for yourself if it isn't something that allows you to use your talents and to pursue your interests and to challenge you so that you keep growing?

Certainly, you go into business to make money. Don't ever forget that one, because as soon as you do, you will no longer be in business. But the focus of the small-business entrepreneur should not be fixed on making money. In a study of 138 entrepreneurs and their businesses conducted by the University of Houston's small-business development center, only eight percent of those who started a business simply "to make more money" were successful. Thirty-three percent of those people who started a business because they had identified a market opportunity were successful. Fifty-four percent of those who started a business because they wanted autonomy and independence succeeded.

Obviously, you are crazy if you get into business to *lose* money. But doing it just to make money may be a flawed approach to entrepreneurship. Counting your profits is the business equivalent of keeping score in sports: You can't play and watch the scoreboard at the same time. If you take care of business on the field and in the office, the score should take care of itself.

DO WHAT YOU LIKE AND MAKE IT PAY

Learning to identify opportunities is one thing, finding the right one for you is an entirely different matter, and a critical one. But it shouldn't be all that difficult. You don't have to hire a team of consultants, go off to a temple in Tibet, or spend weeks in the public library pouring through self-help books. As Severson noted, for him deciding what to do was like "falling off a log."

A simple formula: *Do something you like to do.*

The one addendum that complicates it, of course, is that: *It has to be something that other people, a lot of other people, will pay for.*

Doing what you enjoy and making money at it may not be as difficult to achieve as it might seem at first. As you will discover in the examples that follow, there are already a great many small-business entrepreneurs out there pursuing lifelong goals, and reaping the full benefits of their work and skills and talents.

I don't have any talents, you say? Can you shop? Ten years ago, Elysa Lazar was a young working woman in New York who couldn't afford to pay retail, so she became an avid bargain hunter. She discovered she had good instincts for tracking and bagging designerwear at unpublicized discount showroom sales in which the markdowns are so huge that it makes paying full price seem like a violation of all ten commandments.

With a business degree from Columbia University and a few years in the corporate world, Lazar recognized a market niche that would suit her nicely. She began publishing *The S&B Report*, a sales-and-bargains newsletter that announces the dates and locations of low-price sales of high-price designer items including clothes, linens, and jewelry.

Lazar launched the newsletter not so much because she though it would make her huge amounts of money, but because it appealed to her and she thought others with excellent taste but modest budgets would feel the same way. Like most entrepreneurs, she encountered those who didn't share her enthusiasm initially. "I left my job—my friends and family thought I was crazy—and started a business out of my apartment, funded by me," she said in an interview. "Then it started catching on, and I started hearing from people who really appreciated what we were doing."

Shopping not your bag? Can you walk?

Seth Kamil and Ed O'Donnell were graduate students at Columbia University when they became desperate for cash to live on. In talking about their dilemma to a professor specializing in urban history, he suggested they take something he did for students occasionally and turn it into a business—giving walking history tours of New York City.

Big Onion Walking Tours, which usually employs about 10 other starving grad students, now conducts more than 700 walking tours each year and draws as many as 500 participants a day. The guides, many of whom are historians, often use anecdotes and historical stories gathered in their scholarly research. The business has done so well, that Kamil told *Inc.* magazine that he may not be able to give it up once he gets his graduate degree: "I don't know if I can walk away from this now. We're growing so fast and I'm just not sure I can find another opportunity as exciting as this one."

Most entrepreneurial businesses start with an idea, a flash of inspiration, a desire to make a living doing what you enjoy, or, as in Kamil's case—a desperate need to get groceries. If you choose your opportunities wisely—if you start a business that also fills a need or provides a service that others are willing to pay for—your passion can have a big pay-off. In the case of Elysa Lazar, her modest idea about helping others find bargain buys has had an incredible payoff.

Her first newsletter was seen by Michael Gelman, executive producer for *Live with Regis & Kathie Lee*. He invited Lazar on the show to report on sample sales in Manhattan, which led to an appearance on *Oprah!*, in which she snared a $600 spring wardrobe from national discount stores, and a regular stint on CNBC's *Steals and Deals* cable show.

The *S&B Report*, published monthly, now has more than 12,000 subscribers who pay $49 a year for the tipsheet. Lazar also puts out a weekly listing of exclusive sales, for which 3,000 subscribers pay an additional $104 to receive along with the *S&B Report*. The queen of bargain shoppers has also written three hunting guides: *Outlet Shoppers Guide, Shop by Mail*, and *Museum Shop Treasures*. Not content to rest on her discounted sales receipts, Lazar conducts seminars for corporations and adult-education groups on topics ranging from dressing for success to building a wardrobe on a budget.

Lazar's passion for a good deal is now a business with more than $1 million in sales, and is still growing. We tend to forget that one of the greatest things about this country is that you can actually take an idea that appeals to you and create a business. More businesses are launched with enthusiasm than with skill, and very often it is the business that comes from the heart that endures because the entrepreneur is committed to making it work.

Often this commitment comes from an idea that simply makes good sense. These ideas may spring from the entrepreneur's own need for a product or service, or, as in the case of my ticket-jacket business, from a simple but striking perception.

Many successful entrepreneurs will tell you that they got into business before they even thought about starting a business. How does that work? Dan Hoard and Tom Bunnell of Seattle were clowning around one day while taking a breather during a backpacking jaunt in Australia. For reasons only the entrepreneurial gods may divine, Hoard was inspired to chop off the lower part of a pants leg. He then put it on his head for a cheap laugh. "It looks like a head sock," he proclaimed. He got the laugh; in fact, he and Bunnell thought it was so funny that when they returned to the United States, they drove around the Pacific Northwest test-marketing their *Mambosoks* out of the back of their van. They even handed out five of them to a wedding party, which inspired the bride and groom and friends to wear them while doing the polka at the reception.

The first 1,000 Mambosoks were produced in the spring of 1991. Tom sold them from behind the bar he was tending, and ran out of Mambosok stock in two weeks. Over the next six months, the two accidental entrepreneurs took in $200,000 from head sock sales. Within the first two years, they had sales of $1 million.

Like many entrepreneurs, they never had a formal or written business plan. They didn't dare seek financing for fear of being laughed out of the bank. They had no idea what *cash flow* meant until their bank account dropped below $100, and they figured that they'd better get serious about business and take a look at sales and production figures. When knockoffs began showing up, they diversified into shirts, shorts, and caps. In 1993, the two buddies had sales of about $3 million, and, believe it or not, a real business that started as a cheap joke. "We wanted to do something fun, something funky," Bunnell told *Inc.* magazine. "It turned out to be a business."

What better reason is there to start a business? To do something enjoyable, something interesting, and to make money too? True entrepreneurs enjoy what they do, they have a passion for it. If they don't enjoy what they are doing, they generally sell out and look for something that they enjoy more.

Here are tips on how to get into a business that will be interesting and enjoyable over the long term. As you go over them, remember this. Don't jump into a business simply because you are fed up with working for someone else. Big mistake, folks. If you hate your job, find a new one, and work on your own business ideas on your own time. Don't get into something, commit your time and money, and realize too late that you have made a mistake.

1. Turn your hobby into a business, so that you never have to go to work.

Sonny Hootman of Farmington, Iowa, liked to fish for catfish. Like most catfishermen, a strange and exotic breed of sportsman, he made his own bait out of rotten cheese with other secret ingredients thrown in. Sonny's special blend worked like catfish catnip. It didn't take long for others to pick up the scent. Soon, Sonny was making bait for his friends, and selling some, too. In fact, it wasn't long before he was making 100,000 pounds a year of Sonny's Super Sticky Channel Catfish Bait, and taking it to the bank. I'm not talking about the riverbank either. "We are sort of a cross between the redneck world and the business world," he said.

A warning here. Actually two warnings. Number One: Do not eat Sonny's catfish bait, a mistake that small children, dogs, and the occasional undiscriminating late-night refrigerator raider have made. Warning Number Two: Be aware that if you turn your hobby into a business, you probably won't get to simply enjoy your hobby anymore.

Nowadays, when Sonny goes fishing, it's *field-testing*.

Entrepreneur Greg Rothman's small business was created from an entirely different scent: Chocolate. An unrepentant chocoholic, Rothman became enamored of high-quality Belgian Leonidas chocolates, which sell for $19 a pound, after his parents brought some home to him from abroad. From that point on, whenever he learned of someone going to Europe, he requested the chocolates.

Finally, in 1996, Rothman stopped relying on friends and family and, with partner Rick Ciancuillo, opened up a Leonidas chocolate shop in Chicago—one of only a handful of the franchises in the U.S.

As in the case of Sonny Hootman's hobby turned business, Rothman also has discovered a drawback to turning pleasure into work. When he indulges his sweet tooth now, he is biting into his bottom line.

2. Think about something that you needed or wanted and couldn't find, and then make it your business to provide it.

After growing up in Venezuela, Rostislav Ordovsky-Tanaevsky made his first trip to the homeland of his Russian father in 1984. While on business in Uzbekistan in the Soviet Union, he contacted relatives from whom his father had not heard since 1917. When he went to buy film to photograph the relatives, he couldn't find it anywhere. Later, when he went to have lunch, he found the conditions in restaurants dismal. One had no seats. Another was closed for "sanitation hour."

These deficiencies triggered the opportunity-sensing perceptions of Ordovsky-Tanaevsky, a natural-born entrepreneur who had started his first business in college and his second upon graduation. He found the business opportunities in his father's homeland enticing, particularly after he met and fell in love with a ballerina. He first opened a film store and a restaurant, in response to the opportunities he spotted on his initial visit. His OSP appears to have been right on target. Today, Ordovsky-Tanaevsky, in partnership with Kodak, owns several hundred *Fokus* photo retail stores in the former Soviet Union and he is also Moscow's leading restaurateur. He owns a chain of hamburger and pizza joints, New York style delicatessens, and assorted theme restaurants. His company, Rostik International, has revenues in excess of $100 million and employs about 6,000 people. He is a major business owner today, but he started out with one restaurant and one photo shop, both of which were inspired by what he observed on his first visit.

Noel A. Kreiker of Chicago is another entrepreneur whose small business arose out of a need she perceived while on an overseas visit. When her husband was transferred to Bogota, Colombia, Kreicker packed up their two children like a trouper, since she had once served in the Peace Corps in the Philippines. Still, the one-year stint was a disaster, she said, because the family had no understanding of the language or customs.

To remedy that problem for other transferred families, Kreicker founded International Orientation Resources, Inc., which employs 35 full-time professionals at its Chicago headquarters, and 15 other staff at offices in Detroit; Portland, Oregon; London; Singapore; and Cologne, Germany.

3. Find a problem and fix it.

There was a blacksmith from Vermont who moved to Illinois to farm in the 1830's. When he got to central Illinois, he found it difficult to plow the rich but dense clay soil, so he used his blacksmithing skills to build a better plow. Other farmers asked him to build them similar plows and soon, he had quite the business going: In fact, I'm told it's still going strong, running like a Deere—John Deere.

That farmer-entrepreneur saw a problem, then created a business to address it. He created one of this nation's greatest businesses while fixing that problem, and that is how a great many other enterprises have come into being. Your OSP doesn't have to have a satellite link to spot these kind of opportunities, but you do have to have your antennae up.

Roland Dugas was a hospital administrator in Lafayette, Louisiana, in 1971, when he and two fellow hospital workers, Richard Zuschlag and Rolland Buckner, found themselves discussing the lack of adequate ambulance service in their community and region. Local funeral homes that had once provided ambulances had decided to stop the service, leaving many neighboring communities without any rescue or emergency vehicles.

Dugas and his friends decided that since ambulances were vital to these towns, they would start an ambulance service by asking their clientele to help them finance it. They sold $49 annual memberships through a community telethon that first year. Acadian Ambulance Service has more than 140,000 members and a renewal rate of 90 percent. Their original small business designed to fix a problem has proved to be such a good solution that it has grown to a big one that employees 920 and has revenues of more than $58 million.

4. Start a fad.

As the makers of the Hula Hoop, Silly Putty, and Beanie Babies will gladly tell you, there is nothing that will put a company into the profit column quicker than a toy or product that becomes a major fad. It takes a lot of luck and perseverance to tap into this entrepreneurial market, and there are no surefire guarantees of success, but that doesn't stop a lot of entrepreneurs from chasing the dream. Mike Manisso is a man in search of a fad. This inventor and entrepreneur from Newark, Delaware, is president of Forte Sports, whose first product was the Wild Ball soccer ball. Manisso attempted to cash in on the growing popularity of soccer in the U.S. by marketing soccer balls with zebra and tiger stripes. That shot missed the goal. But he came back with the Bungee Bag, a combination paddle ball and yo-yo, also in zebra and tiger stripes.

Like most small-business entrepreneurs, Manisso didn't have money to market his product in a big way, so he sent boxes of the Bungee Bags to strategic targets—including the casts of trendy television shows such as *Friends* and *Seinfeld*. His greatest results came from an appearance on the QVC television shopping program. His 10 minutes there resulted in 9,000 sales, launched his product nationwide, and got the attention of major retailers like Kay-Bee Toys, Disney Stores, Wal-Mart, Kmart, Target, and Walgreens.

5. Do something good for people.

Peter Yates had a successful business that made catheters used to diagnose medical problems such as heart disease. But he decided what really suited him was creating products that didn't just identify problems, but solved them too. The English entrepreneur wanted to have a profitable company, but he also wanted to create products that benefitted society. He now runs Hyper-Quest, a CD-ROM publisher specializing in entertainment/educational titles for children that teach astronomy, archaeology, mythology, and anthropology in interesting, amusing, and nonviolent ways. "I'm not interested in being a social worker, but I get more excited by products that go beyond filling a need," he told *Inc.* magazine.

6. Beat the big guys at their own game by providing high-quality products and services.

Founded in 1927, Harry W. Schwartz Bookshops in Milwaukee has been battling the Wal-Martization of the book store business for nearly 20 years. David Schwartz, who has run the family business since 1972, has had to take what was once a high-minded literary bookstore in battle with the high-volume chains and superstores such as Waldenbooks, Barnes & Noble, Borders, and others.

Schwartz admitted in an interview that when competition intensified in the early 1980's, "I was totally unlettered in the business part of my profession. I knew how to buy books from the sales reps, and I knew how to sell them to people. And I knew nothing about the business in between." He has learned.

To survive into the 1990's, Schwartz has had to:

- merge with a competitor
- take in a silent partner
- open a mall store
- close old stores, open new ones
- enlarge his stores from 4,000 square feet to 9,000 square feet to 15,000 square feet.
- embrace the "bestsellers" that he once scorned
- reverse past policy and begin encouraging browsing
- discount a whole range of books
- develop a specialty in direct sales of business books
- offer free coffee, t-shirts, audiotapes, dolls, and toys

In general, Schwartz and his partners have had to go to war by becoming professional *retailers* rather than booksellers. They chose to fight head to head with the bigger stores by essentially going back to school and learning how to run their smaller operation as if it was a superstore chain.

7. Steal the crumbs from the big guys and make cake.

Schwartz is not alone in his battle. Everywhere you look, in towns big and small, huge superstores seem to dominate. The giants would appear to rule whether selling hardware, books, groceries, or electronic goods. But if you look carefully, small-business entrepreneurs like Schwartz are thriving under the radar of the big guys. While Schwartz chose to take the superstores on head to head by mimicking their methods, others are choosing to find niches by stealing small bits of their market and building customer loyalty based on quality goods and, above all else, top-notch, even extraordinary, service.

Richard Foos started a business with $3 worth of used records that nobody else wanted, then he and partner Harold Bronson turned it into a $70 million company by producing collections of novelty tunes and oldies music that the major record companies considered unprofitable. Former antiestablishment entrepreneurs Foos and Bronson are the creators of Rhino Records, Inc. While only ten percent of the records produced in the U.S. turn a profit, Rhino beats the establishment by making money on 90 percent of its releases.

I am quite familiar with several small-business entrepreneurs who have created big profits by sneaking in under the radar of the bigger competition. One of my favorites—shared by my wife, I might add—is Atlanta jeweler Haim Haviv who has a tiny, one-room jewelry store hidden away in an office building, but who probably does $20 million in business each year just from the people *I* send to him. I heard about Haim from my secretary; in fact, the *only* way to find him is by word of mouth. Yet, he has thrived in the affluent Buckhead neighborhood of Atlanta, where there are scores of big jewelry stores, because of his high-quality and highly personal service.

When I first went in to shop at Haim's store, I was underwhelmed. He had a very limited selection, but he told me to tell him exactly what I was looking for and he promised to get it for me. A few days later, he called and told me to come back in. "Here it is," he said, "and here is my price. But before you buy, go across the street and price the same product in some other jewelry stores at the Lenox Square Mall."

Not one to turn down a bargain-hunting mission, I did just as Haim instructed. Every other jewelry store that had the product was charging at least three times Haim's price. From that point on, I never purchased jewelry from anyone else. Haim is ethical, and he gives great value, great quality, and great service. If I called him up right now and said I wanted an emerald the size of my fist, he'd have a dozen lined up for me tomorrow morning.

How does he do it? Well, I don't know where he finds such

top-quality jewelry, but I can guess that since he doesn't have an enormous overhead, huge advertising, and marketing costs, or dozens of employees, Haim is able to keep his costs down. But even that wouldn't work if he didn't provide excellent service, too. I hesitate to say he is flying under the radar, though. I would be more inclined to say that Haim flies *over* it.

Small-business entrepreneurs cannot compete head to head with the big chains when it comes to product range or inventory, but if they hone in on a niche market and offer relentlessly good products and services, they can thrive as Haim has, by building customer loyalty.

Another *prime* example of this, if you will pardon the expression, is City Meat Market Inc., in Naperville, a suburb of Chicago. This is a company that has been around for 105 years simply because it has incredible customer loyalty. Current owners Tom and Deborah Klingbeil have owned City Meat Market for 23 years, and even though people are consuming less beef these days, when they do work up a hunger for red meat, they often want high-quality beef.

Although prices are higher at City Meat Market, the level of service keeps customers coming. To cater to on-the-go suburban families, the Klingbeils have recently begun offering fully pre-pared meals, broadening their market and winning even more loyal customers.

8. Create art and a business.

I suppose there are still a great many starving artists out there, but after learning about Christian Riese Lassen from my friends at *Success* magazine, I have to wonder why. There is no reason for gifted and creative people, whether they are musicians, painters, writers, singers, or dancers, to feel they have to sacrifice or suffer for their art. I don't think Pablo Picasso, considered to be the greatest artist of this century, suffered a great deal. A genius in painting, sculpture, etching, stage design, and ceramics, Picasso was also an entrepreneur who knew how to market his talents. He understood that while you should be true to your talents, there is no dishonor in profiting from them. Certainly the great chefs are artists, and they too are well compensated. So why not other artists? While growing up in Hawaii, Christian Lassen always found a way to practice his artistic skills while also profiting from them. As a teenager, he decorated his friends' surfboards with elaborate designs that eventually attracted the attention of one of the top art galleries in the islands. Eventually, though, Lassen grew unhappy with the way his work was marketed. He felt he was treated like "a surfer kid," and, so, he became determined to gain control over the merchandising of his art.

In 1982, he gathered up $1,000 to print a limited-edition poster of his work, which a Japanese distributor snapped up. That was all the confirmation Lassen needed. From that point on, he made prints of every painting so that his work could be sold to and appreciated by thousands rather than by one individual. He also realized that he could extend his market by licensing his works. He made deals with Disney, Panasonic and the American Greeting Card Company.

Considered one of the world's leading environmental artists, Lassen is now known around the world. His paintings sell for more than $100,000, and his Las Vegas company, Lassen International Inc., produces posters, t-shirts and other products bearing his distinctive work. He normally paints half the day and then conducts his $30 million business, which has 150 employees and seven art galleries, during the rest of the day. "For both artists and entrepreneurs, a blank canvas represents opportunity," he told *Success*. "You need unbelievable tenacity and a strong sense of completion to turn your vision into reality."

9. Find gold in a lost market.

Big companies are geared to big markets and, often, it is not worth their time or expense to explore smaller and perhaps difficult to reach markets. That leaves ample opportunities for small-business entrepreneurs like Lyn Smith, a Caterpillar factory worker in Pontiac, Illinois, who has turned his penchant for old Chevy Nova cars into a very good side business run out of his home.

When he had difficulty finding obscure parts for his hot rods and for those he rebuilt and reconditioned for other people, Smitty, as he is known on the drag racing circuit, began searching out parts at car-parts swap meets held across the Midwest. He found many items there that he needed, and also discovered that a lot of the old parts he had lying around his garage were going for good prices. He began attending more swap meets as an exhibitor, particularly after a longtime local Chevy dealer closed down and sold off its buildings and contents. Smitty cut a deal to buy everything in the dealer's parts storage room for a flat low price and for hauling it all away. The room proved to be a swap-meet man's gold mine and Smitty turned a small investment into a major profit in short order.

There were still some parts, like wheel and headlight rims, that were difficult to find even at swap meets, so Smitty began advertising to buy old parts in car magazines. Most came in badly battered and rusted, but he sends them to reconditioners who restore them for him. He sells the reconditioned rims all over the country to a market that big auto-parts suppliers have yet to tap, although most swap-meet goers will tell you that this can be a very lucrative business.

Another market that always seems to have room for small-business entrepreneurs is the college campus. It is estimated that this country's 14.5 million college students spend an estimated $30 billion to $60 billion a year. One of them, Raymond Sozi, was living on a tight budget while attending an expensive Ivy League school when he realized that there was a ripe market for a discount card catering to his cash-strapped peers. He created the Student Advantage card, which offers reduced rates on everything from CDs to train tickets. While this market has been mined before, Sozi took it a few giant steps further by going national with his card, and signing on big brand companies like Kinko's and Amtrak, as well as local mom 'n' pop places popular on each campus.

His Boston-based business has 500,000 members on more than 1,000 campuses. Students pay $20 each for an annual membership, producing annual sales of $1 million, which is expected to multiply quickly.

Chip Paucek and James Rena also found an opportunity among

the student minds and bodies on their campus. The George Washington University graduates came up with a plan to make dry subjects like macroeconomics and statistics more palatable with supplementary course videos featuring comedians and actors. After raising $95,000 in startup capital for their Cerebellum Corp., of McLean, Virginia, they at first marketed their videos with titles like *The Creepy Crawly World of Calculus* or *The Dissected World of Biology.* They succeeded in placing their products in 150 college bookstores around the country and success appeared to be at hand, except for one significant problem. The videos didn't move off the shelves.

Stunned by their lack of sales, Paucek and Rena began interviewing students to find out where they had gone wrong. The word came back that the tapes, priced at $29.99, were too expensive, and the packaging, which emphasized fun more than facts, did not convey that there was valuable information offered on the tapes.

Armed with this information, the two entrepreneurs recalled each and every unsold video, ripped off the old covers, put on new ones, and dropped the price to $19.99. They sold like Jane Fonda's workout tapes. Cerebellum now offers 11 types of instructional videos that are sold at 1,100 bookstores. Revenues now exceed $1 million annually.

10. Take an old idea and use new technology to create a business.

Twins Jason and Matthew Olim were a couple of jazz buffs frustrated by the poor selection in most music stores, so these young entrepreneurs opened one of the first music cyberstores on the Internet. Their CDNow offers every jazz album made in the U.S. and nearly 20,000 imports, as well as thousands of other CDs, cassettes, t-shirts, and other items.

Unlike the typical record store, however, the Olim's business has very little overhead, and no inventory. The brothers take orders at their homepage (cdnow.com) and then contact distributors who send the product out, delivering most within 24 hours. Sales and advertising revenues were around $6 million in 1996, and sales were being doubled every couple of months.

CDNow is what is commonly known as a *virtual business.* The

Olim brothers, who wear ponytails and prefer to go shoeless in their corporate office in suburban Philadelphia, came up with the idea for their business in 1994. Jason, who was then a programmer for a software company, dreamed up the basic concept while talking with friends about the limited selection and lack of music knowledge by sales staff in most record stores. He envisioned a virtual record store where shoppers would not have to leave their homes or offices to search for selections by their favorite artists, albums, or record companies, or to browse through their favorite musical genre, whether it be classical guitar or acoustic New Orleans blues.

Jason, whose previous entrepreneurial experience was limited to a house-painting service that paid his bills while he attended Brown University, figured he could get his CDs and cassettes wholesale, charge a slight markup and do enough volume to turn a profit. He initially planned on having just three employees to run the business.

Jason's plan may have been overly simple, but his timing could not have been better. In 1995, CDNow's first full year in operation, the number of people using the Internet increased eightfold, from one million to eight million. By the next year, it was estimated to have increased to 13 million.

The twins also managed to start their business with minimal funds. Jason used $1,500 he had saved for a guitar to purchase a new computer instead. He spent another $500 for a software license. He later used $12,000 of his own money and a $70,000 loan from a private investor to get the virtual business rolling, but revenues quickly began paying all other costs.

He and his brother built their record store in the basement of their parents' home on weekends and after work. Matthew wrote the thousands of lines of computer code needed, as well as the intricate software necessary to construct and manage an interactive Web site. It is said that Matthew worked so much that he had to brush his teeth in front of his computer.

The brothers sold their first CD in August 1994, six months after Jason dreamed up the idea. Sales in the first month were $392. A year later, they did $189,000 in the first month. In 1995, total sales reached $2 million. By early 1996, the CDNow web page was attracting 300,000 shoppers per month and taking 300 orders a day with the average sale being $40.

Although their profit margin is very slim, about 12 percent, the Olims believe that their business will experience even greater increases in volume as more and more people become comfortable shopping, and giving their credit card numbers, over the Internet. They also believe there is another source of income, one that Jason had not envisioned, to be developed for their virtual record shop—advertising on their web page.

The Microsoft Network selected CDNow as a test site for on-line ads in early 1996. The Olims began charging four cents every time someone clicked on a web page carrying an ad. One hundred thousand clicks were recorded, bringing in $4,000. To tap that source of income, they have launched some ingenious, if unusual advertising. Computers linked to the Internet through colleges and universities were treated to the message "Hey, you! The college kid in front of the screen. Get 10 percent off all Geffen titles." If that didn't get the message across, a few screens later, there was a followup: "We asked you nicely the first time, now get your ass in here."

At last report, Jason estimated that CDNow will be taking in as much as $3 million in advertising revenue. The brothers already are also licensing and selling the technology they developed to create their store to both direct competitors and similar ventures selling videos. They are also planning to offer live concerts online.

The Olim brothers say the key to their success was "vision, drive, and execution." Their motto is "Every week is a revolution."

THE QUESTIONS TO ASK YOURSELF

. . . .

The Olim twins appear to be a great entrepreneurial success story. They took a basic idea and through their own obviously abundant skills they created a dynamic business. Their business will surely face some challenges from competitors eager to match their success, particularly the big record store chains that will surely wade into this new market, so the Olims have to be prepared. Small-business entrepreneurs are faced with a steady barrage of opportunities and challenges every day. The inventive Olim twins seem to be up to these challenges, but believe me, they will be tested. Every company has its unique attributes and its unique problems. That is why even very similar companies, such as Microsoft and Sun Microsystems, grow in very different ways.

When faced with problems and challenges, small business entrepreneurs have to make decisions that are appropriate for their business. They have to learn to analyze situations, establish priorities, and make those decisions wisely. Before you decide what type of business to operate, there are some key considerations to take into account. Every small-business entrepreneur needs to consider the following points while preparing for the challenges of creating, starting, and running a business.

Define your business goals to match your personal goals.

What do you want, not just out of business, but life? You are sadly mistaken if you think your personal life and your business career are separate matters. They are woven so tightly together that you may as well acknowledge it from the start, rather than head off on the wrong lonesome road. I have known people who thought the two aspects were separate and I have known people who did all they could to keep them separate. Both approaches are laden with trouble.

Before you set your goals as an entrepreneur, take time to give careful consideration to how well they match up with your personal goals. As in the case of the airline jacket printing business, I decided in short order that it was not the sort of thing that really matched up with the life I wanted. It was a great and lucrative business, it just wasn't my cup of tea.

Like Charlie Poole, many entrepreneurs say they crave independence and control over their careers, but when you are starting out, you need to be more specific, just as Charlie was. He wanted to be his own boss, but he also had a specific goal to live in the North Georgia mountains and to be involved in a business that was close to his heart as a fisherman and outdoorsman.

What are your more specific goals? Are you a lifestyle entrepreneur or a profit-centered entrepreneur? Are you looking for a business to express your creativity or artistic talents? Do you want to make a big score by exploiting a new technology, building a business, selling it, and getting out? Do you want to be involved in something that contributes to the social welfare of your community over the long term? Do you enjoy a business in which you deal with the public every day, or would you prefer a more solitary pursuit?

Consider whether you are looking for a business that generates a relatively big and quick return or one that has more of a long-term payoff. Are you looking to get in and out of a business quickly to make a profit and move on? Or do you want what Charlie has built, a long-term family business that you can operate, live off, enjoy well into your retirement years, and perhaps pass on to your children and grandchildren?

Remember that each type of business carries risk, demands, and sacrifices unique to it. Charlie spent years living on very little money as he built his business into a more profitable enterprise. There was no guarantee that a bigger competitor wouldn't move onto the lake and blow him out of the water. He tried things, such as a sandwich shop, that didn't work out, and he tried some that he didn't think would work but did—such as his wife's suggestion that they sell clothing items, too.

The small-business entrepreneur may escape long meetings and bureaucratic infighting, but there is no escaping long days and sleepless nights fretting whether the next shipment will come in, or go out. Entrepreneurs often complain that they have to wear many hats, and bear all the responsibility, but those who make that complaint are often people who did not give specific thought to their decision to go into business. Before you commit to starting a business, think long and hard about whether it will satisfy you personally and professionally, if it will demand that you take greater risks or make bigger sacrifices than you are willing to take on or are capable of handling. In other words, make sure your business will provide the lifestyle you want, because owning a small business is a way of life, not a job.

Define your specific strategy for starting and running your business.

The worst situation a fledgling small-business owner can get into is to have a business up and running and then one day be hit with the realization: *I don't know where I am headed with this.* The entrepreneur who wants to have long-term success and a sustainable company has to have a bold and specific strategy that integrates all of your aspirations with well-defined long-term policies about the market the company will serve, its geographic reach, its technological capabilities, and other factors. To attract quality and committed employees, you will need a strategy that clarifies your vision and goals for the company. This clear strategy will also help you make decisions and policies that will move your company in the right direction. Every business needs guideposts. Are you going after a niche market or taking on the industry leaders? Will you have your own sales force, or will you market in other ways?

When you have formulated a strategy, it is important to consider carefully whether it will allow the business to be profitable, and whether it permits for growth. Will it be competitive? A small business such as a neighborhood dry-cleaning store may seem like a good way to benefit from your own hard work but it is difficult to generate the sort of big profits that can free you to hire employees to do most of the work. Mail-order businesses are all the rage because they are relatively easy to start up, but many entrepreneurs discover that there is intense competition and often low profitability.

Before starting, the small-business entrepreneur needs to consider whether his or her business strategy will work over the long term, particularly if the business relies on cutting-edge technology, fashion trends, or government regulations that might change. They were pioneers on the Internet when they launched CDNow, but the Olim twins will soon face a great many challenges that mirror those faced by more traditional retail-business owners. Increased competition, new technology, and changing tastes will confront them as well so, like most entrepreneurs, they will have to adjust and refine their strategy as they go along.

Entrepreneurs like Charlie Poole, who has a more traditional business, also have to refine and change their strategies in order to constantly find new sources of generating income and to serve and expand their customer base. Charlie has done this by offering more boat storage, a wider range of goods in his store, including clothing and videos, and by having on-site boat repair and sales. By broadening his business, he increased profits without abandoning his basic operation.

When developing and refining your strategies it is important also to monitor whether or not you have planned for an acceptable rate of growth. To do this you have to consider the competition and its growth rate, whether the quality of your product might suffer from rapid growth and the impact that might have on your customer base, whether you can fund growth yourself, and whether you are can handle the stress and demands of a rapidly growing company.

Look deep within yourself and consider whether you have the resources, the organizational infrastructure, and the personality to make it work.

Even if you have a clearly defined strategy for your small business, it will never succeed if you, the driving force, don't have resources like qualified employees, a ready market and customer base, or available financial resources beyond your initial start-up financing.

Also vital to your ability to carry out strategy is the strength of the infrastructure of your organization. Are your manufacturing and delivery systems expandable if your business takes off? Do you have too much invested to back down if growth is slower than expected? Can your employees handle rapid growth and increased responsibility? Are there people who will be able to step up to management? Is the company culture compatible with your strategy for either long-term growth or rapid expansion?

Finally, the entrepreneur needs to consider that in starting a business, he or she may have to change with it and take on new duties. It is true also that most small-business entrepreneurs have to wear many hats, especially in the start-up phase. Are you prepared to build a company and its organizational structure and systems while keeping the books, monitoring cash flow and performance, and hiring and supervising your employees?

There is a natural evolution in any entrepreneurial enterprise in which the company founder moves from the role of visionary to actually doing the work and running the company, to then teaching others how to do it, setting goals, and then overseeing the entire operation. For me, when I get a business up and running and then bring in others to manage, it is like going from quarterback to coach. I may not enjoy it in the same way, or even quite as much, but it too has its rewards. I realize, as all entrepreneurs must, that you have to let the business develop and to do that, you have to adapt and grow with it. You have to decide whether you are the sort of entrepreneur who can nurture a business from start to finish by accepting and learning new roles as it changes, or do you prefer to get it up and running and then go seek new challenges?

Entrepreneurs, by nature, are action-oriented, seat-of-the-pants people, but if your business is to succeed over the long term, you need to make certain that the business you choose suits you and will wear well over many years and many challenges.

When you're startin' a business you've got to look ahead and make sure that you have enough money, enough help, and whatever you are gonna need to open that business or you are gonna have to work three shifts. I know because I have had to work those shifts myself.

— RUTH BROOKS

SCRAMBLING AT START-UP

W HEN I began building the Small Business NETwork, I decided I wanted a major telephone long-distance company to be a partner in it, because I wanted our members to have access to the same telephone-service packages available to bigger businesses. In searching for a long-distance partner, I started at the top at AT&T by calling for Bob Allen, the CEO, but I got no further than an assistant who directed me to the AT&T Small Business Group, which seemed like a natural-enough place to take my concept.

I thought they would be all over the idea, because the network I planned to put together had the potential for bringing in a whole lot of business from a market that is notoriously difficult to round up. But I got tossed around and thrown back and forth like a beach ball at a rock concert. I never did crack the fortress of AT&T's Small Business Group. (So much for my "celebrity pass" to the highest echelons of business).

To tell you the truth, I got knocked around a good bit at MCI and Sprint, too. All in all, I think I spent eight months on the phone trying to get a phone company to talk to me. Is there some irony in that? I'm not a literary guy, so I wouldn't know, but as an entrepreneur, I do understand that it is typical of any start-up. It doesn't matter that you have the greatest idea in the world. You are going to run your head into walls. You are going to have doors closed, if not slammed, on you and your sure-thing, sure-fire concept. It happens to us all. The late entertainer Art Linkletter often told the story of how he stood in an orange grove in California years ago while a friend tried to pitch him on this incredible fantasy he had about starting an amusement park. Linkletter told his friend Walt that he ought to stick to Mickey Mouse cartoons. Linkletter figured his decision not to buy into Disneyland probably cost him several-hundred million dollars over the years.

Walt Disney certainly had trouble getting his dream business up and running but, as we all know, it survived, which is better than most. Henry Ford failed at two start-up businesses before his car company took off. Howard Johnson ground his father's cigar store into a stub before he built an empire in the motel and restaurant business. Charles Revson had gone into the dumpster with a business that tried to sell sales-motivational material during the Depression. Then he started his beauty-care products company with four employees—himself, his brother, a receptionist, and a delivery boy.

At any given time, some 7.2 million Americans—about 4 percent of the adult population—are attempting to start a business, according to a report on entrepreneurs done by Paul Reynolds, a professor at Marquette University. Only about 10 percent of those struggling to get a business started get the job done within two years, Reynolds found. Roughly half of all start-ups go out of business within four years, mainly due to inadequate planning, undercapitalization, poor cash-flow management, and indebtedness, according to the U.S. Small Business Administration.

But even smart business entrepreneurs experience failure. In reviewing its 1996 listing of the top 500 businesses in the country, *Inc.* magazine noted that the average number of previous start-ups for each company's founder was 1.9. Henry Graff, founder of the Marque ambulance manufacturing company, had gone through 11 other start-ups. Graff had started up "far more failures than successes," before making his Marque, he told the magazine.

I have never started a company that at some point in the early going I didn't get frustrated and stop and say, *This must be a stupid idea, otherwise, why is it so hard? Why don't people get it? Why aren't they banging on my door and throwing money at me?* Or, *Why do I want to do this? I could be sitting on the dock at the lake house with my kids and grandkids. I could be playing golf with a buddy. I could be on a beach somewhere with my wife.*

Like me, you are going to have doubts when you start a business. It is part of the trial by fire that every start-up involves. Listen to what this successful entrepreneur had to say about start-up fears that afflicted him when he tried to start a magazine and couldn't get financing years ago: "There is one crucial element that doesn't appear in any business plan, as anyone who's ever tried to start a business is aware. I'm talking about fear . . . I realize that the failure may have had more to do with the F factor than with the scarcity of venture capital. Although I didn't admit it to myself at the time, I was actually trying to raise too much money for the launch, in an attempt to take the risk out of something that would have been risky from day one under the best of circumstances. The moral? Better to acknowledge the role of emotions in business and the impact they have on business decisions than to pretend they don't exist." The man who wrote that is George Gendron, who later founded *Inc.* magazine.

CLIMBING THE MOUNTAIN
. . . .

In trying to get my own network of small-business entrepreneurs put together, there have been many, many days over the last three years when I have taken one step forward and two steps back. It has been a challenge and a struggle every day and there have been times when I've thought, *this mountain is too high to climb.* But I don't let those thoughts hang around for long. I don't let the unreturned phone calls or the bureaucratic blockades discourage me to the point that I think about turning back or giving up. I believe in the Small Business NETwork. It's my mission and I know I will probably have to get bloodied, bruised, and banged about some before I can get other people to buy into it, but I wouldn't have begun the climb if I didn't think it was worth the effort.

The challenges of starting a business test your worthiness to be an entrepreneur. Coming up with a business idea does not make you an entrepreneur; taking a concept from idea to reality is the measure of your success. I think that there is a great deal of value in having to struggle at the outset. It focuses me. It hones my instincts and it strengthens my determination. Most of the greatest athletes I've known in my career and since are those who were forged in fire. They encountered hardship or failure early in their athletic careers and emerged stronger and more determined. Michael Jordan's story of being cut from the junior varsity team is now legend. His teammate Scottie Pippen was a benchwarmer who was forced to develop his skills and prove his mettle in a small junior college. The great football receiver Jerry Rice is another example of someone who had to prove himself in the early going.

Although he was drafted out of Mississippi Valley State by the San Francisco 49ers in the first round of the 1985 NFL draft, many questioned Rice's ability to play professional football. He did not have outstanding speed or size, and in his rookie year he had difficulty hanging onto the ball, catching only 49 passes.

But at the end of that first difficult season, Rice decided to spend the off-season focused on his mission to become the best receiver in football. His training regimen that summer, and for the rest of his career, has become legendary. In his second year in the NFL, he caught a few more passes. In fact, he led the league with 86 catches. In his third year, he set a record by catching 22 touchdown passes in only 12 games. He led the league in touchdown receptions for the next three years and today is regarded as probably the best receiver in the history of the game.

Rice's eventual greatness did not come without early struggle.

The same can be said about accomplishing most worthwhile things. Struggle is part of the process. If you remain focused on your mission, and if you are willing to do what it takes to accomplish it, then you can survive the struggle and so can your business.

My mission is to provide the largest single network in the world for small-business entrepreneurs, and every task I set for myself in starting out was intended to make the network attractive to my market. I wanted to offer them a corner shop where they could go to interact and share ideas and find ways to save money and make money and to grow and enhance their businesses.

I did not have a formal business plan at first because my concept was not set in concrete. I wanted to get out and talk to people, and try to figure out the best way to serve the small-business entrepreneur market before crafting a formal plan. Going through this process of starting a business as I was also putting this book together was difficult, but it did serve to remind me of all the challenges involved in launching a new enterprise. There are universal laws regarding start-ups that came to mind:

1. Starting a business always takes more time than you thought it was going to take.

This is not necessarily a bad thing. Our world moves so fast now, we've become intoxicated with the instant solution. We all want to take a pill and lose the 25 pounds that we put on over five years. Instant results is the mantra, whether it's covering up a bald spot or buying stock. Entrepreneurs, whose batteries are often a bit overcharged anyway, frequently are guilty of going after the quick fix, rather than taking their time and doing things right when starting a business.

If it is taking you longer than you thought it would to get all the pieces in place, it is probably an indication that you are taking pains to do it right rather than simply rushing to meet an arbitrary timetable. The start-up period is crucial, and I would much rather see an entrepreneur take the time necessary to do the research and test the product or service before rushing in.

Believe me, there is nothing, absolutely nothing, worse than launching a boat before it is completed. Or a restaurant. Or any other kind of business. Most of them are built around serving a customer or client, and if the first people in the door don't get what they came in for, you might as well close up shop, because it will be a very, very difficult struggle to get them to come back in the door if you disappointed them the first time around. Take your time, do it right. Get everything in place, and have all the backup systems up and ready to roll too.

Sandie Ledray of Seattle started making her own soap because her skin was sensitive to most commercial soaps. Her friends began buying all of her private stock, so she and a friend each pitched in $300 to start Brookside Soap Inc., a small business now grossing over $200,000 a year with eight varieties of bar soap. But between the $600 investments and the $200,000 gross was three years of sudsy research and package design before the first product was rolled out.

In starting your business, you should be aggressive; you have to keep pushing to get things done and to move people along and get decisions made, but the process also requires patience. This is a marathon more than it is a sprint. When you are running for distance, you know that as you start out that you are going to go through performance peaks and valleys. You will hit a wall at some point, and then when all of the really good natural juices kick in, you will get that runner's high that will get you through.

Patience is a difficult virtue for the entrepreneur. Believe me, I know. Most of us are driven, we want to make things happen. You don't want to lose that drive, even if you could, but it has to be harnessed. It's like having a baby at home. You are eager for the child to get big enough to communicate and to play with, but there is no rushing that process.

More than 30 years ago, Everett M. Rogers wrote the classic *Diffusion of Innovations,* in which he explained the process by which entrepreneurial innovations are adopted by the public and the mass market. In the book, he explained why some innovative products are embraced almost immediately while others take decades, and why some superior innovations are rejected while inferior ones prevail. One of the key lessons of this classic work is that many entrepreneurs rush their innovative products to the mass market and fail because they do not recognize a major tenet of marketing. That tenet is that most people buy a product not because they realize it is superior, but because they've seen or heard of other people using it. The majority of consumers are afraid to try something new for fear of being criticized. And so the wise and *patient* entrepreneur doesn't rush an innovative product at the mass market. Instead, the entrepreneur first tests and introduces the product to the most influential and adventuresome consumers for that product, what Rogers calls the "early adopters." If they accept the innovation and embrace it, *then* you know that it will probably succeed in the mass market.

If you were going to come out with a new line of trendy clothing today, it wouldn't be wise to run to the buyers for the major suburban department stores and push it on them. Instead, you would market it to small stores in urban areas where adventurous trendsetters hunt for the next great fashion statement. Then, when they have adopted your clothing line, you can call on the major retailers, but the chances are they already will be calling you.

Too often, the small-business entrepreneur gives in to the driven side of his or her personality, and rushes what may be a great idea or concept into reality without getting the infrastructure in place. Even the best of prospects can be irretrievably lost in those situations. I've seen it happen in business and in sports.

Few quarterbacks come out of college with more natural talent than Vinny Testaverde. He was the complete package, the prototype for the modern quarterback, a six-foot-five-inch, 215-pound Heisman Trophy winner who set records at the University of Miami for both passing yards and touchdown passes. He was the first player chosen in the 1987 draft, going to the Tampa Bay Buccaneers, who desperately needed him. Tampa Bay did Vinny a disservice, however, when they rushed him into the starting lineup late in his rookie season. It was a critical mistake that has had a lasting impact on this great athlete's playing career.

As fine a quarterback as he was at that point, Vinny was not properly prepared for the mental and physical intensity of the

NFL. It was not his fault. Even though I was thrown into action my rookie year and did okay, very few players come right out of college ready for the pros, particularly at the quarterback position. Most teams give their rookie quarterbacks at least a year to learn the system and to adjust to the higher level of play. It's not that Vinny didn't have some great games. In fact, he set a record by throwing for 369 yards against New Orleans in his rookie season but, in his second year, he had problems with inconsistency, particularly with interceptions. In 1988, he set an NFL record with 35 passes picked off. The fans got down on him, and Vinny got down on himself. It was primarily due to the fact that he was rushed in before he had been fully prepared.

After being traded to Cleveland and forced to be a backup quarterback, he eventually recovered his confidence and became a very good starting quarterback, but I have to believe that had he been allowed to develop his confidence and hone his instincts during his rookie year instead of being rushed in before he was ready, he probably would have been a quarterback of the same stature as Dan Marino and Joe Montana.

And now, back to Ahmad Rashad down on the field. Okay, you want a *business* example? Then I'll give you one, even though this is something of an embarrassing story for me to relate. Way back in time, right after the Ice Age, and before there were Golden Arches on every intersection in the world, I got into the fast-food business. This was 1968, I believe and, in truth, Ray Kroc had already been franchising his burger joints for seven years and had enjoyed tremendous success.

Burger King and other imitators were beginning to pop up all over the country, and I thought maybe I could get a piece of the action with my own version.

This was just before I got into the consulting business in the textile industry, so I had too much time on my hands. I was with the Giants in New York and we weren't exactly tearing up the NFL either. I was on the prowl for other opportunities, figuring I might need a backup job. You can probably tell I'm stalling here, because I know that you are going to laugh when I tell you the name of the fast-food franchise that was supposed to make me the Ray Kroc of jocks. Well, here goes. It was *Scrambler's Village.*

Go ahead, enjoy yourself. The name may sound silly now, but the concept was ahead of its time. On your next visit to a Kenny Rogers' Roasted Chicken or a Boston Market, take a look around. What do you see on the menu? Chicken and fish and veggies and all sorts of other food. That's what we offered at Scrambler's Village. It was a fast-food smorgasbord.

I still think it was a great concept, but we rushed into it as if people weren't going to still be hungry unless we opened yesterday. We scrambled all right. My lawyer was my partner on this sure-fire deal and he and I ran right out and bought a piece of choice real estate on Piedmont Road in Atlanta. There, we put up the first Scrambler's Village in what we were certain would be a long, long line of franchised stores across this great land of ours.

I was 28 years old and aggressive and cocky and not the least bit patient when it came to taking time to developing a menu and testing it and creating market awareness before the rollout. We did not spend enough time in planning and preparation and training. Dave Thomas of Wendy's did all those things, but we didn't. The clock ran out on Scrambler's Village very quickly. (In fact, I think I still have some frozen chickens in the freezer if you're hungry.)

We were young and impatient and it cost us some money that, fortunately, we could afford to lose. I think the average *franchise* owner for any fast-food chain spends more time in training than we put into developing Scrambler's Village, which is why I was left to scramble for another way to make my fortune.

I learned a lesson from Scrambler's Village, one that I often remind myself about when launching an entrepreneurial business. You have to be patient. You have to make sure the product or service is ready before rolling it out.

That patience and thoughtful attention must continue after the ribbon is cut on opening day. Those first few weeks and months are critical. It is then that you have to be on top of everything in order to make crucial adjustments and fine-tuning. It is during this period also that you learn how things will really work, and what real customers like and don't like about your operation. If you don't tune into that feedback, you'll be tuned out of business in short order.

The entrepreneur has to put his ego aside during start-up. You can't be so narrow-minded and cocksure that you don't hear what the market is telling you. Too much pride will jam your receivers.

On the other hand, the world is damned near full of people who love to tell entrepreneurs that their ideas won't work, so you have to filter out the voices of those who are negative just because it's easier than being constructive. Then again, if I go to ten people with an idea for a business and nine of them tell me it sounds like a seriously stupid idea, I'd better be listening. The key is to test your idea with people who will be straightforward with you, and to find as many of them as possible. It is important, too, that you talk to people who are knowledgeable in the same business. Their experience can save you a lot of money which, finally, brings me to the second law of starting a business.

2. You are going to need reinforcements.

Entrepreneurs tend to be lone wolves, but in starting a business it helps to have someone to share the burden. You don't have to go it alone, and it doesn't necessarily take a huge salary to lure top-notch people to your team. To lure top talent, you can consider offering them equity in the company. Before you do that, however, you'd better be sure the person is as dedicated to the business as you are.

This is one of my tactics, and it has worked well for me over the years in bringing in talented people for far less money than they could be making elsewhere. Some of them have made millions and they have deserved it, because they brought talent and energy and expertise that took my idea farther than I could have taken it on my own.

"The days of the gunslinger entrepreneur are dead; you need to surround yourself with experts and reward them with equity. To get rich today, you must make others rich," noted Jon Goodman, director of the entrepreneurial program at the University of Southern California, in a *Fortune* interview. To get the best people, you have to be willing to share. Microsoft, one of the most successful companies of modern times, has made millionaires of many of its more than 16,000 employees, because Bill Gates understands the wisdom of offering equity to his best and brightest. George Perrin, founder and CEO of Page Net, a Dallas company that operates the nation's largest paging network, shared equity with his staff when he was struggling to get it started. When he took it public, ten others became millionaires.

Another way to get expert advice, and some good networking contacts is to put together a board of advisors, who also may be rewarded in shares for lending their expertise and contacts to you in the development of your business. Candidates for your board could be active or retired executives with experience in the field or market you have targeted, bankers or investment professionals or anyone with experience in raising capital, and academics with extensive knowledge of your business area, and a marketing or sales professional.

Here are some other good sources for advice and information that can help you in the critical start-up phase.

- Suppliers and vendors connected with your business. Even if you don't end up dealing with them, you will find that those whose businesses are linked to yours are often willing to share their advice and experience in order to help their market grow and flourish.
- A growing and valuable resource for expertise in starting a business can be found on college campuses. Small-business development centers funded by the Small Business Administration often offer seminars, books, and videos on market research and business plans. The SBCD Connection (800-633-6450) can help you find a center in your area. Other industrial and business development assistance is usually available in most communities and can generally be found by contacting the chamber of commerce or city hall.

- Business and professional organizations and trade groups. These may range from informal networks in your community like the Jaycees, Rotary Club, or Engineering Society, to state and national organizations.
- Don't count out friends and colleagues who are knowledgeable about business. They are familiar with your strengths and weaknesses and may be more likely to tell you what you need to hear rather than what they think you want to hear.

3. You must be willing to broaden the concept of your product or service.

When I first bought into the software business that became Knowledgeware, I quickly became frustrated and nearly bailed out. It was a high-tech product that was difficult to explain and difficult to use, even though it worked very well. It was simply hard for me to sell something that, while a great product, was so complicated to demonstrate or explain to the customer.

Just as I was beginning to think this business was not for me, along came a new technology that made our product simpler to use. As a result, it was easier to sell, too. I leaped on the new technology, merged with the company that made it and, suddenly, I was back in business in a big, big way. The lesson here is that if I had not been willing to broaden my concept of my product, I never would have latched on to that new technology that, in truth, became the basis of a very lucrative business.

Have you ever heard of John Wesley Hyatt? No, he didn't found Hyatt Hotels. But he did invent an early form of the roller bearing in the 1890's. The problem was that Hyatt was fixated on using his invention for the axles of railroad freight cars. In his time, however, the railroads took care of friction in the wheels by stuffing the wheels with rags soaked in oil. It wasn't exactly high tech, but it was effective. Hyatt went bankrupt trying to convince the railroad men to try his roller bearing.

Then along came Alfred Pritchett Sloan, a draftsman for Hyatt Roller Bearing Co., who asked his father to buy him the bankrupt firm because he had a broader vision for Hyatt's invention. Sloan thought the roller bearing would be perfect for the product that

Henry Ford was just starting to manufacture, some sort of horse-less carriage. Within two years, Sloan had a thriving business with Ford as his leading customer. Sloan, by the way, later led another automobile company, General Motors, to the top of the heap.

Too often start-up businesses fail because the entrepreneur is unwilling to change his initial concept of his product or service. The inventor of novocaine, a German chemist named Alfred Einhorn, conceived it as a surgical anaesthetic but surgeons found it unsuitable. Dentists, however, loved the product, but Einhorn tried to stop them from using it for that "mundane purpose." He lost out because of his refusal to broaden his vision.

Would you like a more modern example of a company that *did* broaden its vision? Well, have a foam peanut. Tom Martin and Jerry Sullivan began experimenting with grain sorghum in the mid-1980's with the idea of creating a snack food. When that marketing plan didn't work out, they broadened their thinking and began pitching their product as Biofoam, an ecologically friendly, biodegradable packing material replacement for the polystyrene "peanuts" that are filling up landfills at the rate of 50 million pounds annually.

This altered concept for their product attracted high-powered entrepreneur and investor Ed Alfke, founder of the Rent-A-Wreck company. He invested $5 million and bought a controlling interest in Biofoam. Alfke then brought in other big-money investors, and is now running with the concept, making frequent stops to deposit money in the bank. Sales of Biofoam topped $2.5 million in 1996, five times those of the previous year. Alfke projects sales of $80 million by the year 2000.

Stanford Business School professor James Collins studied 18 visionary companies from a cross section of industries and compared them with a more narrowly focused peer group. "We kept seeing that these great companies weren't architected from a single, great idea. That means entrepreneurs should have a vision for their company first, then experiment, sometimes unsuccessfully, with ideas," he told *Fortune*.

Take for example, Bill and Dave, who were a couple of young engineers who decided to start their own business but who had no clear idea of what they wanted to do. They considered manufacturing a number of items, including a clock drive for a telescope, a shock machine to help people lose weight, a bowling foul-line indicator, and a sensor to make urinals flush automatically. In the end, they settled for building computers with a company that today bears their surnames, Hewlett and Packard.

4. Remember, it's not profit that counts. It's cash flow.

One of the unrelenting truths of starting a business is that it always costs more than you think. You have to treat your start-up business in the same way you treat a newborn baby. If you want it to grow, you have to feed it. In the case of the business, you feed it with cash. (Not that babies don't consume a lot of money, too).

As you are starting your business, you are going to need to invest more and more money into it. Be prepared for that. As soon as you get the business up and running, start the process of finding additional financing, because I guarantee you will need it.

Billionaire Warren Buffett, who is generally regarded as the most astute investor in the country, has said that if he wants to find out how a company is faring financially, he doesn't talk to security analysts because they are only concerned with profits. Instead, he talks to bank-credit analysts who understand cash flow. You have to have ready access to money to pay your bills and to feed your company in its early stages.

5. You should begin building your management team early on.

One of the primary problems small-business entrepreneurs encounter during the first few years is that when their businesses begin to grow, whether rapidly or even moderately, they don't acknowledge that they need help at the top.

The small-business entrepreneur may start out as director of sales, employee relations, manufacturing, accounting, legal affairs, chief accountant, and public-relations director, but if the business is to succeed, sooner rather than later, the owner will have to bring in expert help in key areas. Ask Willie King of Washington, D.C., who started a photography business in 1993 after working as a counselor for troubled kids. Willie leased an office and paid out some serious money for equipment to process color film, but after spending $20,000 in savings and only nine months in business, he was broke. He had to close his business. Willie tried to do it all, including keeping the books, which he had no training for. "I lost my behind," he told the *Wall Street Journal.*

Willie went back to a small business development center to get better training and plans to try again. His first try fell short because he tried to do more than he could handle. It's the old saying: Just because you can cook doesn't mean you can run a restaurant.

Usually, by the fourth year of a typical entrepreneurial business, the owner begins to respond to new opportunities as burdens because he is trying to do too much by himself. Once you get 30 to 40 employees, you need to begin searching among them for management candidates. If you can't afford to hire a management team from the outside, you can afford to identify the three or four people who appear to have talents in certain areas such as customer service and personnel or marketing and sales. Give them additional duties to test their ability to grow in a job, and see what they can do.

6. Once your business is doing well, step back and ask if it really needs you anymore.

The entrepreneurial ego and drive can be incredible assets during the early phases of starting a business, but down the road, when the business is up and running and doing well, the entrepreneur needs to ask the vital question, *Am I giving this business what it needs at this point in its development?*

This is a major pitfall for entrepreneurs who may have worked long hours for years to build a business, and will probably be reluctant to step aside or to at least share decisions with someone else who can bring a fresh perspective. Many companies flounder a few years into operation because the entrepreneur's vision and drive have diminished but his or her ego won't allow letting go of the reins.

If you keep these rules in mind as you start your small business, you can avoid a lot of trouble. To give you additional help in determining whether your start-up is headed for trouble, here are Twelve Early Warning Signs of Start-Up Distress:

1. You are having difficulty paying the bills.
2. The product for your market seems to be shrinking rather than growing.
3. More and more customers are looking but not buying.
4. Customer complaints are increasing.
5. Inventory is growing faster than sales.
6. Your bank has more at stake in your business than you do.
7. Your company success is overly reliant on one person.
8. Employees complain about "poor communication."
9. Your managers complain that they don't have enough information about sales levels, accounts receivable, and inventory levels to make sound decisions.
10. Your company is late in producing financial statements.
11. The company experiences sales growth, but no growth in net income.
12. Your company is committing to expenditures before cash to pay them is available.

If any of these warning signs crop up during the start-up of your business, you had better pay attention and move fast to remedy the problem. I've found, and other entrepreneurs will tell you, that these problems don't go away, they only get worse, and bigger.

A feller was interested in buying my corner a few years ago and he offered a good price but I said 'What would I do with all that money?' He said he had a friend who would help me invest it. I told him that if I had enough damn sense to make all that money, I sure had enough damn sense to spend it too.

— RUTH BROOKS

CASH POOR, MONEY SMART

IN THE 1960's, I got into a money crunch when I became involved in a company that provided supplementary learning programs to school systems. It franchised learning centers that served people who were having difficulty learning to read or write. It seemed like a good service that offered a good return while helping people get on track with their lives, but it ended up throwing me for a loss.

I had a partner who had encouraged me to sign for some bank loans to finance the business and, regrettably, I did it without paying enough attention to the repayment schedule and my level of exposure. When the loan came due, I wasn't prepared to cover it. The amount due was $250,000. My NFL salary was about $50,000 a year at the time, so I wasn't exactly swimming in it. The bank was not at all understanding when I didn't write them a check for the full amount. They threatened and harassed me and my family. They didn't care that I was a hotshot football player.

They wanted their money. They were all over me. It was my own fault. I had not paid enough attention to the business. I had spread myself too thin financially and otherwise.

It reached a point where the bank said if I didn't make a $50,000 payment in two days they were going to start foreclosure procedures on my house. At that point, I was scrambling both on and off the playing field. Fortunately, I had a friend, an *angel*, or private investor, usually someone you have known, who loans you money. His name was Buddy Kauffman. In exchange for a percentage of the business, Buddy made the payment for me. That business, by the way, eventually grew into Behavioral Systems Inc., my national consulting company, and Buddy's rescue investment paid him off handsomely over time. He saved my bacon and he is still a friend of mine today, but I was lucky to have him to call upon.

It's nice to have angels. No, it is wonderful to have them. But you shouldn't count on them bailing you out every time you need help. The small-business entrepreneur needs to develop his own ingenuity and creativity in financing business start-ups and growth because, too often, investors are less angelic and more like the other guys with the horns and pitchforks.

I got lucky with Buddy. You might not be so lucky. William E. Wetzel, a business professor at the University of New Hampshire, has studied the so-called "angel market" of investors, and estimates that these private lenders lend tens of billions of dollars in increments ranging from $50,000 to $500,000. Often these investors have their own agendas. If you are trying to run a start-up, you probably don't need some nervous, nail-biting investor calling you every day, or popping in to check on *his* investment. Nor do you need your angel sitting on your shoulder, offering advice, and demanding you run your business his way.

In most cases, those who invest in your business are going to feel that they have the right to be in on every decision. Sometimes they demand that you constantly show gratitude to them for bailing you out of trouble. There are angels out there who give you just enough money to keep your business going so that they can have the opportunity to take it away from you. That has happened more than once. A savvy investor will buy into your business and then pull the rug out from under you, so that he or she can then step in and take over. There are sharks out there, and some of them use money as bait.

If finding an angel appears to be your only option, here are a few heavenly hunting tips that, if nothing else, may at least keep the devils at bay and out of your business.

1. *Look first to your own flock.*

My friend Buddy was an entrepreneur too. He understood the pitfalls of starting a business and keeping it running through the early stages. Because he had been in my position, he was also less likely to interfere once I had accepted his money. Experts say that the most common and best angels are experienced entrepreneurs who share the spirit. One extra tip: Move to Redmond, Washington. That is where all those Microsoft millionaires live, and it's said that a lot of them are looking for entrepreneurial ventures to invest in.

Not fond of the rain? Move to South Dakota. *Inc.* magazine reported a few years back that South Dakota was home to a million more small-business loans (1,452,737) than the second-place lending state, California.

2. *Don't deal with the angel on your own.*

As I noted earlier, savvy and unscrupulous private investors have been known to eat the unwary entrepreneur alive, then swallow up his business. Never negotiate a deal without a lawyer and an accountant and, just in case they turn out to be fallen angels, take along a cross and a jar of holy water.

3. *Check out others who have flown with your angel.*

When you are considering dealing with an investor, ask the names of others who have dealt with him or her. Contact those individuals and get their perspective. Find out how the investor responds in difficult circumstances.

4. *Don't sell your soul, or even a piece of it, if you can help it.*

Keep in mind that while a loan may be difficult to repay, at least once it is paid you are rid of the investor. If you trade equity in your company, the investor may be more difficult to shake loose. Although I frequently give equity to investors, I make sure I know who I am getting into bed with first.

5. *Be very careful about dealing with angels in the immediate family.* I know of a developer who had a surefire plan for a housing development in Chicago. He needed money to purchase the land and get the deal going, so he went to his parents and brothers and sold them on it. But when he began building his own house in the development, and then bought a new car too, his family angels turned on him for cashing in on the deal before he had paid them off. As a result, this developer was not invited to either Thanksgiving or Christmas dinner.

It is tough to do business with family members because it is so difficult to draw the line between what is personal and what is business. Don't rule it out entirely, if the right situation comes along, but know that having an angel in the family can be hellish.

LOOKING FOR CASH IN ALL THE RIGHT PLACES

David Blundin, a 29-year-old MIT graduate, had already spent $150,000 to develop the concept for his start-up software business when he realized he was going to need even more cash. At first, he considered a venture capitalist group, but they offered him just $600,000 for a 30 percent stake, and wanted the option to take majority ownership for only $1 million. They also made it clear that they had a more narrow vision of his company than Blundin did. To his credit, he turned away from the big-money guys and instead signed a $200,000 deal to lease his product to a software firm, which gave him the money he needed without giving his company away.

I can't stress enough that while venture capitalists can save your butt, you need to be on alert because they can also kick it. They can seem like angels, but if you enter into the arrangement hearing nothing but harps, you can get into deep, very deep, trouble. These are savvy opportunists, who are capable of snatching your hard-earned small business right out from under you. They can rescue you, if you are willing to pay their rate, which is usually five to 10 times their initial investment within three to five years. Some also can offer good advice and expansion, management, and alliances, but be prepared to have them poking around in every aspect of your business, and know that if you give them the chance, they are ready to step in and take it over entirely.

If you end up with a real investment angel like Buddy, you are extremely lucky. You have to be very careful when bringing in angel investors, most of whom are looking for returns up to 50 percent. Make sure both of you understand the role you want them to play in the actual operation of your business.

To attract any loans, whether from a bank, an angel, a government agency, or a venture capitalist, you will first need a comprehensive business plan. There are hundreds of books that offer detailed descriptions of how to write a business plan, and there are also scores of computer-software guides to business plan writing. You will find the specifics there, but remember that while writing a business plan is hard work, the time you spend doing it carefully and thoughtfully will prepare you to better handle all aspects of your business down the road. It will also ready you for the grilling you will receive from potential investors and money lenders.

No matter who you approach about a loan, you can pretty much be assured that the potential lender will, at the very least, want these five questions answered, so make sure you are prepared to respond.

1. *How much money do you need?*
   Be prepared to be specific. This is no time to beat around the bush. Once the lender knows exactly how much you need, he knows how well you understand your own business. You can be assured he or she has done the homework, and may know it better than you do.

2. *What do you plan to use the money for?*
   After all, you *are* asking them to take a risk by lending you money, so they have a right to know exactly where it is going. Each lender has his or her own specifications, and you

have to let them know why you are looking for a loan. Your answer gives them a grasp of your priorities and approach.

3. *How will this money improve the business?*

It had better lower your costs, expand your capability, or move you closer to having a self-sustaining business, otherwise, the investor may see himself pouring money into a dark, deep hole. Good luck finding investors if you can't answer this one.

4. *How are you going to pay me back?*

Another perfectly logical and reasonable question. Most bankers and other lenders will want to know that you are going to pay them out of cash flow, backed up by business or personal assets. Investors wanting a piece of your company will also be interested in knowing how soon you expect to be profitable and self-sustaining as a business.

5. *Do you have a Plan B?*

If you can show that you have a number of options for generating revenues and financing, potential lenders will be more willing to join the party.

In general, I'd advise you to consider financing methods and partnerships that aren't based on someone giving you money to bail you out. Ever since that early experience, I have been leery of borrowing money, which is not to say that no one should ever do it. Many people have done very well by borrowing from banks or venture capital companies. Most of the modern leading-technology companies were started with venture capital. It has worked well for them. It just isn't for me. It's not that I never borrow money—sometimes it makes sense. But believe me, I always know exactly what I am getting into, and I never do it unless it is absolutely the best way. I still have nightmares about the guys in suits standing at the front door, holding my home mortgage in their hands.

Now, in fairness, many financial institutions and venture capitalists are far more interested in lending to small-business entrepreneurs today than in years past. But they aren't doing it because they think we are swell people.

The market for big corporate and consumer loans has very nearly been tapped out, so the money people are turning to an area they have long neglected, the credit-hungry small-business market. Major banks, financial services companies and brokerages, and government lenders, such as the Small Business Administration, are vying for the small-business market, eager to hand you money in exchange for getting a hand in your pocket.

Business lenders have lessened the risk of making small-business loans by adopting the computerized, statistics-based methods, known as *credit scoring*, that were developed by credit-card companies for analyzing and evaluating individual borrowers. With this method, lenders measure an entrepreneur's ability to repay the loan by studying a number of key indicators, such as the individual's credit history or personal debts. Some institutions, such as Wells Fargo Bank in San Francisco, are even "prequalifying" small business owners and issuing them lines of credit at 13 percent annual interest.

The credit-card companies themselves have jumped on the small business bandwagon. Diane and Wade Butler, owners of B&B Plumbing, Electrical & Gas Co., a small business in Corinth, Mississippi, used a $15,000 lease line from their American Express Co. business charge card to purchase a computer, a desk, and two drain-cleaning machines. No banks would loan the Butlers the money, even though they'd been in business for 10 years. The catch, of course, is that they must pay a hefty 18 percent interest on that money.

ANGELS FLY IN THE STRANGEST PLACES
. . . .

Aside from finding the perfect angel, another relatively benign source of funding can often be tapped at the state and local government level. Many communities and states have programs to encourage business growth. Colleges and universities increasingly offer economic-development programs and incubators.

Phil Rubin and Molly Bondhus were just a couple of Minneapolis hipsters throwing "rave" parties and making a few bucks in the underground economy, when they hit on a line of alternative clothing that rapidly found a receptive audience among the cool crowd. Originally intended for skateboarders, their Thump line of clothing became all the rage, mostly by word of mouth among generation x-ers. Catalogs were only shipped out on demand. There was no advertising, but business took off when a Thump t-shirt got prominent play in a video for the rock band Soundgarden. Shortly after that, a *Playboy* centerfold model was depicted wearing a Thump and not much else, and Johnny Depp wore one for a photograph in *Interview* magazine.

When they sensed their clothing line was about to take off, Rubin and Bondhus went to a local bank to get a loan, but they were turned down flat. A local reporter who saw the potential of their company put a good word in for them with a friend who was a bank president. He would not give them a loan either, but he sent them to the Minneapolis Community Development Association.

As with any loan, this one came with plenty of strings attached, but nothing that the alternative clothiers couldn't weave into a deal. Thump Inc. was required to move into an inner-city business incubation center, which made them eligible for a one-year line of credit guaranteed by the city of Minneapolis. The city also guaranteed fifty percent of their loan as long as the money was used to purchase inventory or machinery. In order to get the $25,000 loan, the young entrepreneurs also had to prove that they would create jobs. They created eight jobs within the first year and, at last report, were racking up sales of more than $2 million a year, with a huge market in Asia.

To hook up with an investment angel, you might try the following connections:

- The Capital Network Inc. (512-305-0826) *Success* magazine calls this "the nation's largest capital network" for connecting entrepreneurs with investors.
- Investor's Circle (630-876-1101) This is a national network of private investors who are most interested in businesses that benefit society.
- Seed Capital Network Inc. (423-573-4655) For a $299 hookup, this network will link you to wealthy private investors.

- Technology Capital Network at MIT (617-253-7163) This nonprofit link brings together investors and entrepreneurs.
- Accelerate (714-509-2990) This program is run by the Small Business Development Center at the University of California-Irvine. Its Pacific Venture Capital Network has a database that matches investors with high-growth, high-tech businesses.

For general and specific information on public organizations offering loans and lines of credit or small business incubators, try these contacts:

- Center for Entrepreneurial Management (212-633-0060) This is the world's largest organization of entrepreneurs and CEOs.
- National Association of Development Companies (703-812-9000) This group promotes small-business expansion through SBA loan programs for fixed-asset financing.
- The Small Business Association Answer Desk (800-827-5722). Call for information about SBA programs.
- SBA Investment Division (202-205-6510) This government office manages programs that provide debt and equity financing to small businesses.
- National Business Incubation Association (614-593-4331) The NBIA provides contacts, training, and group insurance programs. It also sponsors an annual national conference.

CALLING FOR CASH ONLINE
· · · · · · · · · · · · ·

Former corporate attorney Andrew Klein went to the Web after traditional methods of raising interest for a stock offering to attract capital for his Spring Street Brewing Co., a New York microbrewery and pub, fizzled out. What happened there has become the stuff of legend. Spring Street, brewer of Wit beer, spent $200 to develop a home page, plus another $150 a month to maintain it.

Then, Klein conducted a do-it-yourself, initial public offering on-line and brought in $1.6 million from 3,500 investors, most of whom tapped into his Internet home page.

In 1982, the U.S. Securities and Exchange Commission (SEC) introduced regulations that allow small companies to go public without an intermediary broker or investment banker, but they were widely ignored because investment bankers and lawyers didn't see how they could make money from small company offerings.

As small-business entrepreneurs came to realize the potential of the Internet for marketing their do-it-yourself IPOs, however, more and more have tried it. There is still some confusion about regulations and how they affect small companies using the Internet to offer stock—the seller has to be registered in a state in order to accept investments—but most questions are being addressed.

Most of the companies that have been successful using the Internet for stock offerings are high-tech companies or businesses with understandable concepts. Investment experts caution that there is a lot more to doing this than creating a home page and rolling out the red carpet. Here are things to keep in mind if you are considering this option for raising capital:

1. *Get their attention online, secure the deal in person.*

   Use the Internet to lure investors, but talk to them and meet with them before accepting their investment, if possible. In most small businesses, you have to live with your investors as well as their money, so it pays to get to know them and to get a feel for whether or not you are going to want to deal with them over the long term.

2. *Check them out.*

   The Internet is a very democratic entity, which is good, but if you are going to be doing business with someone, you need to know more than their online moniker. Ask for references and check them out.

3. *Make sure they understand the deal.*

   Online investors may not be as experienced or as informed as other lenders. Make sure your new "partners" understand all aspects of your operation, and the deal.

4. *Don't forget other avenues.*
   Your online search for investors should be part of a bigger strategy that includes placing advertisements in major newspapers and talking with bankers and other investment groups.

Here are a few online resources for finding investors:

- The Fran Tarkenton Small Business NETwork (http://www.ftsbn.com) Everything you will ever need; just ask me.
- Money Hunter (http://www.moneyhunter.com) This site offers an award-winning business plan as a model for entrepreneurs, as well as advice from managers and financiers.
- Capital Quest (http://www.usbusiness.com/capquest/home.html) Small-business entrepreneurs can place an executive summary of their business plans on this site, which is checked out often by private investors.
- FinanceHub: Venture Capital on the Web (http://www.financehub.com/vc/vctab.html). This site includes a database of 11,000 investors and links to dozens of venture firms. It guarantees four funding sources.
- Foundation Center (http://fdncenter.org/) This is a non-profit organization that helps individuals and organizations find funding from foundations and philanthropists.
- Capital Venture (http://www.capitalventure.com) Members include venture capitalists, entrepreneurs, investment bankers, and others.

There are a million other sources and books out there that tell you how to get financing to start your business and to keep it going, so I won't get into any more of the nitty-gritty of obtaining money from outside sources here. The way banks, government-loan programs, and venture capital firms operate changes from week to week anyway, so I'll leave that to others. I'd rather tell you how to *avoid* borrowing money by using your creativity and street smarts to leverage your noncash assets, to look for other opportunities that won't put you in debt, and to come up with innovative and creative strategies that allow you to provide your product or service at the lowest possible cost. Rather than taking on debt, in many cases it is far wiser to take on a partner or to work in cooperation with others, so that your business can grow from a solid foundation, rather than a debt-laden house of cards.

HORSE-TRADING
. . . .

I have yet to hear a small-business entrepreneur, or any sort of entrepreneur for that matter, complain about being up to his ears in cash with nowhere to spend it. Every business has a cash crunch at one time or another. That is why I think it is so vital to develop your financial horse sense early on so that you do not have to rely on money, money, money to keep your business alive. Even if you have the money and don't have to borrow it, relying on constant infusions of cash to stay alive can be a deadly thing. I think having an abundance of cash to start your business is more of a curse than a blessing. If you raise $10 million for a start-up, you will spend $20 million, but if you have to scrap to get your business going, you will develop the mindset and the commitment that will help you find the most efficient and economical ways to operate it over the long haul. I don't think it does an entrepreneur any good, particularly in the early going, to be able to buy his or her way out of problems.

Paul Galvin proved that he had what it takes as an entrepreneur when he ran into a serious problem during the start-up of his electronics company, Galvin Manufacturing Corp., in Chicago. With only $750 and a lease for half of the first floor of a six-story building, he opened his business. He couldn't even afford desks for his five employees. Obviously, with so little capital, he was in for trouble, and it hit when his first big order came in but he had no place to put the people he hired to fill it.

Frantic, Galvin didn't run out and borrow huge sums of money, or go begging on the street for investors. Instead, he got creative. He checked out the floors above his office space and discovered they were either empty or only partially occupied. He didn't have enough cash even to rent that space, so Galvin and his brother came up with a plan to "borrow" it by secretly wiring it for their use, setting up worktables each morning, sending workers up during the day, and disassembling the whole operation—wiring and all—each night to avoid detection. The Galvin brothers also set up worktables in the men's washroom. The landlord caught on, but by that time, the brothers were able to pay the rent and their company, which later changed its name to Motorola, survived the pangs of start-up. I'm told it is still in business today.

The best businesses I have been involved with are those, like Motorola, that weren't built on bank loans or huge cash investments, but instead, had founders who were creative and innovative men and women who built them with hard work, guile, and street smarts.

Personally, I usually have had no choice but to bootstrap my own businesses, even though I have had considerable financial and career success. Bankers are more likely to ask me to sign a football than a loan application. When I first tried to get my software company going, the banks wouldn't loan me a dime, even though I had run and sold a couple of successful businesses already. My response was to finance the $3 million start-up out of income from my other businesses. I got my revenge a few years later, when I took the company public at $12.50 a share and made several million dollars. After that, every banker in town wanted to be my buddy. The entrepreneurs who succeed over the long haul are those whose primary weapon is ingenuity and energy, rather than a ready supply of borrowed cash and the debt burden that comes with it.

STARTING UP AND CLEANING UP

Andy Appelbaum and Cliff Sirlin cleaned up with a start-up even though they had no cash and no collateral. The two New York lawyers, whose business was profiled in *Success* magazine, spotted an opportunity for a business that provided exceptional service to harried professionals like themselves, who didn't have time to go to the dry cleaners, let alone do their own laundry. So, they started Cleaner Options with two employees—themselves—and a lot of shoe leather. They put out fliers and advertised that they would pick up laundry, get it done, and bring it back to the doors of their clients. Within 18 months, their company, based in Greenwich, Conn., had revenues of more than $1 million and a 30-percent profit margin because of their low overhead.

Their bootstrap operation illustrates several key methods for the small business entrepreneur who, like them, has more energy and creativity than cold cash.

Their "bootstrapping battleplan" included these money-saving maneuvers.

- *Contract out the dirty work.* The primary service that Appelbaum and Sirlin provide is pickup and delivery. They did not have the desire, or the money, to get into the actual cleaning business. They did find, however, that there is a lot of downtime for most dry cleaners, who generally operate at only about 55 percent capacity. The two astute entrepreneurs negotiated deals with a number of dry cleaners that allowed them to get wholesale rates, thus cutting their costs.
- *Take your customers hostages.* The Cleaner Options boys managed to wipe out one of the biggest concerns of the bootstrap start-up entrepreneur when they signed their customers to long-term service contracts, thus guaranteeing a market and giving them a 90-percent retention rate. They sold their clients on the fact that they needed long-term contracts in order to set up their pickup and delivery routes. If you can find a way to secure your market over the long haul, it helps all aspects of your business, as well as making it easier to sleep at night.
- *Carry a light load of inventory.* Appelbaum and Sirlin had no inventory other than the canvas bags they used to haul their client's dirty laundry in. Keeping inventory costs low is vital to the bootstrapping small-business entrepreneur and even if you need a lot of equipment, say, for your fitness center, you probably have the option of leasing rather than buying it.

• *Join forces with your supplier.* If you can convince the companies that you will be buying supplies from that you are going
to be a long-term customer, they may be willing to extend
you credit or allow you to stretch payments out over time to
reduce your start-up costs and help you build your business.
That is essentially what Appelbaum and Sirlin did when they
cut deals with their dry-cleaning services to give them wholesale rates by doing their client's laundry in off-peak periods.

COOPERATIVE ENTREPRENEURSHIP

The history of business entrepreneurship in this country generally
offers far more stories of cut-throat competition and bitter rivalry
than cooperation and mutual support, but the history being made
today is another story. While competition is still intense, as exem-
plified by the global war being waged between Coca-Cola and
Pepsi, there are increasing examples of companies big and small
looking for ways to join forces with other businesses, and even
some rivals, in partnerships and alliances that make incredible
sense.

These strategic alliances, as they are often known, are rooted
in another American business tradition: The extended-family
Business NETwork. A few months ago, I gave a speech to employees of the Best Western Hotel chain, and one of the hotel
franchise holders I met was a gentleman who had immigrated to
the United States from India. People of his nationality have
moved into the hotel franchise business in a big way, and I asked
him why. He told me that hotel franchises had proven to be a
great port of entry for him and his family members and other
Indian immigrants, because they were able to buy franchises by
forming partnerships and leveraging their assets. They didn't get
bank loans. Instead, they started out with entire families getting
jobs working in the hotel chains, saving their money, and then
pooling it to buy a franchise and open their own hotel. Then they
would all work together in that hotel, pool their money from it,
and buy another one. Each hotel they bought went to another

family in the group, until each had their own. Then the process began for each member of the individual families to get their own hotels.

This is, in fact, a very traditional American way of building wealth. From the English to the Germans, to the Irish, and the Asians and the Hispanics, each new wave of immigrants has built wealth by creating mutual support systems and alliances. While it is true that financial institutions are, learning to serve the small-business entrepreneur, it is still true that banks are most eager to lend money to people who don't need it. Debt is still a burden and additional pressure that the small-business person is better off avoiding if at all possible.

That may mean sharing in the profits of your company by bringing in partners. It may mean that it will take you longer to realize the full benefit of your business creation. But more and more, partnerships and mergers—even between former rivals—are seen as a wise strategy. As I was putting this chapter together, business-news pages across the country were reporting that two fierce competitors, Boeing and McDonnell Douglas, had decided to join forces. While stunning at first because of the longstanding rivalry, this merger makes perfect sense. With the aging of the nation's fleet of commercial aircraft, Boeing had received a record number of 618 orders for new planes in 1996, worth $46 billlion in contracts. McDonnell Douglas, on the other hand, had been concentrating on small model jets and had gotten out of the production of widebodied airliners—the most common commercial planes—and, as a result, had missed out on the building boom. It was faced with laying off many of its well-regarded engineers and technicians. Now, many of them will go to work under contract to Boeing, helping the former rival meet its obligations, while keeping their jobs.

In days gone by, you never would have seen that happen. In the past, it was every man for himself. Boeing probably would have watched McDonnell Douglas suffer while picking off its best and brightest. Today, both companies realize that it makes sense to work together for the benefit of all. Smart business entrepreneurs everywhere realize that throwing money at problems only creates greater problems. Instead, they are looking increasingly for opportunities to form mutually beneficial partnerships, alliances, and mergers.

PARTNERING IS BETTER THAN BORROWING

Partnerships are my preferred method of financing both start-ups and growth for my businesses. The formation of my airline-ticket-jacket printing company serves as an example of partnering up to pay for a start-up. Rather than lay out a lot of money to hire a printing firm to produce the jackets, I partnered with one instead. Believe me, I slept a lot easier knowing I had a good partner than I might have knowing I had a huge loan.

Sure, I gave up half the profits of the company, but that should never bother an entrepreneur. There is an old southern saying that covers that: *The hogs go to slaughter but the pigs get fed.* There was plenty to go around and I needed them more than they needed me.

When I launched the Small Business NETwork, I wanted to hit the streets like a Rose Bowl Parade. I felt we needed to announce it in a massive rollout and, of course, I didn't want it to cost me much, if anything. True, I have some money in the bank, but like most entrepreneurs, I prefer to keep it there for the lean times. If I buy a four-page color spread in *Forbes* magazine, prime-time television commercials, and billboards in Times Square, I may make a big splash, but I'll also empty the pool.

Like most people, I only had so much money available to finance this start-up. To protect my cash reserves, I had to look for other ways to make my splash. There are always other ways. I believe if you use your creativity you can find ways to market your product or service without spending hundreds of thousands of dollars that you may need down the road to expand your business.

When starting a business, my goal, as in all my ventures, is to leverage what I have as best I can to maximize my dollars, to get the biggest bang for minimal bucks. In the end, I got my Rose Bowl Parade rollout for the Small Business NETwork, and I did it at very little cash outlay. How? The trendy guys call it *guerilla marketing*, but back in Georgia, it's more likely to be known as good old-fashioned *horse-trading*. I leveraged like a madman, which is the way small-business entrepreneurs have to do it if they are going to keep their businesses alive.

CASHING IN ON STRATEGIC ALLIANCES

One of my primary tactics for marketing the Small Business NETwork without spending a great deal of money was to leverage my relationship with a wide assortment of affinity partners, which are generally major corporations eager to tap into the small-business market.

As a small-business entrepreneur, you have to learn not to limit yourself or your thinking when it comes to marketing and advertising your business. You cannot be parochial or narrowly focused. You can't operate in a protective crouch while all of those businesses around you, both big and small, are reaching out and joining forces wherever possible.

In launching the Small Business NETwork, I targeted a market of 46 million men and women. To reach that massive market through conventional advertising and marketing would cost millions and millions of dollars. We did not have that kind of money in our budget, so our only option was to form alliances to expand our market reach.

It took months and months of travel and presentations to sell our concept to these big corporate partners. They had to be entirely convinced that our product was going to add value to theirs. Believe me, there are no easy sales any more. Just getting to the right people and getting those people to listen is a challenge when dealing with large corporations.

If you are up to the challenge, the rewards can be great. Among those who signed on as affinity partners with the Small Business NETwork were Prepaid Legal Services, Forbes, Intuit, Kinko's,

Hertz, Sir Speedy, Office Max, and Federal Express. Each of those partners will have an icon on our web page, and the Small Business NETwork will be featured on their web pages. By forming partnerships with the Small Business NETwork, I offer them access to their target market and, in exchange, our network gets to plug into their much larger marketing and advertising campaign budgets through cooperative advertising. They market the network for me in exchange for giving them links to our home page on WebTitan and, for other considerations, the vast majority of which did not involve any money changing hands. It is a win-win situation for all parties, including network members who receive hundreds of dollars in coupons and lower rates from the affinity partners when they join. The result is greater value for everyone involved.

While many small-business entrepreneurs go into business because they want to be independent, there are very few Lone Rangers out there today in the business world. Even the giant corporations know the value of forming mutually beneficial partnerships. You see it every day. Take a look at your frequent flyer club, for whatever airline you fly. Today you get frequent flyer miles for renting a car, staying in a hotel, and using a charge card. Why? Because the airline, the rental-car company, the hotel chain, and the charge-card company are all after the same consumer—the business traveler—and so each has become an affinity partner.

Being a resident of Atlanta, which is also corporate headquarters for Delta Airlines, I can remember when Delta was flying high as the nation's number-one airline a few years ago. In the 1960's and 1970's, Delta was flourishing and, because it was so successful, it developed a case of tunnel vision. They didn't believe in hiring people who had worked for other airlines because they felt they could develop their own talent better than anyone else. Their corporate culture developed a smugness, as if they had mastered the game and didn't need to heed what any other airline or business was doing. Then, in the 1980's, the wake-up call came. Deregulation shook the entire industry. Delta's employees became disgruntled. Along with that, Delta made a move into the international market by purchasing Pan Am Airlines but, as a result, Delta incurred debt and went through difficult times. Today, Delta has a whole new attitude. When you fly their airline today, you can charge it to a Delta credit card created in partnership with American Airlines. You can get frequent flyer miles on Delta when you buy stock, because of its partnership with the Charles Schwab investment brokerage firm.

Now, Delta recognizes that it pays to partner with other businesses and to pay attention to what is going on outside its own corporate headquarters. Its leaders realize that what worked 20 years ago doesn't work today. In forming strategic alliances, Delta brings more value to its customers and to its corporate culture.

ONE MORE SPORTS ANALOGY

When Jerry Jones needed more cash to pay Deion Sanders and his other high-priced talent in Dallas, what did he do? He formed alliances with Nike, MCI, and others for advertising rights at his stadium. Jones and other modern-day team owners have spent hundreds of millions on their franchises—far more than previous team owners and, in order to stay competitive, they have to pay their players what the market is demanding they be paid. (Do you think it's too late for a comeback? Even for a guy with a bionic shoulder?) To stay in the game, Jones felt he had to have fresh sources of revenue, and thus made alliances with Nike, MCI, and others. He realized that he had to change in order to remain in business.

The beauty of this era of business is that there are no limits on forming partnerships. Every company, big and small, is looking for ways to leverage its assets to create more value and to expand its market reach. In the past, businesspeople were narrowly focused. They did not consider sharing resources for fear of having to share profits or secrets. Today, the mindset is to open up and reach out in order to create more value for customers by leveraging on a wide field. In the old way of thinking, Delta Airlines might look at Marriott Hotels and say, "We have no common interests. We fly people, you give them shelter." Today, however, businesses big and small are increasingly looking for ways to form alliances and partnerships in order to leverage collective strengths.

This trend is particularly noticeable in the small-manufacturing sector, where independent companies that serve major industry leaders like General Motors, Boeing, and Caterpillar are working together to assure quality and on-time delivery. These looseknit manufacturing networks pool their resources for short-term contracts in order to take on jobs that they would not be able to handle individually, forming what some call *virtual corporations* or *flex-nets*. *BusinessWeek* reported that there are as many as 250 manufacturing co-ops scattered across the country. Some have 100 members or more, others have five to 15 businesses joined together. In Wichita, the Kansas Manufacturers Inc. group, is an alliance of 20 odd-job shops working together. Previously, only one of the shops was handling multimillion dollar contracts but shortly after joining forces, KMI landed a $1.7 million order for auto parts to be supplied to a Swedish manufacturer. In Athens, Ohio, ACEnet is an alliance of 40 food companies. In Columbus, Indiana, the FlexCell Group represents 10 metalworking shops.

POSItech Manufacturing Group is an alliance of nine small companies in West Virginia that was formed in order to bid collectively on defense contracts that were too big for the individual members to take on themselves. A team effort by six of the nine companies produced 12,000 tank-tread parts in a contract worth several hundred-thousand dollars. In Erie, Pennsylvania, a similar alliance, EBC Industries Inc., was formed by a large company joining forces with a dozen local machine shops that each offered specific metalworking skills. Sales and employment have tripled since the alliance was formed.

The flex-net flurry is in part due to downsizing and outsourcing by major companies. In Seattle, the Pacific Manufacturing Group is a collection of eight small job shops. It bolted down a $500,000 contract for bulkhead doors in Navy ships just one year after forming, and the next year was awarded a $300,000 followup contract.

GROWING THROUGH PARTNERSHIPS
• • • • • • • • • • • • • • • • • •

While forming partnerships can be a highly effective and cost-efficient way to market your new business, they are also a great way to *expand* your existing business. Early in the life of my software business, we were just sort of plugging along, struggling to find our niche, when the folks at IBM decided that our Knowledgeware software was a perfect match for their mainframe computers. IBM bought 8.5 percent of the company for $10.5 million and set us off on a great course, because it also opened up a huge market for us. I never would have been able to raise the money to travel all over the world and reach the markets that IBM had already developed through its sales force. When we partnered up, IBM's salespeople became my sales staff, and their existing relationships with customers in government and Fortune 500 companies became avenues for my product to be sold. In return, my product served a need that IBM's customers had, and IBM got a percentage of each sale. It was a sweet deal for all of us: IBM, Knowledgeware, and the customer. That partnership really took us to a new level, from $6 million a year in sales to $129 million, and helped me expand the company I had started from scratch into one worth more than a hundred million dollars.

When you form a partnership with another business that is going to market your product, you have to first and foremost make certain not that *you* are going to profit, but that *they* are going to profit. Why? Because if there is not a substantial incentive for them to recommend your product to their existing clientele, they won't do it. The partnership has to be at least as rewarding for them as it is for you, because there is no guarantee at all that their sales force will share in your entrepreneurial zeal for the product. It can be difficult enough for salespeople to work up enthusiasm for their own company's products and services, so if you are the new guy on the block, you are going to have to win them over. Salespeople are very bottomline oriented. It is the nature of their work. If you don't give them a big enough piece of the pie, they won't push for you, even though they may have signed on with an eager smile and promises galore.

In these situations, most people greatly underestimate how much of the profit they need to dole out to the selling partner. I have had products priced at $199, of which 50 percent of my profit went to my selling partners. In doing that, I make a far more modest profit myself, but it is still a lot cheaper over the long run than having to hire a sales staff and establish your own marketing and distribution network. Consider that if you have your own staff, you have to pay them even when they are not selling, but if your partner is handling the sales, you only pay for product that is out the door. The costs of hiring and providing benefits for a sales, marketing, and distribution network is generally prohibitive for most small-business entrepreneurs looking to expand their businesses.

Keep this in mind, too: The person who tries to reap a huge profit off each unit sold is generally in it for the short haul. You want to take a modest profit per unit, say 15 percent or less, and go for high-volume sales. Those who go for the high profit are generally run out of business by the high-volume opportunists who slide in with a lower profit per unit and undercut them in pricing, but outdo them in volume of sales. If you don't believe me, go to the hundreds of businesses that have lost out to Wal-Mart. The formula I just gave you is the lifeblood of Sam Walton's creation, which is no little business today but, not so long ago, it was a small business just like yours.

We just put a sign out for our restaurant and put some flashing lights on it and you wouldn't believe how much business it brought in. But we can only seat 28 people at a time. The other day I looked out and saw all those people waiting and I said, 'Lord, lock the door and don't let nobody else in.' That made everybody laugh and time went by and people acted like they didn't mind.

— RUTH BROOKS

MARKETING LEVERAGE

MY YOUNG daughter Hayley came home in an unusually good mood recently, considering where she had been. "Daddy, I had the greatest time at the dentist. I can't wait to go back," she said.

For a minute, I thought my little girl was still under the influence of some laughing gas. Like most children and adults, she generally has nothing good to say about a visit to the dentist. But, as it turned out, my daughter is only one of hundreds of young patients who love going to see Dr. Michael Healey, a pediatric dentist in suburban Dunwoody, Georgia, because he has an old-fashioned merry-go-round attached to his office.

His young patients are allowed to sit on the genuine antique carousel, a 1928 C. W. Parker model with 20 handcrafted horses. It is one of only about 100 operating antique carousels in existence. Dr. Healey's carousel is both a marketing tool and an investment. "Some people put their money in the stock market, I put mine in collectibles so that I can enjoy them, too," said the dentist, whose carousel has proven such an effective marketing tool that he has been able to cut out costly Yellow Pages advertising with no negative impact on his business.

"The carousel is part of an entire package that we offer to attract children to our practice," he noted. "We have a sitting area that is like a day-care playroom and we have attendants to watch the children in it so parents can leave their other children there while they accompany the patient child during treatment. We have postured this as a nurturing practice because dentists have been getting a bad rap for 300 years, and we have to do something to fight it."

Three times a year, Dr. Healey hosts parties for his patients and, on these occasions, he actually runs the carousel, giving rides to several-hundred young people over the two-hour party. A photographer takes pictures of each child on the carousel and Dr. Healey sends the photographs to their parents. "The parents put the pictures of their kids on the carousel on their refrigerators and people see them and want to know about our practice," Dr. Healey said. "It really spreads the word."

Since introducing the carousel to his dental practice, Dr. Healey's patient list has grown to more than 2,000 young people.

"It intrigues the kids and they learn to associate our office with fun rather than the usual images of a dentist's office. It is a good way to get people in the door so that they see all of the special treatment we offer," he said.

As Dr. Healey obviously understands, the key to marketing your business's service or product is not how much money you spend on marketing, but how *well* you spend it. The small-business entrepreneur generally does not have tens of thousands of dollars to spend on marketing, maybe not even hundreds of dollars are available, but there are ways that smart small-business entrepreneurs can leverage modest marketing budgets by directing their limited funds to the right place—the most profitable customers or markets—at the right time.

MARKETING ON THE CHEAP
. . . .

One of the things I love about small business entrepreneurs is that they are wizards at finding cheap marketing techniques to get their product or service out in front of the public without giving away the store. Although I want to focus primarily on some of the new high-tech, but relatively low-cost marketing methods, here are a few of the proven, low-tech standard methods that small businesses have employed over the years.

- *Street-corner gorillas and/or giant chickens handing out coupons.* It's funny, you see this cheap marketing ploy done mostly in big cities, even though it has a small-town flavor to it. It may not be high-tech or reach a vast audience, but it certainly gets the attention of people on the street. It is also an inexpensive marketing ploy, particularly if the suits fits you.
- *Great giveaway gambits.* It's amazing what people will pay for in order to get something free. Beauty products have led all others in this marketing ploy, throwing in a whole bathroom cabinet full of soaps, scents, and deodorants just to get you to buy their primary product at an inflated price. Computer makers are quickly catching up, though, tossing in software packages, modems, and other extras to lure you to their line. Any added value that you can offer your customers will enhance your product. You see it everywhere you go today, from hotels that offer concierge floor service and office space to frequent guests, to bookstores with reading chairs, free coffee, and snacks.
- *Preferred customer status.* My friend David Wesley got sick of being asked by his grocery store checkout clerk if he is a "preferred customer," so he finally responded: "Yes, they said they'd prefer I shop somewhere else." Funny guy. But it does seem like this marketing trick is used by everything from banks to bookstores and beyond these days. In fact, another friend of mine went on one of those riverboat casinos in the Midwest a while back, and reported that the line for

regular customers had only five people in it, while that for "The Gambler's Club" preferred customers had at least 1,000. The day is fast approaching when we will all be somebody's special customer.

This is simply another marketing method for tightening the bond between your business and your best customers, but in making them "preferred" you had better be prepared to actually offer something of value for the title, otherwise people who see through the ploy may become insulted and take their business elsewhere.

- *Scratch and win.* The modern marketing contest has apparently rubbed merchants the right way because you see these "scratch-and-win" games everywhere, from the grocery store to fast-food chains to video stores. Contests of any and all kinds can be used as cheap marketing devices, and they can be a lot of fun for all involved, but make sure you cover your bets. A few years ago, a young fellow in Chicago made a half-court shot at a Chicago Bulls game on national television and claimed the $1 million prize. The problem was, this guy had once played junior college basketball, and the insurance company that had covered the bet refused to pay, citing a clause that prohibited anyone with that level of playing experience from competing. Knowing that to refuse to pay would have been a public-relations disaster, the two sponsors paid up.

- *Make news.* Business-news editors for newspapers, magazines, and television shows are not easily fooled by business owners trying to drum up sales by planting stories in the newspaper. On the other hand, if you can find something of legitimate public interest about your business—and there had better be something or you will soon be out of business—then this can be a very effective way to bring people to the front door.

Although editors and reporters can be hard to sell, they are also often hard up for stories to fill their newspapers or time slots. I'll give you a tip here. Around the Christmas holidays, newspapers have huge amounts of space to fill around all of the retail ads and, because many of their regular staff members are on vacations, they are hungry for stories, particularly those that are not about tragedy, violence, or death.

Never underestimate the power of the press to capture the public's attention and put your product or service in the public eye. Remember, too, that there is a media feeding chain in which the major media outlets use the smaller ones as tip sheets. So, while it may seem hardly worth the effort to get the local *Daily Bugle* to write about the giant venus fly-trap that ate a mouse in your flower shop, remember that the story could go out on the Associated Press wire, which reaches hundreds of newspapers and television editors around the country. Who knows, old Venus could end up on *Entertainment Tonight* or *Late Night with David Letterman*. It has happened before.

- *Celebrity events, tent sales, and charity benefits.* I have never understood why anybody would come to a book store or car lot to see me standing there, but I've been asked to do all sorts of appearances over the years. Then again, can someone please tell me what the psychological explanation is for a tent sale? What is it about a tent that makes people want to buy a car? These events are time-proven draws for customers, as are charity benefits, which give the client another reason to feel good about coming into your business.

- *Free first consultations.* If you need to broaden your customer base, whether you are an attorney, a chiropractor, a masseuse, or a witch doctor, this seems to be a popular marketing ploy to bring new faces through the door. It gives you a basis and a point of contact for building potential long-term clients and customers. Once you get them in the door the first time, half the battle is won.

There is no guarantee that any marketing or advertising method will put money in the cash register, which is why you have to watch these costs closely. Occasionally, you do see a business that has succeeded primarily because of clever advertising or marketing, but no business survives over the long-term solely through advertising and marketing. Sooner or later, people get weary of hearing "Where's the beef?" and begin asking, "Well, where the hell *is* the beef?"

Too Good's to Be True

• • • • • • • • • • • • • •

I heard recently about a furniture store in central Illinois that illustrates this point. Good's Furniture, owned by a family of the same name, is located in Kewanee, Illinois, which is a small farm community about 200 miles southwest of Chicago. To give you an idea of how rural this place is, the town is proud to call itself "Hog Capital of the World."

About 20 years ago, the astute owner of the furniture business, Phil Good, began running television ads featuring his very nice wife Mary as the spokesperson for the store. Mary has a friendly down-home manner and the ads began attracting people from a wide area. The problem was that since they had seen the ads for his store on television, people came to Good's expecting something special. Good's was a nice store at the time, but there was not anything special about it, other than its appealing spokesperson. While the store carried very nice furnishings and offered competitive prices, it was much like any other. When customers told Phil and Mary that they had expected something more, the owners decided that they had better make sure their store lived up to its advertising.

How many times have you seen a movie trailer that made it seem like a great film, but then you went to it and realized every good part of the movie had been in the two-minute ad? Movies like that die a quick death at the box office because, while the marketing may be great, the product is lousy. Word of mouth wipes them out.

The Goods did not want to make that mistake with their furniture store, so they began pouring money into making their store special. Today, Good's Furniture still has a big television advertising budget. Their folksy ads can be seen across central Illlinois and people sometimes drive for more than 100 miles to shop there. They are not disappointed.

Good's Furniture Store now covers two city blocks in downtown Kewanee and, along with thousands of pieces of furniture, you'll find it includes a German wine-cellar restaurant, a bakery, an ice-cream parlor, a gift shop, a hair-styling shop, and a bed-and-breakfast inn. As many as seven tour buses stop have stopped per week at Good's, and people have been known to try and stuff furniture they've purchased into the luggage compartment of the buses.

Phil and Mary Good have done well by spending big on advertising, but they have also had to spend a lot of money to live up to their advertising. They have been able to do it because their store has become something of a destination in this rural area, and Mary is one of the biggest celebrities in that part of the country. Theirs is a unique success story. In fact, other furniture stores in the same area have tried to duplicate their strategy and come up short either because their commercials were not nearly as appealing, or because they have not been willing to reinvest in their businesses the way the Goods did.

Most business owners feel they simply could not afford to do what the Goods have done. I've seen people blow all their careful planning and hard work by spending their cash reserves on huge advertising and marketing budgets that did not provide an adequate return. It isn't necessary to do that and, in most cases, it is just plain dumb.

GETTING THE MOST BANG FOR YOUR BUCK

As Ruth Brooks knows, but too many others forget, the true measure of success in business is not how big your office is or how many people you have working for you, it is how much *more* money comes in that goes out.

One of the quickest ways to cut into your profit margin is to go hog wild on advertising and marketing rather than formulating a strategy that gives you the most bang for your buck and doesn't clean out the checking account. No small-business person can afford to advertise if it is not going to have a definite and *measurable* impact.

I certainly don't recommend them as a tool for small-business owners, but I have had a lot of success with infomercials over the years. Then again, I never air an infomercial in a big way until I test it and test it and test it to make sure it will pay its own way and then some. To slap a $150,000 infomercial on the air without knowing for certain that it is going to work would be foolish. The same holds true for most forms of marketing and advertising.

No one is infallible. Not every idea you have is a great one. You have to be willing to test and probe and know whether you are spending wisely, otherwise, you won't have a business to market for long. If there is not some way to measure the results of your advertising dollar, don't get out the checkbook.

Is it necessary to advertise and market your product or service? Certainly. But there are plenty of ways to do that without giving away the store and everything in it, and without going into debt by borrowing a lot of money.

My arrangement with Sir Speedy is a useful example of leveraging for small-business enterpreneurs. Sir Speedy's primary clientele is the small business, so I approached them to be an affinity partner because I can help them reach that market. In exchange, they add value to our membership package by offering a Sir Speedy coupon. They also offer membership sign-up for the Small Business NETwork in their more than 800 shops around the country. No money has changed hands, but both the network and Sir Speedy will benefit from our relationship, and the members of the network who are Sir Speedy customers will benefit most of all.

Most entrepreneurs are natural born horse-traders. When they need something for their businesses, they are far more likely to look for a trade than to reach for their wallets. I've been bartering all my life. In my rookie season in the NFL, we got a couple tickets for each game to give to family and friends, but for one of my first games I traded my tickets for a sofa and some chairs for our apartment. Most of our vacations were actually trips paid for by companies who footed the bill in exchange for me playing a few rounds of golf with their executives or giving a speech to their seminar or convention group. Most athletes today make so much money that they wouldn't consider that sort of trade-off but, back then, it was a great way for us to have some nice trips together.

I probably barter more today than I ever have, not so much because I need to do it, but because it makes good business sense to leverage your assets rather than throwing money around that you may need in tight times. My oldest daughter, Angela, who has a very entrepreneurial mindset, started a speakers' bureau a few years ago to handle my speaking engagements and those of some other clients across the country. She thought it would do her business and her clients good to advertise in *Entrepreneur* magazine, but of course she didn't have a big enough budget to advertise in a national magazine. As it happens, I know Barry Rupp, the founder of that magazine, who at the time was still publishing it. To help my daughter out, I provided her a leverage tool. I went to Barry and offered to write a monthly column for his magazine. Part of the deal was that my daughter's company would get to place an ad in the magazine each month. My daughter got exposure and I wrote them an article and there were negligible costs for each party.

Granted, you may not have a celebrity dad to leverage in trade for an ad in a national publication, but I'll bet you do have *something* you can leverage to market your product in some way that will help bring business to your door. Maybe the publisher of a local shopper or advertising publication would trade an ad for your product or service, whether it is a car tune-up, a little landscaping or a free limo ride for his daughter's prom date.

If you are going to succeed as a small-business person, you have to learn to think of your business not only as an income generating tool but also a leverage tool, something that has value that can be traded to create greater value.

THE WORLD BAZAAR IS ONLINE

When you think of small businesses that are quick on their feet and savvy marketeers, you probably don't think of companies with names like Bulk Handling Technology Inc. But this small business based in Winchester, Ohio, had three employees, $1 million in annual sales, and a knack for finding a niche in a highly competitive field dominated by giants such as Dresser Industries. Like many small businesses, Bulk Handling has survived by carving out a niche and focusing on being better and smarter than the competition. This company has flourished by crafting customized conveyor belts, rock crushers, and other industrial strength tools for mining operations and industry. Also like most small businesses, however, Bulk Handling didn't have the bulk to handle a big marketing campaign to get the word out about its nifty niche products.

Until the summer of 1996, that is.

One of the employees at Bulk Handling was an early Internet junkie who volunteered to create a Web site for the company. He learned how to do it at a $1,500 class offered by AT&T and, for that, and the price of a modem and Windows 95, Bulk Handling jumped on the net. For an investment of less than $2,500, this small business attracted $2.5 million worth of contracts in its first few months on the Internet. Among the potential clients it attracted were a pineapple-processing plant in Western Australia and a copper mine in Chile.

Here is a warning to all of the business Goliaths out there: Put on your protective eye wear because the Davids of small business have got themselves a whole new sling. It's called the Internet and, with the unleashing of sophisticated but inexpensive tools for electronic commerce—for data interchange, telecommuting, groupware, and for the World Wide Web—the small business entrepreneur can be a contender.

Twenty years ago, the technological developments that occurred—mainframe computers, industrial robots, and semiconductors—were primarily tools of big business. Today, the majority of technological growth is in products that can be used to make small businesses more competitive. Laptop computers, cellular phones, the Internet, networking systems, and the massive amount of data now available to small businesses has helped drive a modern small-business entrepreneurial revolution in this country.

Your small business may actually have an edge over the giants because, as a small-business entrepreneur, you can target niche markets, make adaptions, and change strategies with market shifts more readily than ponderous big corporations. The Internet is rapidly becoming the world's shopping bazaar, and it is a perfect place for the small-business entrepreneur to set up and reach a huge market without racking up big costs. Aside from thoughtlessly pouring your own money into a startup, the dumbest thing you can do as a small-business entrepreneur is throw money out like bait, hoping the customers will bite. Marketing can be a deep hole that many small businesses fall into. You can't depend on marketing and advertising to bail you out if your product or service is not a value to the customer. And, if it is a true value, you shouldn't have to throw a lot of money at marketing and advertising in relation to your sales and profits.

A WORLD OF LEVERAGE ON THE NET

I think the Internet may prove to be the greatest leverage tool for the small-business owner to come around in a long, long time. It is far less expensive and far more accessible to the small-business entrepreneur than many other forms of marketing and advertising. Many small-business people have no idea that right now it is possible for them to market their products to the world, at a very low cost, without an expensive or elaborate infrastructure.

Winfield Jones of Boise, Idaho, is a precious-gem broker, who can offer his clients very competitive prices on diamonds and other gemstones because he doesn't have to spend huge amounts on advertising, retail-store space, or other costly overhead. He sells by word of mouth and on the Internet. "Having a Web site means that I am open for business to the entire world. I am available to customers 24 hours a day, seven days a week, and 365 days a year," said Jones, who was one of the first entrepreneurs to use our WebTitan product to design his own Web site and link up to the Small Business NETwork.

Atlanta attorney Charles Robertson said when he began using the Internet as a resource in his business strategies, it was "like going from pencil drawing to oil painting." The Robertson & Walker law firm was one of the first to see the value of the Internet and to create a home page, which is linked to the Small Business NETwork at www.ftsbn.robertsonlaw.com. The site has become an invaluable tool, and is used to communicate with clients via e-mail, to do research, and to link up electronically with a wide variety of sources. In the first two months of being online, the law firm attracted 12 new clients directly through its Web site, which has been receiving more than 50 hits a day.

The Internet allows small-business entrepreneurs like Winfield Jones and Charles Robertson to fling their marketing messages out to the global market in ways that only the giants like Coca-Cola, Procter & Gamble, and General Motors have done in the past. Understand that as it exists now, the Internet is in no way a sure-bet, end-all, guaranteed way to market your business or product, but I believe it will soon become the best bet, particularly for those entrepreneurs with limited resources but an unlimited market. I believe also that in a very short time, most small-business owners will find it necessary to have an Internet strategy, because if they don't market their products and services on the Internet, their competitors will. It is also true that the large corporations doing business with smaller vendors or suppliers increasingly demand that they be plugged in, if not to the Internet, then to electronic networks such as EDI (electronic data exchange) systems or LAN (local area network) systems.

NETREPRENEURS ARE WIRED

Like most people, including even Bill Gates and the folks at Microsoft, I was wary at first about jumping on the Internet bandwagon. The business world in general was cautious and still is, to a great degree, about how the major players will be able to cash in. One of the things that I really like about the Internet is that while many chest-thumping big businesses have failed to make money online, after some very showy efforts, hundreds of small-business entrepreneurs have stepped in and come up with incredibly creative ways to sell, market, publish, and advertise on the Internet.

Time Warner's flashy "Pathfinder" Web site was such a flop when it was introduced that the CEO of Time Inc. called it the "new definition of the term black hole." AT&T pulled the plug on its ballyhooed "Health Site" before it was officially launched. MCI Communications Corp.'s shopping mall on the Web had trouble finding tenants. The big dogs of business have been tangle-footed in their efforts to capitalize on the Internet, mostly because they have tried to integrate it with their existing marketing and distribution networks. Well, that dog won't hunt on the Internet.

This is a whole new medium, and the race here will go to those businesses that jump on and adjust to it without trying to make it fit preconceived strategies. Robert E. Johnson had conceived his InfoSeek Web page as a subscription service that would help people find online publications and databases for a $9.95 per month fee. But people weren't willing to pay for his search engine, particularly when there were others that didn't charge. Instead of giving up, Johnson dropped the fee and stayed online because he believed his search engine was a good one and that eventually he would find a way to make money with it.

He was right. InfoSeek attracts millions of visitors, and is also attracting advertisers who are paying more than $5 million a year to ride on Johnson's Web page. In turn, Johnson pays $5 million a year to advertise *his* product on Netscape's home page. Johnson is still refining his product, and, at last report, was still not making money, but he is pioneering in the development of advertisement and products tailored to consumers. For example, InfoSeek was the first search engine to sell ads linked to the keywords used by net-surfers. If you search for "golf" on Info-Seek, the results will probably come on your screen accompanied by an ad for a company selling golf equipment or other golf-related items.

Before you jump on the Internet with your small business, you should first consider your approach. It may often seem like the wild, wild west of marketplaces at this point, but there are four distinct ways to open up shop.

1. *On the global village square*

   This is the new-fangled, old-fashioned approach to operating a business. You find a space on the main drag and hang out a shingle or put some product in the window. That's what having a home page on the Internet is like. You get out there so that anyone using an Internet Web browser can find you by punching in your Web address or using keywords to find you while searching the Web. Once they get there, you show them either a sampling or your entire catalog, and you give them a toll-free number to call or an order form to fill out.

2. *The virtual shopping mall*

   As with the real thing, when you open a shop in the mall, you are tying your fortunes to those of all of your mall neighbors but, in general, you are counting on the drawing strength of your combined numbers. The same holds true with the Internet version of a shopping mall. In this form, a group of businesses locate at a single Internet site in hopes that together they will draw more visitors than if they were separate.

   Hawaiian coffee-bean peddlers Bob and Arminda Alexander hitched their store to six different virtual malls after expenses on their real store in Maui shot sky high. For a few hundred dollars each month (instead of $12,000 each month at their Maui location), they could link to the half-dozen virtual malls including Downtown Anywhere and Planet Hawaii. After they started getting $15,000 a month in orders from their virtual mall sites, the couple shut down their real store.

3. *Cyber-billboards*

   Better than the roadside kind, and not as likely to be cut down by environmentalists or hit by lightning, electronic bulletin boards are commonly known as *newsgroups*, and they cover every topic you've ever dreamed of, and a few that might give you nightmares. Posting information about your business or service in these newsgroups generally costs nothing more than the price of being online. You do have to be selective because some newsgroups ban commercial solicitations, while some have no bans and others allow discreetly worded ads like "If you need help with your resume, call BusinessAdvisors."

4. *Electronic newsletters*

If many of your clients or customers are online, you can mass e-mail your newsletter to them at the fraction of a cost, and in half the time of publishing and mailing a regular newsletter. And you don't have to lick the stamps.

Jesse Briggs, owner of the Yellow Strawberry Global Salons chain of 37 hair salons, uses an e-mail autoresponse service known as *mailbot*, which works like fax-on-demand systems in which customers request faxes by calling an automated phone system. Based in Fort Lauderdale, he markets to new clients around the world from his Web site, which gets 25,000 visitors a month.

To set up a mailbot, you need e-mail access and existing customer information easily obtainable over the Internet. Customers send you either a blank e-mail message or request specific data. The mailbot will find that preformatted message and send it back almost immediately. Internet service providers charge between $10 and $50 a month for mailbot service. There is also a one-time setup fee.

Briggs sends out specialty hair-care tips delivered to clients' e-mail and the mailbot adds prospects' names to an e-mailing list for salon products and updates. Mailbots work for both business owners and customers. They are much less expensive than regular mail, faxes, or 800 numbers.

Another mailbot marketeer, high-tech products retailer, Halted Specialties Corp., in Santa Clara, California, set up a mailbot system to send special sale information to its customers and owner David Joseph reported that the mailbot significantly increased mail-order business.

THE HOTTEST MARKETING TOOL GOING
. . . .

How hot, hot, hot is small business on the Web? Try hothothot. com, the home page for a little Pasadena, California, shop called Hothothot that had a nice local business selling hot sauces with names like *Satan's Revenge* and *Scorned Woman*. After running into the president of a Web page design company, co-owner Monica Lopez decided to give the Internet a try. At last report, their home page featuring 150 different hot sauces was drawing more than 1,500 visitors a day and generating 25 percent of the store's sales. "Above all, the successful Web trailblazers share the ability to adapt—to scrap what's not working and improvise a new business plan on the fly," *BusinessWeek* reported. Many small and agile businesses and a growing army of *netrepreneurs* are leaping online and, in many cases, experiencing incredible success. I think this is one of the most exciting business developments to hit in my lifetime. Although I had been reading a great deal about the Internet and how people like Bill Gates were slowly coming to view the Internet as a new business frontier, I first realized its marketing potential personally as I was helping my daughter Melissa start her sports-memorabilia business. I am not a technocrat nor am I an engineer, and a good deal of the high-tech talk is way over my head, but when you talk about a medium that can help anybody reach 40 million people, it hits my entrepreneurial antennae hard enough that I tune in and listen.

When we were getting Melissa's business going a few years ago, a friend offered to help her build a home page for the business because so many sports fans are on the Internet. I had no idea how to build a Web page, but Melissa's friend had started a Web page building business with a group of guys who had been downsized by Lockheed. I paid them $5,000 to build Melissa's Web site and it was fantastic. The best thing about it was that within a week or two, Melissa began getting orders from all over the country and beyond, including a $400 order from Singapore. I may not be a technological wizard, but even I can understand those results.

That was just over a year ago and, since then, technology has rapidly progressed to the point where people can now build their own Web pages for a fraction of what I paid. In fact, our WebTitan CD-ROM includes a Web building program that helps you create as many as 20 pages on your Web site. It then hooks you up to the home page of the Small Business NETwork and gives you access to our high-speed Internet connection. Since many people still are not well-versed as to how Web pages and the Internet work, we also included a comprehensive instructional segment on the WebTitan that demystifies it for the regular, low-tech businessperson.

LIVING AND DYING WELL ON THE WEB

I would call the Internet the wave of the future, but by the time this book is published, the future will have arrived. Most of the estimated 250,000 businesses that are online at this point have been there less than two years, and most businesses don't reach profitability for at least the first six months to a year.

In 1995, it was said that about $70 million in commerce was conducted on the Internet. In 1996, that figure was $518 million. Some predict that by the year 2000, there will be $6.6 billion in business done in this manner.

The Internet is already proving to be particularly valuable to bootstrapping small businesses. Most of those operating on the Internet are on tight and tiny budgets. In June of 1996, market researcher ActiveMedia surveyed 1,100 businesses online and 31 percent claimed to be profitable, while 28 percent predicted they would be within one to two years. Those surveyed reported total revenues of $130 million, just for the month. So, if you have a product or service that can serve a wide audience, the sooner you get on the better. Just ask funeral home owner Carlos Howard of Norfolk, Virginia.

A funeral home? How can the Internet benefit that sort of business? Well, Carlos wondered the same thing when his friend Rodney Jordan, an early home-page designer and netrepreneur, began trying to convince him that he needed to get on the net.

Jordan noted that as far as he had been able to determine, there were no other funeral homes on the Internet back in 1995. He said that it was true, you couldn't sell funeral services over the net. But you certainly could sell the primary product of most funeral parlors—caskets.

As you may have suspected, there is an *incredible* markup on caskets in the funeral home industry. There have been investigative reports into allegations that some unscrupulous funeral-home operators take advantage of grief-stricken family members by charging outrageous prices for caskets. After talking to his friend about the Internet, Carlos realized that there was a great opportunity to turn the tables and to take advantage of those funeral homes that overcharged for caskets. He had a home page built and, true to his motto "The Priority of People Taking Priority Over Profit," he began selling caskets on the Internet for $200 over his cost.

His burial business went through the ceiling. In fact, one of the first responses to his Internet marketing campaign came from a buyer in Korea, who began ordering 200 caskets a month from Carlos Howard's funeral home.

The great thing about marketing your product on the Internet is that you don't need to have a huge inventory on the premises. You don't even need a premises. You can take orders and then arranged to have products shipped directly from the manufacturers to the customer, or, in the case of Peter Ellis's business, you deliver the customer to the dealer.

Ellis lost $15 million during the California recession in the early 1990's, which forced him to sell or close his 16 car dealerships. He has found automotive rebirth, however, on the Internet, where he no longer is burdened with real estate, inventory, and a huge sales force. Ellis's new company is Auto-By-Tel, which sells sales leads to auto dealers around the country for a monthly subscription fee of $250 to $1,500. He provides the dealers with the names of people who have walked onto his virtual car lot on the Internet (autotel.com) and agreed to buy a car at the no-haggle price. More than 1,400 dealers have signed on to the system and Ellis was anticipating revenues of $6.5 million in 1996.

SMALL-BUSINESS NETREPRENEURS GO BIG

Along with opening up the marketplace for existing businesses like Bulk Handling and the Carlos A. Howard Funeral Home, the Internet has inspired a whole new breed of netrepreneurs such as

Ellis, for whom the Internet *is* essentially their business. Although some big businesses with massive marketing and distribution systems already established have had trouble figuring out how to adapt them to the Internet, these pioneering netpreneurs have jumped on and taken off with virtual businesses.

Amazon.com is a virtual bookstore that offers more than a million selections—five times that of the standard book superstore, while discounting bestsellers by 30 percent. Created by Jeff Bezos, a former hedge-fund manager, Amazon.com has no reading chairs or espresso, but it has successfully created a sense of community for its customers. Amazon.com operated in the black after just six months online, and reportedly has sales of more than $17 million a year, and climbing. While convenience and low prices are a major lure for online shoppers, Bezos claims the secret to his success as a netrepreneur is personalized service. Visitors to Amazon.com are asked to fill out a profile listing their reading preferences and when new books on their favorite subjects or by their favorite authors are released by the publishers, they are notified by e-mail. Amazon.com also hosts book club forums, chat rooms on all varieties of topics, and online visits by authors.

Amazon and other netpreneurial businesses also hold regular contests to bring customers back. Smart Games Inc., a Marblehead, Massachusetts, netpreneurial business, offers cash prizes of up to $50,000 to visitors who score well on its *Smart Games Challenge* CD-ROM game. Its Web site, smartgames.com attracts more than 500 visitors a day, and helps generate $1 million in sales for just that one CD, according to *Business Week*.

But there is *more*. Netpreneurs have also discovered that if they have a popular home page on the Internet, other businesses want to link up to them in order to attract visitors to *their* pages. Both Microsoft and Lands' End have begun paying the Olim twins to advertise their products on the CDNow.com home page, bringing in advertising revenue reportedly in excess of $100,000 a year. Internet advertisers pay according to how many *hits* or visits, a Web site gets. A really popular home page, such as that for ZDNet, a computer shopper's site, commands more than $100 per 1,000 impressions or visits. Less popular sites get about $30 per 1,000 impressions.

Although ad revenues on the Internet are nowhere near those of television, most market researches believe it will grow rapidly. Some predict advertising will generate $5 billion a year on the Web by 2000.

SETTING UP SHOP IN CYBERSPACE

Naturally, I would like to tell you that the absolute *best* and *only* way to open up shop on the Internet is to use our WebTitan product, which helps you build your own home page step by step, and then, with the push of a button, links you to the Fran Tarkenton Small Business NETwork home page. I'd like to tell you that, but, well, there are other ways.

The good news is that you probably won't have to pay nearly as much as I did to set up my daughter's home page for her memorabilia business. There is an entire industry of home-page builders now, and it no longer demands that you master the highly technical HTML, or hypertext markup language. Like WebTitan, there are many programs available that make creating your home page as easy as any other desktop publishing task, like creating a newsletter or a brochure. I'm not going to provide you their names here because the products are always changing and, besides, why help the competition? I'm not *that* big a guy.

There are also Web business and city directory services that will put your business online with pre-formatted Web pages. They operate similarly to WebTitan in that they put you on their home pages and help draw people to your business.

If you are a real technophobe, you can hire a Web site development company, which is often run by a couple of high-school or college kids who seem to have been born with special Internet genes. Typically, they charge about $50 an hour, or around $1,000 total for your basic custom-created site. If you include a downloadable product catalog, video, or Java programs, the building cost can climb to $5,000 or more.

Like finding a house plan you like, once you have a home page, you have to find a home site to locate on. Running a Web server computer is generally too much for the average businessperson and it is expensive. Luckily, there are scores of Internet service providers just dying to put you online for a setup fee of around $200, which covers registration of your home page name, and a monthly fee depending on how many pages you have. Generally that fee is $50 or less.

AT&T has an elaborate Web hosting service. It charges $295 a month which buys you name registration, 100 megabytes of server storage, and up to 200 megabytes of data downloaded to visitors each month. For an additional charge, AT&T will process credit-card transactions, and even alert you to all those visiting your site as soon as they click on the designated button.

HIGH TECH FOR SMALL BUSINESS

While the Internet can open the global marketplace to small-business entrepreneurs, there are many other high-tech products that level the playing field and allows them to compete more readily against bigger businesses. There is now software that allows the small-business owner to gather and manipulate market information on a regular personal computer. Custom mailing lists can be created by even the small-business owner using easy-to-operate software sold by dozens of companies. MarketForce from Software of the Future Inc., in Arlington, Texas, allows you to manage your own direct-mail and telemarketing campaigns. CD-ROM software offers incredible access to market and consumer information, including nationwide telephone lists that can be searched by name, business type, zip code, and area code, for less than $100.

It wasn't long ago that if you wanted to send out faxes to a thousand customers overnight, you had to pay a fax-broadcasting service as much as 25 cents per fax. Now, you can do it yourself with faxing software programs on your office or home computer that allow customers to request fax-back information on products, and can be customized to blanket thousands of customers with a single product pitch.

INTERNAL NETWORKS WORK, TOO
· · · · · · · · · · · · · · · · ·

Along with the Internet, which helps your small business reach the outside world, several new *internal* networking technologies have been developed, such as *local-area networks* (LANs), *client-server systems*, and *electronic mail* that can make the small shop much more efficient, and profitable, at a relatively low cost. Even the one-person operation can benefit from technology that has already been used by the big operations like Caterpillar, 3M, and Citibank to bring products to market more swiftly, increase productivity, and improve customer communications.

At the Kim Dawson modeling agency, in Dallas, employees once tracked their model's assignments with bulky flow charts tacked to their office walls. It was a messy system that not only looked bad, but was also inefficient and often resulted in double-bookings. The modeling agency spent $50,000 to purchase and install 12 personal computers and a Novell Inc. networking operating system that linked its 11 agents to a software program enabling them to check their model's assignments on computer. Not only did efficiency improve, but sales increased by 50 percent to more than $8 million.

Koch Supplies Inc., a $70 million butcher supply business in Kansas City, Missouri, experienced similar success after spending more than $200,000 for a customized network and software, but immediately realized the benefits. The system allowed the company to greatly increase the number of orders it could process in a day, from 1,000 to 50,000, and it also saved Koch Supplies $200,000 a year in inventory and labor costs.

Although many small-business owners are wary of installing expensive computer networks, in some ways, they have an advantage over larger companies that may have existing systems. Smaller companies don't have to worry about integrating a new system with the old one, and they can customize a network to suit their needs, often by hiring a consultant.

Even a relatively simple and inexpensive e-mail account can give a small company a boost by improving communications with customers and suppliers. It can also eliminate much of the cost of doing newsletters and mailings by allowing employees to send all of the material and information via e-mail directly to the customer.

PLUGGING IN NETWORK HARDWARE

Business Week reported in 1996 that there were more than 30,000 consulting firms just waiting for the opportunity to install network software for your business, and fierce price competition from superstores on basic products has kept costs down. Hourly fees generally run from $100 to $150 a month. You can find these services from networking vendors, the Yellow Pages, and word of mouth. Small businesses may be better off using a small operator sympathetic to your specialized needs. Some of the superstore chains, such as CompUSA have packaged deals including hardware, software, and system installation.

Hiring people that is out of the family is just askin' for trouble. You got to forever be not trustin' them and watchin' them all the time.

— RUTH BROOKS

TEAM INC.

I T W A S 1975, late in the fourth quarter, and I was running out of options against the Iron-Curtain defense of the Pittsburgh Steelers. I must have tried 99 percent of the 300 plays in the Minnesota Vikings' offensive playbook while looking for a way to get the points we needed to win the game. Up to that moment, all we had on the scoreboard was a pitiful three-point field goal. The Steelers had one touchdown and the point after. The score was 7–3, their lead.

In the huddle, I racked what remained of my brain after a long afternoon of being trampled and thrown around like a rag doll by one of the biggest, toughest, and most talented defensive lines in the history of the game. Finally, I decided to go with the one play that we had yet to try. "Boys, I've got a winner: *Twenty-nine Reverse.*"

It must have been an odd sight for the fans in the stands to look down upon the playing field and see the entire offensive huddle of the Minnesota Vikings, with the exception of me, the quarterback, falling to the ground laughing.

It was not that my teammates didn't have great respect for my leadership, my ability to win a game in the closing seconds, or my absolute mastery of every nuance of the great sport of football. It was just that they had never seen me throw a block before.

Twenty-nine reverse called for me to hand off to Ed Marinaro, our halfback, who then handed off to our John Gilliam, our speedy wide receiver, on a reverse. To make this play work, it was up to me to then clear the way by knocking down a defensive lineman. For those who are not football fans, defensive linemen are exceptionally large human beings whose idea of a hamburger is a steer stuck between two loaves of bread.

Once my teammates had regained their composure after hearing the play I had selected to win the game, we went to the line of scrimmage. I took the snap and handed off to Marinaro, and moved stealthily toward the sideline to lead the sweep. I had hoped against hope that I would encounter an exceptionally small defensive player. Maybe an influenza-depleted tight end who had lost his way, or a rheumatic punter who'd run onto the field by mistake.

But no, fate was not that kind.

As I ran ahead of Gilliam, who had the football and the game in his hands, I spied a looming, ominous figure blocking out the sun. This wasn't just any defensive lineman. It was one of the best defensive linemen ever to play professional football.

I'm not sure if it is his Christian name, but he was known then, and still is today, as *Mean Joe Green*. Six-feet-four, about 270 pounds. He resembled your average freight train on legs. Only faster.

Many people have asked me over the years what went through my mind at moments like this, and I generally acknowledge that fear is a primary consideration; that and the image of my bones and cartilage being shattered and ripped beyond repair. But I did my job. I did not want to let my team down. I knew it was going to hurt, really hurt, but I refused to be a coward.

I derailed the mighty freight train. Well, in truth, I closed my eyes and dove for his ankle tops. I think I tripped him. Mean Joe went down, somehow, and we scored. The problem was that though we had scored and won the game, I was still on the field, lying within reach of a very angry Mr. Mean Joe Green.

"Was that you?" he growled.

"No, Joe," I said. "I don't know how I got here."

My story changed as soon as I was safely out of his range. I did the victory trot, waving to the fans, as I strutted into the locker room and all the way home. The next morning, driving to our team meeting and a review of the game film by our coach, Bud Grant, I was fully prepared to be lauded as a national hero. I couldn't wait for my teammates to stand and applaud me for my unselfishness, my bravery, and, of course, my blocking artistry. As I parked my car and walked into the Vikings' training headquarters, I wondered, in fact, if there was a Nobel Prize for courage in sports.

When Bud got to the key play, he slowed the film and carefully and incisively broke down every aspect of it, praising the near-perfect execution and noting the role of every player involved. Except me.

It was there on the film, so it wasn't just my imagination. You could see me throwing my puny 185-pound body in front of the thundering might of Mean Joe Green and you could see the entire stadium shake as he went down.

But Bud didn't give me so much as an honorable mention. Not a tip of the cap or a pat on the back. I was devastated. I didn't say anything until the meeting was over and everyone else had filed out of the room. Then I went up to this coach for whom I had the greatest respect.

"Great game wasn't it, Coach?"

"Yes, Fran, it was a great win."

"Coach, how come you didn't mention my block?"

"I saw your block, Fran, it was a great block. If you hadn't made that block, we would have lost the game. Of all the things you have done for this team, all the passes you have completed, all of the touchdowns you have scored, that block was probably the most important play you have made for us."

"But, Coach, why didn't you say all that in the team meeting?"

"Well, Fran, you are such a self-starter, such a highly motivated and positive guy, I didn't think I needed to say anything to you in front of the other guys. Should I?" asked Coach Grant.

"If you ever want to see me block again, you damn well better," I replied.

In football, perhaps more than any other sport, there is no getting around the fact that you cannot get the job done by yourself. To succeed, you need your teammates to work together, to share ideas, and to do what it takes. And when the members of your team do their jobs, I believe they should share in the rewards.

I believe that if you expect your employees to work as hard as you do, you damned well better share the rewards with them. Teamwork has always been vital in sports, but it is increasingly just as important in business, particularly in small businesses that need a small but reliable and skilled team in order to survive.

Customers expect more from business today than ever before. They demand service and performance and attention. Your small business is only as strong as your links to those customers—your employees, whether they are taking orders over the phone, filling them over the counter, or preparing your product for delivery in the back room. Your employees have to have guidelines that instill in them a sense of responsibility to your business and to the customer or client but, more than that, they need to know that you want them to succeed at and enjoy their work in an environment that encourages and rewards them for their efforts. It is up to you as the small-business owner to establish that culture, which reflects the values, beliefs, and attitudes that drive your business.

BUILDING A STRONG COMPANY'S CULTURE

Think about Disney, Ben & Jerry's, Southwest Airlines, and Coca-Cola. Immediately, the distinctive corporate cultures of these leading American businesses come to mind. All are different, sometimes vastly different, but all share the common goals of service, quality, and an unwavering emphasis on exceeding the customer's highest expectations. People who work for companies with well-defined company cultures always know what is expected of them, even in times of rapid change that can necessitate difficult adjustments. "A strong culture is a sort of an anchor for letting people loose to create a lot of change," not impede it, said Harvard Business School's Rosabeth Moss Kanter, in *Inc.* magazine.

When I was starting out in business, I read a book entitled *The Human Side of Enterprise* by Douglas McGregor. It influenced my perceptions of management then, and it remains every bit as insightful and on target today. McGregor believed in *humanistic* management. He felt that a business's success was tied to how well its managers developed the talent and creativity and enthusiasms of the people working within it.

The most successful entrepreneurs I know have learned that their role is not to put controls on their employees so much as it is to help them achieve their goals and use their talents within the framework of the business. The real role of the leader is to turn loose their people and let them put their unique skills to work. The leader's job is to put together people of diverse skills who mesh as a team, just as a football team is made of specialists, kickers, punters, blockers, runners, and throwers. The top team at Coca-Cola includes a Cuban immigrant, a Mexican immigrant, and a native of Georgia. They are a diverse group with diverse talents, but they are a great team. You put a team of talented people together and then let them play and build on each other's talents and weaknesses. It won't work if everyone has the same skills, and it won't work if the coach or boss won't let them apply their talents.

The day of the entrepreneur dictator is doomed. The fact is that you get the best out of your employees by rewarding them— not only with financial incentives and promotions but primarily with helping them achieve their goals, allowing them to grow, and to contribute and to use their talents and gifts.

I saw a terrific news story recently about a group of blue-collar workers in central Illinois who had worked day and night for months to create a giant air cannon that could shoot pumpkins, yes, pumpkins, nearly three-quarters of a mile. In order to compete in a local fall festival, which had a pumpkin-tossing contest, they created this device they called "the Aludium Q 36 Modulator" (named after a television cartoon character's weapon of choice).

These young guys had to master some complex technical problems and measurements in order to build it, and most of them were the type who would rather ride a Harley through a hailstorm than go to the public library. But they did it, and they won a national competition later. They did it out of pride and the pure joy of doing it. That should tell you something right there about the value of creating a positive and rewarding work environment for your employees.

EMPLOYEES AS PARTNERS
. . . .

Anyone who feels compelled to monitor his employees' every move will not succeed over the long term. There are too many other options out there today for people in the job market. Savvy entrepreneurs view their employees as partners and team members. They don't focus on compensating for a worker's weaknesses, instead, they look to develop the employee's strengths and, increasingly, they value employees as vital team members to be protected as the assets they are.

"The average American wants industry, the modern CEO and modern corporate America to treat the worker as a human being, with consideration and thoughtfulness," Aaron M. Feuerstein told the *New York Times* at the end of 1996.

Mr. Feuerstein was speaking from the heart, in an article that inspired people around the country. A year earlier, his family-owned textile company, Malden Mills in Lawrence, Massachusetts, was hit by a devastating fire that left nearly half of the company's 3,100 employees out of work. As newspaper and television reports noted, Feuerstein, 71, could have easily taken the $300 million in the plant's insurance coverage and gone off to enjoy retirement with his wife. Or, he could have taken the opportunity to move the thriving plant, which had $425 million in sales the previous year, to a developing country and its much cheaper work force. But Mr. Feuerstein did not do that. In fact, he did quite the opposite. He stayed and rebuilt and, during the rebuilding period, when his company was not making any money, he kept most of his employees on the payroll for 90 days and began bringing them back as quickly as possible.

"The mensch of Malden Mills," as one newspaper hailed him, was widely respected by his workers even before he acted so honorably. His company nearly went bankrupt in the early 1980's because Asian manufacturers had taken over the market for imitation fur, which had been Malden Mill's leading product. Although many business owners might have used the hard times to extract pay cuts from $10-an-hour laborers, Feuerstein blamed his own marketing mistakes for the problems and left wages alone.

His employees responded by coming up with a new product, Polartec, a fluffy polyester fabric with the thermal properties of wool. It became the insulating fabric of choice of major coat makers such as Lands' End, Eddie Bauer, and L.L. Bean, and opened up new markets, allowing Feuerstein to hire more employees.

Since word got out of his paternal approach to his workers, he has been invited to the White House, honored and feted all over the world. His favorite award, though, came from a Hebrew day school, whose students created a quilt made from strips of Polartec. It is embroidered with eleven panels depicting different biblical phrases of encouragement to do good including "Who is honored? One who honors others."

Feuerstein is a living example of that. He told the *Chicago Tribune* that he believes that "everything rests on our ability to produce quality products for our customers. That's the ballgame. And that quality, when you're done with your state-of-the-art buildings and your engineers and your research and development, depends on that worker on the floor. If he wants to give you quality he will. If he wants to destroy you, he will. The average worker in all corporations wants to give loyalty. Once that is torn apart, I don't think you can ever put it together again."

Feuerstein is a deeply religious man, whose ideas about teamwork and sharing the profits are not just some pie-in-the-sky management fad. Nor is he alone in recognizing the value of treating employees as partners in the business. From giant corporations to small businesses, owners and managers are doing all they can to build a sense of teamwork. Some of the trendier and more adventurous companies send their employee teams on Outward Bound excursions or corporate sports competitions, even paintball-war games, trying to foster the team spirit and build trust among coworkers. There is even a "Synergy through Samba" workshop in which employees pound and shake exotic percussion instruments to promote communication, and team work that has a good beat and is easy to dance to.

From calling in Chicago Bulls' coach Phil Jackson to lecture on Zen and the art of teamwork, to asking their employees to become paintball warriors and samba shakers, corporate managers and business owners are trying all sorts of things to build teamwork. Why? The downsizing epidemic created an atmosphere of distrust and nearly destroyed any concept of loyalty in modern business. In a backlash, more and more employees, whether downsized or just fed up, are leaving big business to start their own enterprises, and those who have remained tend to think of themselves more as independent operators under contract than as part of a team.

In addition, the labor pool in this country is at one of its lowest points in history. Across the country, small businesses are struggling not because there is no market for their products and services, but because they can not find qualified employees to fill the orders and meet the demand.

I don't put much stock in most stereotypes, particularly those about athletes and entrepreneurs, but if it is true that many entrepreneurs are guilty of focusing on profits rather than people, then this chapter is critical to your success as a small-business entrepreneur.

A TOUGH TIME TO FORM A TEAM

· · · · · · · · · · · · · · · · ·

I've been out talking to a great many small-business entrepreneurs in the last year as we've been putting the Small Business

NETwork and this book together, and this is one of the greatest problems they cite to me time and time again. Management experts say that for every employee who leaves a company, at least $50,000 in lost productivity goes out the door, too. Small companies that can't afford training programs and employee orientation are the worst hit, because it takes them so long to restore that lost productivity.

The labor shortage has been compounded by the fact that so many people are involved in starting and running their own small businesses today that there are fewer people willing to work for someone else. Downsized Xerox employee Michael Diener thought he could recruit from his former coworkers when he became customer-services director at Helysis Corp., a machine-tool maker in Torrance, California. But he quickly discovered that nearly everyone he knew that had been laid off at both Xerox and IBM had already started their own businesses.

Half of the 434 entrepreneurs interviewed by Coopers & Lybrand in 1996 cited a lack of workers as their biggest obstacle. *BusinessWeek* reported that service companies complained of a shortage in high-tech workers, marketing and sales executives, scientists, and statisticians. Blue-collar-business owners are also begging for crafts workers and tradespeople.

Two years ago, Hughes Missile Systems laid off 6,000 people in California. Small business entrepreneur Kamrin Benji of Los Angeles told *Business Week* that he figured the layoffs would benefit his start-up business by sending scores of highly qualified job applicants his way. Instead, the computer-parts exporter is still having to recruit at colleges and on the Internet, and it is harder now than ever before to find employees, he said. "I ask myself all the time: 'Where are all these people who lost their jobs?' " he said.

Benji is not alone in his search for employees. Across the country, small businesses have to compete for employees with the huge wave in new business start-ups as well as with bigger businesses that are now rebuilding to put the muscle back in their operations after having downsized to the bone. When Boeing, which laid off 40,000 people during the recession, announced plans to rehire 8,200 workers by the end of 1996, Bill Pritchard, president of Wichita Tool Co., knew he was in trouble. He lost the half-dozen former Boeing workers he had hired, along with a few other workers who went with them. Worse yet, the Boeing people had bragged so much about the wages and benefits of their old jobs, they demoralized those who they left behind at Wichita Tool. The competition for workers has driven up wages even for small businesses that have traditionally lagged behind, but the little guys are still at the bottom of the wage scale, which makes it even tougher to lure employees into the fold.

Some small business have been forced to turn away customers and contracts because they don't have the workers to fill orders and meet demand. Pritchard reported that he had to decline $700,000 in orders in 1996 for that reason, even though he had raised wages by 10 percent and joined a small-business training alliance.

Business forecasters say the labor shortage will probably get worse, with the small business boom occurring just as the generation behind the baby boomers, which is much smaller in numbers, is entering the labor pool. To deal with the shortage of available team members, entrepreneurs who might have been swamped with job inquiries just five or ten years ago, are paying headhunters to find them people, and recruiting relatives, temporary help, and even retirees and welfare recipients. In addition, small-business owners are pulling out the stops to try and keep their employees, offering them everything from job-sharing to flextime. Even car washes and fast-food restaurants have taken to offering signing bonuses and other unusual incentives. Jay Brodsky, president of Ran-Paige Co., a machine-maker in Sellerburg, Indiana, reported that he rented a Long Island conference center in order to recruit workers for his North Carolina plant. He did that only after installing $750,000 in robots to do what had been manual labor, and then offering a 17 percent pay hike to fill the remaining jobs.

KEEPING GOOD EMPLOYEES HAPPY

It is a worker's market out there, so retaining good people is extremely difficult. True, downsizings and layoffs flooded the labor pool for a brief period, but most of the major corporations and industries are now re-engineered and rehiring their best and brightest.

In a survey conducted by Arthur Anderson's Enterprise Group and National Small Business United, 23 percent of the 1,000 small-business owners interviewed said they are sharing profits with employees in order to keep them. Corey M. Rosen, executive director of the National Center for Employee Ownership, told *BusinessWeek* that incentives such as a strong stock plan at a small company can cut turnover in half. His center found that there is a strong correlation between the amount of money a company puts in its stock plan and the number of workers who said they planned to look for other work in the next year.

Another study, this one by the Consortium for Alternative Reward Strategies Research, analyzed the effectiveness of reward plans like profit-sharing and bonuses at 663 companies, about a third of which were small businesses. Those companies that quantified performance reported productivity gains produced a 134 percent return on what they paid out to employees.

Sharing the financial success of your business can be a great way to keep valuable employees, but I believe you have to also create a *culture*, or work environment, that recognizes their importance in other ways. Talented people, whether professionals or not, want to work in a stimulating atmosphere that allows them to contribute and gives them opportunity to grow. A study by the Center for Creative Leadership in San Diego indicated that businesses whose CEOs scored high on employee development, communications, ethics, and motivational skills, also enjoyed the best retention rates, as well as 20 percent higher profits.

I believe that if you are going to survive as a small-business entrepreneur today, you have to share all of your business with your key employees. That means not only the profits, but also the decisions and the responsibility.

I have always loved to brainstorm with the people around me —or even strangers. Whether in the huddle, the conference room, or on an airplane, I get charged up when people are willing to share ideas and strategies. I have tried to maintain the team spirit in business. I may be the president and the ultimate decision maker of my businesses, but I work at involving all the people who work with me. I ask for their thinking and their impressions and ideas. I used the same approach in football. I was always looking for any information, any insight, that would give me an edge. On my teams, everybody contributed and, in my businesses, everybody is a player.

Everyone wants to feel that even if they don't own the business, they at least share in the ownership of ideas. To build this team culture, I think it is also essential to share in the profits of the company in order to reward employees and to encourage them to continue to contribute.

Here are recommended methods for retaining employees:

- *Stock plans.* Most small businesses cannot match the pay of larger corporations, so one method for overcoming that handicap is to give employees stock, or at least the option to buy shares at discounted prices. Management experts recommend that stock grants be made based on performance and vested over several years to encourage employees to stay.
- *Pay for performance.* The happiest people are those who see a direct correlation between how hard they work and how much they make. Financial incentives like profit-sharing and bonus plans can be tied to individual or company performance in order to reward your employees. Often, performance pay is based on a percentage of base pay or profits. In the early 1990's, many companies faced with foreign competition attempted to boost productivity by offering pay for performance to all levels of workers but, in recent years, many companies have preferred to reward all employees rather than recognizing specific individuals.

Pat Lancaster, founder of Lantech, a small manufacturer of packaging machinery in Louisville, Kentucky, told *Fortune* that his attempt to offer incentive pay to some of his 325 employees was a disaster. It resulted in intense rivalries among his employees, favoritism, and manipulation as well as "secrecy, politicking, and sucking noises that you wouldn't believe," according to CEO Jim Lancaster, son of the owner. Lantech scrapped incentive programs for individuals and instead instituted a profit-sharing system in which all employees get bonuses based on salary.

There are management experts who feel also that it is a mistake to give stock options to employees because that makes them, in essence, partners in the business. The more partners you have, the greater potential for problems.

- *Value points.* This is the option recommended by those who feel stock options are too laden with potential for trouble. In a value-point system, employees receive a share of the company without sharing in getting stock or ownership. Value points are claims to a piece of a company's growth in value, as measured by its profits. In this system, employees are rewarded according to how much the company's value increases and also according to how much each employee has contributed to that increase in value.

The total value of your company can be measured by multiplying its net earnings by a standard number, usually 10. An employee can calculate his value-point total by first calculating the company's value at the time he was hired. This is done by taking the net aftertax profit of the company at that time and multiplying it by 10. He then establishes the current value of the company in the same manner. Next, subtract the first value from the second to measure the growth, then divide the growth by however many value points have been awarded.

The value-point system gives the small-business owner more control if an employee leaves, because it allows the owner to tie value-point payments to compliance to noncompetition clauses, paying the points out through the life of the clause.

- *Inclusion.* Management studies show that the employees who stay are those who feel that they are a part of the company, and that their talents, opinions, and suggestions are valued. By allowing your employees to make decisions and to share in the control of your company, you build a culture that says "It's us against the competition" rather than "It's us against the boss."

- *Employee-friendly environment.* Ask your employees what you can provide to make their lives easier, whether it is day care, flexible hours, an employee lounge with snacks, college courses, or professional-development seminars. If your employees feel that you are interested in *their* career development, they will be more inclined to look for ways to help your company get better.

In my new company, the Fran Tarkenton Small Business NETwork, I'm giving all my key employees a piece of the business. I can't stand the idea of not sharing the profits with the people who help my businesses succeed. They are all getting paid salaries to live on, but if these companies do make it big, they will make substantial amounts of money.

I have always tried to create an environment that encouraged my employees to think of themselves as partners in the business. In my software company, I'd set sales goals, and those who reached them got to join me and my family on a Hawaiian vacation. The problem was that I would get to feeling guilty about leaving other good employees behind, so usually we'd end up taking a bunch of other people too. We also had regular picnics and holiday parties and other events to create a strong corporate culture.

I think it is better to spoil your employees a little than to be guilty of neglecting them or of simply trying to milk them for their talent and energy, without ever making the effort to get to know them or to recognize their contribution to your company. Sooner or later, there will be some employees who try to take advantage of that benevolence, or those who are never satisfied no matter what you do for them but, for the most part, an environment in which employees are made to feel valuable and appreciated will result in higher productivity and higher profits. It will also be a much more satisfying business for you to operate.

I am an entrepreneur because I take joy in creating jobs and wealth, and bringing value to my customers and clients. I enjoy business, but not when it has to be conducted on the sharp edge of a razor.

A Poisoned Work Environment
· · · · · · · · · · · · · · · · · · ·

I once worked under a boss who made life miserable for me and everybody else on the team, and I vowed I never would treat people that badly. When you are a football player, the head coach is your boss, and he has more power and control over your life than probably any other type of boss. In truth, most football coaches are more dictators than bosses. Some are fairly benevolent dictators, others rule like tyrants. There are not many bosses in the business world who can set curfews that determine what time you have to be in your hotel room at night. There aren't many who can make you run windsprints or go one on one with monstrous-sized men capable of cracking your skull with a forearm shot. There aren't many football coaches who abuse the power they have, but there have been some, and I had one of them when I played for the Minnesota Vikings.

He had an explosive temperament that had served him well as one of the great quarterbacks in the early days of professional football. It didn't serve his players so well. He was a yeller, a screamer, a guy with a brilliant football mind, but with absolutely no idea of how to manage people so that they did their best because they wanted to win for you. He terrified and terrorized his players instead.

In my rookie season, we had a guy on the team named Red Phillips, who had been a great college player at Auburn University and had then played for the Los Angeles Rams. He was a great wide receiver, tenacious and hard-nosed. After he had been traded to Minnesota, Red contracted a rare blood disorder that weakened him and actually contorted his hands, causing his fingers to gnarl up—a tough disability for a wide receiver, whose job is to catch the football.

Red's weight dropped from 205 to 170 during training camp, but he hung in there. He wanted to keep playing even though he got sick after every practice. Red started for us that season, doing it mostly on courage and willpower. It sure wasn't due to any break that this coach gave him. I'll never forget when, early in the season, we had a tough loss in which Red dropped a pass in the end zone. It would have been the winning touchdown for us and he tried to hang on to it, but his gnarled hands were just not up to the job. The following day, after the coach showed us the film clip of Red dropping that ball, he shut off the projector, and stared at poor Red. The rest of us didn't say a word, we were so mortified. Finally, after glaring at him, this coach said, "Red, I never thought you would come here just to pick up a paycheck."

Red didn't respond; you didn't talk back to the coach in those days. But at that point, I lost all respect for that coach, as a professional and as a human being. I was just a rookie, and there wasn't much I could do about it. I put up with him for my first five years and he made my life—and those of most of the other players— miserable for a good part of those years. I couldn't sleep at night, he'd get me so angry. Finally, before my sixth season, I told team officials that I preferred to be traded rather than to play for him. I was 26 years old, and I had no desire to spend another minute of my life around this abusive coach. As it turned out, I was traded to the New York Giants, and he was fired. I had nothing to do with his firing, at least directly, but I did not feel bad about it either.

You will never get the best out of your employees or your business if that is the environment you create, or allow. In business and in sports, I've been involved in meetings in which the guy in charge ripped apart members of his own team and, believe me, I have seen more of it in business than in sports. I can't function in that sort of environment. It's like asking me to work with a 50-pound load on my back.

GIVE TRUST RATHER THAN TITLES

I believe that the small-business entrepreneur needs to cultivate a sense of teamwork and sharing. I don't have much use for job titles in my businesses. We all have job functions and responsibilities, but I don't need an executive vice president in charge of fax paper, or anything like that. Seriously, I think of every one of my employees as a fellow entrepreneur and I think that is the best way to do business. I want everyone in the organization to be concerned about delivering the best possible product or service to our customers. From the receptionist to the bookkeepers, we are all focused on doing whatever it takes, and share the responsibility for getting the job done.

The best coaches I had were like that. Bud Grant, in particular, was great at sharing leadership without giving up any authority. He had the smallest number of assistant coaches in the league. One time, we were playing the Philadelphia Eagles and Dick Vermeil. I looked across the field and there must have been 14 coaches in green jackets. Bud looked over there and he said, "Fran, see how many coaches they got? You know why that's not good? You have to figure out something for every one of them to do."

He was a common-sense, organized guy. He may not have been a great field tactician, but he was the consummate leader, manager, and enabler. If you couldn't play for him, you couldn't play for anybody. He was great. He was demanding and he set high standards. There was no question that he was the boss, but he always allowed his players to be leaders too. He knew our strengths and weaknesses and he allowed us to contribute. He was not a yeller and a screamer or a dictator. He was one of the truly great leaders I had ever been around. He had authority because the players respected him. I called my own plays, when it wasn't in vogue to let your quarterback do that but, 99 percent of the time, I called the plays that I knew Bud wanted. I can remember many times in the final minutes of play, I'd call a time out and go to the sidelines and ask him what he thought we should do. He would lay out the situation as he saw it and wouldn't tell me what to do, but would let me know what he considered to be the best play. He gave me the information I needed and let me make the call. He was a wonderful facilitator and coach and he knew how to take a bunch of diverse people and make them into a team.

The goal of a business is to win, to win over customers and to beat out the competition, and it should be exciting and fun for everyone involved. Whenever I start a business, I try to look at it as an opportunity to build a culture in which people will be able to put their talents and skills to work so that they will enjoy coming to work every day.

I really don't see how a small business can operate any other way. There is no hiding from animosity and mistrust in a small business. It infects and influences every aspect of your operation. You have to establish a culture of good will. You have to share ideas and successes. I think the worst thing that can happen in a small business is for your employees not to be able to express how they feel and what they think of your ideas. I don't have any desire to make decisions by myself and then have my employees tell me they knew I was headed down the wrong path. That would drive me crazy.

FINDING TALENT

The first thing I look for when hiring employees is character. I want a person who does what he says he will do, a person whose word is her bond. I don't care if someone went to Harvard or Georgia State. The most important credential is honesty and responsibility. Second, I want to make sure the person has the talent required to do the job, because I do not want to put anyone in a position to fail. I want to see everyone in my company succeed and grow. Third, all of my employees have to be team oriented.

When I started the Small Business NETwork, I went after the best and brightest people I could identify, and I told them I would give them a working salary to maintain their lifestyles, but that I also would give them the opportunity to make millions. I also told them that they wouldn't be working for me, they'd be my partners. I gave most of them equity in the business so that their earning potential is unlimited. I think that is the only way to do it, in spite of some of the problems I have had in the past.

I remain convinced that the best way to develop your business is to make your employees an integral part of it. When the success of your business brings real value to their lives, too, it becomes a mutual effort. This also encompasses sharing ideas and decision making with your employees. I believe in an open architecture that connects employees to the business, and helps them feel and be more involved in its success. I call this *ownership of mind and money*. I may be the owner in fact, but I share that ownership. It's risky, to some degree, but it certainly makes it more enjoyable because it is more democratic. There is less *I'm the boss* and more teamwork.

EXPERT OUTSOURCING

Too many small-business entrepreneurs forget the "small" part. The idea is not to hire as many employees as possible so that you can brag about all of your "people." The idea is to have some money left over after you pay everyone's salary. Why should you build a huge infrastructure that weighs down your company? I believe in building a solid core and then outsourcing as much of the work as possible. That way, you eliminate the need for huge offices that cost you $20 a square foot, and all of the furnishings and equipment you need to run them.

Outsourcing is more than a way to save money, although it certainly can work that way, too. Small-business owners are finding that outsourcing can also be a tool to free them from the burden of management tasks that, while essential, are not their areas of expertise.

Tempur-Pedic, an orthopedic mattress importer and distributor in Lexington, Kentucky, had grand plans of rolling out its mattresses in ten regional markets in six months, but owner Bob Trussell didn't have the resources to quickly find and hire an entire national network of salespeople with medical sales experience. Instead, he brought in Sales Staffers International of Danvers, Massachusetts. The salespeople were outsourced, but Trussel set the pay rate, created goals, and conducted evaluations. Those who did not meet sales expectations were replaced by Sales Staffers at no charge. Although half of the first 25 outsourced sales people were replaced, Trussell told *Inc.* magazine that outsourcing "makes sense when you're small and growing, because you can't get bogged down trying to recruit a sales force." Outsourcing firms can handle your accounting, recordkeeping, pay your bills, manage your 401(k) programs and pension plans, as well as control inventory, customer service, and advise you on tax and legal matters, among other services.

Janet Wittes, owner of Statistics Collaborative Inc. in Washington, D.C., turned all of her accounting procedures over to BusinessMatters Inc., which not only did her books, but also discovered that she was underestimating the cost of each employee, sometimes by as much as 75 percent. BusinessMatters began offering tax and personnel help as well as keeping the books, and Wittes's company profits have doubled.

A Coopers & Lybrand study a few years ago found that fast-growing companies with revenues of $1 million to $50 million used outsourcing to achieve savings of 7.8 percent over in-house services. Sales Mark, a sales-rep firm in Little Rock, Arkansas, has more than 100 salespeople scattered over 40 states. Most of them were unhappy that it was taking their company three weeks or more to reimburse their monthly expenses. The company tried giving out cash advances to alleviate the problem, but that created even more bookkeeping woes. Finally, Sales Mark outsourced their reimbursement problems to Gelco PayNetwork, of Eden Prairie, Minnesota, and, as a result, cut the reimbursement cycle to three days.

In the Coopers & Lybrand study, companies that outsourced reported revenues that were 22 percent greater than those that didn't. They also had healthier margins and cash flows. Some outsourcing service companies, like Symmetrix, an information systems provider in Lexington, Massachusetts, guarantee that clients will save money. If they don't, their fee is waived.

It is important that you set specific and clear performance criteria for the outsourcing firms, just as you do for your regular employees. Some small businesses have complained that outsourcing companies don't give them as much service, or the level of talent, that they assign to larger clients

One of the toughest lessons for a young entrepreneur to learn is that you cannot do it all. Most entrepreneurs are go-getters. Most have no lack of self-confidence. And most make the mistake of trying to do more than they are qualified to do. I am an entrepreneur. I can envision a company. I can sell people on my vision. I can market that vision. But I cannot read a contract to save my soul, and I have no desire to keep the financial books or pay the bills, and I do not like to hire or fire people. Those are tasks beyond my ability and I know it. So I hire people to do it for me. I don't necessarily put them all on the company payroll, because I may not have enough full-time work for them to do, but I make sure I have people on retainer who can complete those specialized tasks.

Big businesses can afford to have lawyers and accountants on staff and, in most circumstances, they pay for themselves in a large-scale operation.

As a small-business entrepreneur, you probably cannot afford high-priced full-time experts on financial and legal matters so you may well have two teams: those who are in house and those on the outside. You need to develop relationships and trust with these outside experts, as well as those inside your company, so that they understand you and your business ethics and goals. It would be a mistake to throw your legal work and accounting work to a number of different law and accounting firms. You don't need everybody in town in on your business. You have to know them well enough to trust them with your confidential material. You really have no choice, since you have to trust somebody. The key is to be careful in the people you bring into your company, whether you are talking about lawyers and accountants, or executives and other personnel.

Two outsourcing sources are:

- Outsourcing Institute (800-421-6767). For an annual fee of $399, members receive a newsletter, a list of outsourcing vendors, a CD-ROM with reference material, and discounts on education and training seminars.
- Clearinghouse for Strategic Alliances, Trade & Equity Investment (614-593-4331). A joint venture between Coo-

pers & Lybrand and the National Business Incubation
Association, this clearinghouse helps small businesses locate
potential outsourcing partners for a $300 annual fee that also
gives access to a list of 1,000 companies that provide outsourcing help.

I want my employees to feel that working with me is more fun
than playing golf or going to Hawaii. I want them to look forward
to coming in and using their skills and their training and their
minds. I want them to work in an environment that is not threatening, one that is more like play than work: an environment of
sharing and caring. That is the kind of environment that great
companies are born from and that great things come from. That is
the kind of environment you want to build whether you have two
employees or four employees or outsourcing partners. A value-
based culture creates great things.

It is somethin' all the time in a business, if you just came in and had a day without nobody messin' with you it would be good, now wouldn't it?

— R U T H   B R O O K S

REALITY CHECK

SHORTLY AFTER I returned to the Minnesota Vikings, Bud Grant announced during a team meeting that a lot of the players were trampling all over an area where the groundskeepers were trying to get grass to grow. "There's a sign there that says *Keep off the grass*, so, keep off the grass," he growled.

I thought it was strange that the head coach would make such a big deal about a little grass. After all, we were Super Bowl contenders, the Team of the 1970's (this *was* during the 1970's), and here he was talking about keeping off the grass. But the next day, Coach Grant let me in on his little test. Before it was time to go down to the practice field, he pulled me aside and said he wanted me to come to his second-floor room when everyone else headed out. I found him standing in the window, watching my teammates walking from the meeting hall to the practice field.

"Let's see who listened yesterday," he said.

Sure enough, most of the players walked around the area near the *Keep off the grass* sign, but a few walked right through it. "The guys who went ahead and walked on the grass seed weren't being defiant," he told me. "They didn't see the sign either because they weren't paying attention to me yesterday, or they weren't paying attention as they walked today.

"Those are the players who will make mental mistakes in game situations because they don't pay attention to the signs around them," Coach Grant said.

He was right. Over the course of the season, I kept a watchful eye on those players, at least the ones who stayed on the team, and they were the guys who most frequently made costly mistakes because they were not alert to the things going on around them.

SEEING THE SIGNS
· · · · · · · · · ·

Failing to see the signs will hurt you in sports and in business, too. Missing things like changes in government regulations that affect your business, creeping competition, rising costs of raw materials, shifting technology or consumer needs can trip you up. Today, small businesses can be every bit as complex, competitive, and cruel as big business. The small-business entrepreneur, then, has to be just as agile, alert, and informed as the CEO of a megacorporation in order to survive in this environment.

What makes it so tough today? Intense competition is a chronic headache. It comes from all directions thanks to falling trade barriers, huge disparities in labor costs, and money that can be moved in split seconds. Offshore multinational companies can sneak into the smallest niche markets and steal away customers with high-quality, low-cost goods. Black-market operations nibble away at profit margins. Well-informed customers and clients demand the best for the least and in haste. Do you know anybody who is not looking for a better deal, whether on the job, in the market, or at the mall? Everybody out there seems poised to sue anybody who comes between them and their right to get the best possible deal.

In the meantime, your local, state, and federal officials are busily writing laws and rewriting rules intended to bring order, but that often create more tax burdens and vexing regulations.

Ca-Ce-Len Manufacturing Co., of Granger, Texas, was one of those companies that seemed to do everything right. Though it was in the highly competitive women's apparel industry, it produced high-quality clothing while paying above-average wages and offering better working conditions for its 125 employees than many of its sweatshop competitors. Better yet, its owners, the Benad family, made healthy profits for 20 years, posting revenues of $1.5 million in its best year, 1979.

But when trade barriers began to fall and the underground economy arose, revenues began to plummet for this family business that cared so much for its employees that it ran from 7:30 A.M. to 4 P.M., so working mothers could be home with their children after school.

The passage of the North American Free Trade Agreement in 1993 and the General Agreement on Tariffs and Trade caused shifts in the labor market that were beyond the control of the Benads. Suddenly, huge 8,000-piece orders were lost to foreign manufacturers with lower labor costs, and smaller orders were often snapped up by illegal home-based garment-makers in Dallas, which has about 40,000 illegal workers doing piecework out of their homes, according to a Labor Department study.

In the case of Ca-Ce-Len, fallen trade barriers and the underground economy have made every day a struggle for survival. At last report, the Benads were fighting the good fight, hoping to preserve the family business for the next generations, but with buyout offers and intense competition dogging them, much of the joy of doing business has been extinguished. It is sad, even tragic, but it is also a reality of doing business and, as the movie title a few years back suggested: *Reality bites*.

I don't want you to go into business wearing rose-colored glasses and end up singing the blues because you didn't pay attention to the signs around you. This, then, is a reality check. It's no cakewalk to own a small business, but I strongly believe that for every good thing involved in working for someone else or working in a large corporation, there are five times as many good things about being an entrepreneur and owning your own business. But you have to have both eyes wide open going into it. Picture the Little Entrepreneur sitting on your left shoulder and the Little Employee perched on your right shoulder. When you daydream about owning your own business, each of them gives you an earful:

Little Employee: *You shouldn't give up your corporate job. It provides you a regular paycheck, health benefits, backup support from fellow employees, sick leave, and paid vacations.*

Little Entrepreneur: *True, but I wouldn't be starting my own business if I didn't think it has the potential of providing me a much bigger income over the long term, which will easily pay for my health benefits, my own employees, and even better vacations.*

Little Employee: *What about all of the recognition you get around the office for your good work? All the esteem you have built up with your coworkers and bosses. Who is going to pat you on the back when you are the boss? Where are you going to go to share ideas and industry information? On top of that, who is going to pay for your phone calls? Your phone? The desk it sits on?*

I am a cheerleader for small-business entrepreneurship. I preach the gospel everywhere I go. But I'm not going to lie to you. There may well be things you'll miss when you set out on your own. Here are things that many people claim to miss after starting their own businesses.

- *An occasional pat on the back.* If you do a good job while working for someone else, often you are rewarded in salary, but also in the admiration and esteem of your employer and coworkers. In your own business, odds are nobody will be patting you on the back.
- *The office crowd.* Believe it or not, people often find their best friends among their coworkers. Small-business entrepreneurs sometimes find it lonely going, particularly if they have worked previously in corporations that emphasized a family atmosphere by offering perks such as club memberships or private recreational facilities for employees.

- *Office infrastructure.* When you open up your own office, you quickly realize that there were a lot of things you took for granted back when you worked for somebody else; things such as office supplies, regular and express mail service, janitorial service, photocopy machines, fax machines, printers, and computers. The secretarial pool? Jump in, it's you!
- *The power of the company name.* There are certainly benefits to being with a company for many years. When you work for a major company such as Coca-Cola, AT&T, or NBC, the corporate identity opens a lot of doors to perks and prestige. Owning a small business may not carry quite the same clout and, if you aren't ready to step down a notch or two, it may take you a while to adjust. But there is also a problem that if you leave a big company with a powerful name, you may feel like you have lost your identity and sense of self-esteem. I think that can be dangerous. If you are an entrepreneur, you always are secure in your identity and your skills.
- A *more regimented lifestyle.* Entrepreneurs and would-be entrepreneurs often boast about the freedom of owning our own businesses, but everyone has his own definition of "freedom." Some people can feel freer even if they are working twice as many hours in their own business. Others may not feel so free. There is no such thing as a nine-to-five job if you own the business. Your work is your life. Time is money, your money. Often, people talk about wanting the freedom of owning their own business, but some discover that they've only traded one slavedriver for another—and the new slavedriver looks back at them from the mirror every morning.

  There are also those "free" small business owners who find themselves chained down by debt or demanding bankers. Hopefully, your business will involve doing something that you love, so that balance will come from that, and also from your ability to walk away from work in order to spend time with those you love and in pastimes that are not work-related.

You must understand that it isn't always going to be easy, and that there are some very big challenges involved in starting and operating your own business successfully. You may still need the bottle of aspirin, but at least your headaches will be of your own making, and you will be able to take action to resolve problems rather than having to go through channels or wait for someone else to get around to addressing them.

Although it is estimated that nearly 900,000 new businesses open each year, it has also been reported that there are nearly 800,000 companies "terminated" each year; most of them go voluntarily, if reluctantly, but an estimated 70,000 go down owing money to creditors. Failing companies left nearly $30 billion in unpaid bills, and forced thousands to join the unemployment lines in 1994, according to Dun & Bradstreet. Not a pretty picture, but more than half of the business failures leave less than $25,000 each in liabilities while the headline-making collapses with liabilities of more than $1 million account for less than 5 percent of all failures.

Why do small businesses fail? Why do any businesses fail? In many cases, the business climate is the determining factor, at least statistically. Business failures go up in recessions and down in boom times. In 1992, which was gripped in recession, nearly 100,000 companies went down for the count. In 1995, a relative boom year, Dun & Bradstreet counted 71,000 failures.

Your business's location can be a factor in the rate of failure. The Midwest's failure rate in 1994 was one-third lower than the national average, according to *Inc.* magazine. The Pacific Northwest's was two-thirds above the national average. California's rate was three times that of North Carolina and twice that of New Jersey.

Dun & Bradstreet reports that the riskiest time in a business's life is within the first five years, when 40 percent of businesses fail. Twenty-seven percent fail within the first six to 10 years and 33 percent go down after more than 10 years. Some industries are also more prone to failure. Coal mining, for example, sees 251 failures for every 10,000 companies, while apparel manufacturing has 86 failures for every 10,000. Industries less prone to failure include oil-pipeline companies, funeral homes, and membership organizations.

In a free-enterprise economy, failure is part of business. Broad economic trends such as the statewide recession in California in 1994 can take down a lot of small-business entrepreneurs who thought they were doing everything right. Not coincidentally, California is considered one of the riskiest places to do business. Sometimes it is the industry as a whole that is suffering, taking businesses with it—as has happened in recent years in the commercial fishing business. Global competition has been tough on many small-business entrepreneurs, particularly those in the clothing industry.

Sometimes, then, businesses do all the right things and still fail because of outside influences. All you can do is take care of those factors that you do have influence over and, believe me, there are plenty of those.

In this chapter, I am going to lay out for you some of the primary reasons businesses fail. The purpose is not to frighten you or make you decide to go back to the Acme Corp. fold. This chapter is simply intended as a cautionary exercise, to help you be aware of problems that can occur, so that you can either head them off or find solutions. I will offer suggestions for those solutions either in this chapter or later in the book.

Why do companies fail? There are the general reasons and common afflictions such as lack of a market, poor management, lack of capital or financial controls, poor pricing, overwhelming competition, uncontrolled growth, and poor location. But rather than give you the usual generic reasons, and then offer the sage advice of "Don't make these mistakes," I have played business doctor and drawn up a list of common ailments. The doctor is now in. Learn the early warning signs. Understand how they afflict a business, and know the treatment. Above all else, remember Ruth Brook's rule, tattoo it to your forehead if you must: *You have to have more money coming in than going out!*

1. Lost identity.

Some companies are found wandering the streets dazed and confused because of a sudden attack of amnesia. They forget what they are. They undergo an identity crisis. Then, they collapse. It happens all the time. Just when the business seems to be running itself (if you hear yourself saying that, sound the alarms!), you find it floundering.

I think it is a myth that entrepreneurs are not good business operators. Ted Turner has done okay. So has Bill Gates. They are smart enough to hand over the nuts-and-bolts stuff to the MBAs, while doing what they do best—keeping the vision alive. In many cases, the reason businesses fail is not because they are run by entrepreneurs, but because they *lost* their entrepreneurial spirit. IBM nearly toppled after the Watson brothers, who had steered it to greatness through their entrepreneurial and visionary leadership, had stepped down. When these guiding geniuses left, IBM lost its vision, it got greedy and became inbred, and along came Apple and Microsoft and the wake up-call is still being answered.

Some entrepreneurs lose track of their vision. They allow their employees to run the company, and somehow trust that they share the vision that made it work in the first place. Big mistake. Every business has to have someone who wears the placard and shouts the question at every opportunity: *What is our core expertise? Why have we been profitable in the past?*

Those are the key questions that should guide your decision making every day. They keep you from allowing your business to stray. Jostens, the class-ring company based in Minnesota, had a 34-year record of consecutive sales and earnings increases, until the late 1980's when it diversified into computer systems, which its senior executives knew very little about. By 1993, it was reporting a $12 million annual loss. "Nobody was taking a hard look at what was going on—nobody seemed to be asking the right questions," noted an equity analyst who had followed Jostens' fall.

Business owners and executives are like anyone else, when they forget who their companies are, they begin fumbling around for anything they can grab hold of. If you find yourself, or your top executives, going to management seminars, making pilgrimages to management gurus, and doodling quadrants, quality circles, or matrixes on message pads, take it as a warning sign that the vision has been clouded, if not lost. Employees grow weary of these fads quickly and, when they balk, it creates frustration and seemingly desperate efforts to motivate workers or to revitalize the morale. The preachers around the campfire again serve as a good example of a bad example.

There is also the tendency among business that are dazed and confused to latch on to inappropriate things, such as other businesses. Jostens did this, as did Eastman Kodak, which did very well for many years in the camera and film field but then suddenly grabbed onto the pharmaceutical and consumer health-product business, nearly bringing itself down in the process. *Fortune* magazine once noted that Borden was perhaps "the most egregious recent example of a company that forgot its *raison d'etre.*" Between 1986 and 1992, the magazine noted, Borden's management made over 90 acquisitions, snapping up, among other things, a whole group of small regional food companies. As a company built on the chemical business, Borden was lost in the food marketing department and sales plummeted for 15 straight, nightmarish quarters before Borden was itself the target of a "fire sale" takeover.

2. Blinded by success.

Ignaz Schwinn led his Chicago bicycle company through boom-and-bust waves at the turn of the century, when 300 other bicycle makers went under. But he was no longer around when his descendant Edward Schwinn, Jr., was unable to extend the long-term success of one of America's great brand-name companies. In the early 1980's, the U.S. bicycle market, of which Schwinn once controlled 25 percent, had been hard-hit by foreign competition. China and Taiwan, in particular, captured huge chunks of the market not only by selling their own brands, but also using their cheap labor costs to win contracts to make bicycles for U.S. companies, including Schwinn. Specialty-bike makers, such as Wisconsin-based Trek USA, also cut into Schwinn's market share.

Schwinn's management missed the market shift from reliable, single-gear bikes to faster racing models and mountain bikes. And, sooner or later, blind companies hit the wall just as Schwinn did. The heirs of the founder sold out to Scott Sports Group.

Commerce Clearing House, like Schwinn, was a long-time winner. It was a darling on Wall Street in the late 1980's, a top ten Fortune 500 company in earnings per share and return on equity, but its management's vision became clouded with success. No one looked ahead and saw the development of electronic databases coming. The majority of CCH customers were accounting and law firms that jumped on the new technology. One top executive told *Fortune* magazine that the switch to electronic databases caught CCH unprepared. "It's like we were sitting there with our feet in cement," he told the magazine. Or their heads.

Business history is full of similar examples. Companies become successful and arrogance sets in. It happened to IBM. It happened to Apple. It happens to any business that does not pay attention to what is going on around it, and I am talking about all the way around it. Who ever would have imagined ten years ago that cable television companies would be competing against Baby Bells, and now against Internet-access providers too?

Andrew Grove, CEO of Intel Corp., the world's dominant maker of microprocessor chips, including the Pentium, is an advocate of business "paranoia." As a rather extreme preventative measure to business blindness, he advocates never sleeping, leaving the lights on all night, and an elaborate alarm system.

This Hungarian-born high-tech entrepreneur holds that CEOs and top executives are often the last to recognize major and even revolutionary changes coming to their businesses. He cites movies with sound, the personal computer, and Wal-Mart as examples of major developments that caught industry leaders by surprise— and cost most of them millions and millions of dollars.

Grove isn't just theorizing. In the mid-1980s, Intel Corp. had to abandon its core business—manufacturing memory chips, which was being taken over by the Japanese—and build an entirely new business producing microprocessors instead.

During that period, in which he had to lay off thousands of employees, "I learned how small and helpless you can feel. I felt confusion and frustration that comes when the things that worked before no longer do. And how hard it was to get our people to realize that we had to change."

"Paranoia, to me, means being prepared for—and expecting—the worst," Grove told the *Chicago Tribune*. "It's an attitude toward business in which success always means being a target for competitors. That's not bad, it's how we improve and get more powerful. But if you're responsible for maintaining success, you can't stop to smell the roses. You have to be constantly aware of that natural law."

As Intel, Apple, and others have evidenced, very few businesses, particularly small businesses, can afford to focus so intently on their own operations that they don't pay any attention to what is going on around them, or coming straight at them. The pace of change is so rapid today that no one can afford to let their guard down, let alone to go about business blindly.

3. Too bulked-up to do business.

Many successful businesses fall victim to their own success. They find themselves in great shape, running smoothly, building wealth, and, suddenly, someone tempts them, or they make the decision to go for even greater strength by adding bulk. They go on a buying or spending spree, acquiring another company or expanding product lines or adding to their real-estate holdings—all with visions of greater profits coming their way.

It *can* happen that greater profits are realized that way, but it is also possibile that the added debt load or increased demand on production will make a previously nimble company less able to respond to fluctuations in their market or to increased competition. It happens in companies big and small.

USG Corp., the giant Chicago building-products company, bulked up in the 1980's out of fear of being targeted by corporate raiders with eyes on its $150 million cash stockpile. To fend off a perceived takeover attempt, USG undertook a $3 billion, highly leveraged recapitalization that made this once-strong company vulnerable on another front—a recession. When it hit in the early 1990's, the bulked-up USG had losses over two years that totaled $350 million. Although it briefly declared Chapter 11 so that it could restructure long-term debt, USG's new management has survived, but many companies that get too heavy with debt do not.

Maytag, the quality-brand appliance company, was cleaning up with all-time earnings of $88 million before it took on heavy debt in 1989 by purchasing Chicago Pacific for $1 billion. The plan was to improve long-term health by securing Chicago Pacific's lucrative Hoover Co. and its European markets, but, as *Fortune* magazine noted "the cure was worse than the company's ills." Maytag fell into serious disrepair during the recession of the early 1990's, and is only now beginning to return to health.

USG and Maytag are not small businesses, but the same rules apply to small-business entrepreneurs who get in over their heads with debt, then discover that it cripples their ability to respond to market changes and competition.

Penny's Pastries in Austin, Texas, was a small business cooking along nicely with sales of $160,000 in 1994 for its decorative cookie wholesale business. Then, when owner Penny McConnell landed a $500,000 account with Southwest Airlines, she thought her success and profits would multiply accordingly, but she couldn't keep up with Southwest's production demands of five-million cookies a year. The increased production required her to create a new recipe, new packaging, new equipment, more employees, and a bigger plant to hold it all. A year after winning the big contract, Penny had to file for bankruptcy.

4. Going gray and afraid to admit it.

I can relate to this one. As I moved into the latter third of my playing career, I had to abandon a playing style that had made me one of the most successful professional quarterbacks of all time. I just couldn't scramble as efficiently and as effectively as I had in the past. Some people dared to suggest that maybe I had slowed down. I prefer to think it was that the younger players had speeded up. Whatever it was, I realized that I was going to have to change my playing style if I was going to continue to be effective for my team. So, I became a pocket passer, although I'd still scramble outside every now and then just to prove I could do it.

I have seen many once-successful companies refuse to change their approach, even when it is painfully obvious that the old ways have become outdated or ineffective. These companies are like the Soviet Union in the years before it disintegrated; everyone had a guaranteed job, but the nation was falling apart because no one was doing much.

A prime example of a big business fallen prey to this ailment was General Motors under Roger Smith in the 1970's and 1980's. It's said that there were top executives who recognized that GM needed to rejuvenate its strategies, but it was so burdened down with bureaucracy that change was extremely difficult to bring about. Often, the only cure seems to be to lop the head of the company off—its management team—and put in a more dynamic team. It has happened at Kodak, Apple, Goodyear, GM, and IBM; don't let it happen to your small business.

Wolfgang Schmitt is the CEO of one of the most successful corporations in America, Rubbermaid Inc., yet he is a huge advocate of change as a tool for continuous growth. Rubbermaid is legendary for rolling out 400 new products each year, with one-third of its annual sales coming from product that are five years old or less. How does Rubbermaid keep up this small-business entrepreneurial pace? Schmitt has created teams, nearly 30 of them, that act as miniature Rubbermaids. The five members on each team are in charge of their own sales, marketing, financing, manufacturing, research and development, and profits. The teams give the employees a sense of ownership and entrepreneurship and create a hunger even within such a large and successful corporation.

A Rubbermaid team in search of new-product opportunities and ideas may go into the field for weeks, and work in a McDonald's restaurant or a hospital kitchen—either in the U.S. or abroad. Schmitt calls this "rubbing up against the end user," and he is known for sending his employees all over the world in search of ideas—they bring back up to 4,000 a year—and he allows them to "go with the gut" when choosing which ideas to pursue. Schmitt's favorite quote is from Italian author Giuseppe Tomasi Di Lampedusa: "If we want everything to remain as it is, it will be necessary for everything to change." That is an excellent motto for creating hunger in any entrepreneur, whether the business is big or small.

5. *Customer abandonment.*

It's hard to believe that in this day of nearly obsessive attention to customer service and needs that companies still make the mistake of forgetting or neglecting their customer base, but it does happen. *Crain's Small Business* in Chicago conducted a consumer survey on attitudes toward small business in 1996 in which it reported "One message came through loud and clear . . . Whether it's a corner store or a downtown supplier to corporate America, lousy service is the greatest sin a small company can commit. And when it happens, owners get the blame, because customers think service problems can be traced back to management and a lack of operational controls." On the positive side, the same survey found that "When small businesses hit their stride by providing service and satisfaction, customer loyalty zooms."

How can small-business owners fail to realize this obvious point? Some entrepreneurs are so in love with their product or service that they feel certain the customers will find them. They might, or they just might find someone else. Do you want to leave that up to chance? Any business that isn't constantly seeking new customers and new products to offer their existing customers is probably headed on a downward slide and picking up speed fast.

You cannot expect customers to find you. In fact, you have to give them overwhelming reasons to buy your product, and to keep buying it, if you are going to stay in business and keep growing. Rubbermaid obviously understands that, as do most successful long-term businesses.

Small-business owners need to remind themselves even more than big businesses, because they are far more vulnerable to shifts in customer needs and desires. Instead of "Remember the Alamo" they should put up posters saying "Remember IBM and its mainframes?" and "Don't forget how Wal-Mart sneaked up on Sears."

Small businesses dealing in retailing, fashion, high-tech, and entertainment are among the most vulnerable to sudden shifts in consumer demand, trends, and swift advances. How do you stay in touch? It isn't as easy as it might seem. Marketing surveys and focus groups are probably not enough. Do what the networks do come election time; conduct exit polls. Track down former customers who have stopped coming around. Find out why they defected or stopped using your product or service.

Management experts say that businesses big and small would do well to make their salespeople two-way sources of information. Instead of simply training them to sell your product or services to the customers, you should train them also to gather information from the customers to bring back to you. Would your customers recommend your business to their friends? What brings them to you? Location, advertising, product line? This is valuable information that could be readily gathered if your salespeople are trained to receive as well as sell.

6. Employee indigestion.

Internal problems can cripple business just as easily as outside forces particularly in small businesses, but in big ones, too. Many attribute the fall of Eastern Airlines to widespread employee revolt. More and more large corporations are finding their top executives under attack from within by employees who are hit by downsizing and salary cutbacks, while the top guys in the executive suites are taking home huge bonuses and stock options.

Small businesses rely even more on their employees than big companies, and a disgruntled workforce can drive off customers who may never return. Take your lead from The Olive Garden restaurant chain, which recruits its managers from within the communities they serve, or the Leo Burnett advertising agency in Chicago, which works hard at linking pay to performance and providing stability to counter the often-chaotic work atmosphere at other advertising agencies.

At a time when company loyalty—and respect for employees—is nearing an all-time low, you can attract high-quality people without paying exorbitant wages by creating a work environment based on rewards and respect and stability.

7. Lack of contract-itis.

It is estimated that half of the business partnerships in the country are conducted with no formal contract, or with a contract that is outdated. A partnership without a contract is like a common-law marriage—and we all know how much trouble those can get you into. Did you know that in most states if one partner leaves the partnership ceases to exist? Your leases could be canceled, banks could call in their loans, and you might be required to pay off the partner who is leaving you. Partnerships without contracts are disasters waiting to happen.

You should go into any partnership cautiously, and only after first sitting down with your potential partner, analyzing the business thoroughly, and determining whether it would be better to form a partnership or a professional corporation. Many small businesses go with the professional corporation option because it protects them from being held personally liable for the actions or debts of their associates. Partnerships, on the other hand, often are easier to set up and dissolve, and they have some tax advantages over professional corporations.

Either way, make it an official agreement, legal and binding, that lays out how many new employees will be added, how others can become partners or stockholders, and just what will happen if one partner retires, dies, becomes disabled, or runs off to join the circus.

8. Harebrained business.

I get approached with a lot of ideas, some of them good, others that are harebrained. Overexcited entrepreneurs sometimes get deep into start-ups, pouring a lot of money and time into a project without thinking it through. Worse yet is the entrepreneur who starts out with a fatally flawed idea but sticks with it anyway.

John Y. Brown, the former governor of Kentucky, is in no way a foolish guy. He made hundreds of millions after buying Kentucky Fried Chicken from Col. Harland Sanders, and he married former Miss America Phyllis George.

Although he is a shrewd guy, he came to me a few years ago

with a bit of an odd idea. He called me one time from an airplane and asked me to meet him at the Atlanta airport to discuss this incredible, wonderful, fantastic, can't miss idea he had for a business.

I drove out there thinking I'd probably be able to buy my own island if John Y. cut me in on this deal that was such a sure thing that he refused to tell me what it was over the telephone.

I found him in the airport, and he started out by telling me that he'd seen how well I had done with my entrepreneurial business putting advertising on airline-ticket jackets. "I thought that was ingenious," John Y. told me.

Then he pulled out his beautiful four-color ads and revealed his idea. He wanted to put advertising boards inside bathroom stalls in public restrooms and sell the ads to major companies.

I nearly fell on the floor laughing! It was a creative idea. It had some appeal. He definitely had a captive audience in this particular market.

I admired the fact there here was a guy who had already made millions and millions of dollars but he still had the old entrepreneurial fires burning. But, man, what a plan! Mind you, John Y. had put a lot of money into this already. He had beautiful frames made up and he had signed on some of the major office-supply companies as advertisers, but this brings up another reason that businesses fail. John Y. had what appeared to be a reasonably sound idea, at least at first blush. Without a doubt, he had an open field. It wasn't going to be crowded in the latrine market. But there was one bad flaw. The delivery system. How was John Y. going to sell that product? He couldn't just take the National Director of Public Restrooms out to lunch and cut a deal to stock every stall in America with his billboards.

I asked John Y. about that problem. Are you going to have someone go out and sell from building to building? Are you going to hire someone else to put the ads in every stall in every building and to keep updating them for you? He did not have a good answer.

You can have a reasonably good idea, but if you can't have a cost-efficient way of delivering it to the market, then you've got a business going nowhere. John Y. got back on his plane and I drove back to my house still dreaming about owning my own island. His ads-in-the-privy project went down the can, where it belonged.

But bless him for thinking of me, and for thinking like an entrepreneur, even with all that money in the bank. He is still having fun in business.

As long as you learn a lesson, I figure you come out ahead.
— RUTH BROOKS

WHAT LOSING
TAUGHT ME
ABOUT WINNING

ONE OF the things I most admire about Ruth Brooks is that she will always tell you that she has never run into any serious problems in her businesses. She will tell you this even though she most certainly has had problems and challenges, just as every businessperson does. But Ruth's entrepreneurial spirit is strong enough to endure the hardships and to move on.

I know of one particularly serious problem Ruth had because she mentioned it to me one day in passing. A few years ago, a power failure in the middle of the summer knocked out all of the fans that cooled the chicken houses at Ruth's farm. She lost 18,000 chickens that were to have gone to market the next day. She and her husband had been feeding those chickens for months. They had some serious money invested in the poultry, and they saw no return on their investment.

This problem nearly wiped out one of her businesses and, yet, Ruth told me, "That is just the way with farming. You can't count on nothin'. It was a disaster, but I don't let stuff like that worry me. I don't sit and say 'Oh Gawd, we lost all that money.' We just went on and tried to make some more as best we could. You can't measure hardness on how hard you have to work."

True entrepreneurs never expect to fail, but they also have no fear of failing because they don't see failure as terminal. They see it as a natural part of the process of learning and growing and developing their ideas and their businesses. They believe that if you haven't failed, you haven't been trying very hard.

Bill Gates, one of the world's most successful entrepreneurs, has offered that he considers failure a good trait in job applicants because it shows that they have taken risks. The way people handle failure offers a measure of how they deal with change, he theorizes.

In his book *The Road Ahead,* he writes that "Success is a lousy teacher. It seduces smart people into thinking they can't lose. And it's an unreliable guide to the future. What seems the perfect business plan or latest technology today may soon be as out-of-date as the eight-track tape player, the vacuum-tube television, or the mainframe computer."

As Gates notes, while success is what we all strive for, failure can have benefits too. Yet most of us fear failure to some degree. If you have a healthy fear of failure, you won't rush into things and you will take care in your business decisions. And if you have a healthy perspective on failure, you won't roll over and die when something you try fails; instead, you'll learn from the experience and try again. I have come to understand that failures are part of the process of success. Far too many people think of failure as a finality: *I screwed up, I'll never get another job. I lost my business; now I'll have to go to work for someone else.* But those who achieve lasting success in business are very often people who have failed, learned from the experience, and bounced back because they didn't personalize the failure. They didn't see it as a chronic condition that would never go away.

The Failure All-Stars includes many familiar names in business. Walt Disney was fired from an ad agency early in his career because he appeared to have "a singular lack of drawing ability." Both Disney and Henry Ford experienced bankruptcy before they came up with ideas that today continue to make millions and millions of dollars. More modern examples of one-time failures include General Electric's Jack Welch, who was blamed when a plastics plant that he was managing blew up. Welch, now recognized as one of the best CEOs in the country, thought that he would never get another job in business.

I have certainly had my own share of failures in losing three Super Bowls. I had a chance to put lessons from my football losses into practice in business just a few years ago, when the software company I started from scratch and built into a $150 million business hit hard times. The lessons I learned from this experience were, to a large degree, the inspiration for many of the ideas and advice in this book.

TAKING A HIT
. . . .

In 1980, after hearing a great deal about a hot new area of technology called CASE (computer aided software engineering), I bought into it. I am not a computer wizard by any stretch of the imagination, but I know a good entrepreneurial opportunity when I see it. By 1980, it was obvious that computer technology was going to be a hot area for business development, and my contacts in the business told me that CASE was a cutting-edge process being used to make computer programming more efficient. After researching the business potential of it, I bought into the CASE technology by acquiring rights from a New York company to build and encode data-analysis systems. No banks would loan me the money I needed, so I put up $3 million of my own money, which came from the cash flow generated by my other businesses. I called my company Tarkenton Software, and I had visions of it becoming a leader in the high-tech field.

After several years of building the business and learning more about the market, we merged Tarkenton Software with a highly regarded Michigan company called Knowledgeware and adopted their name. Our goal was to help give small-business owners access to mainframe computers. We provided products that were widely hailed as leading-edge tools for programmers that wanted to customize their own mainframe software.

In the summer of 1989, we got a big boost when IBM signed a licensing deal to use our technology, and to work with us to develop the next generation of programming tools. Big Blue even bought a 10 percent stake of Knowledgeware for $10.5 million.

I felt we were on our way to become the next giant high-tech company, particularly after we went public the following October at $12.50 a share and raised $37.5 million. After a strong year in 1990, the stock climbed to $25 a share and we were ranked No. 2 on *Business Week*'s annual ranking of hot-growth companies in 1991. Within a few months of that article, revenues doubled again and the company I had built had grown to a $129 million operation.

It was a heady time for me. I had been involved in business all of my adult life. I had done very well, but I was always tagged with the "jock" image. There were certainly worse things, but I had fought long and hard for respect as a businessman, and Knowledgeware, a company that I built virtually from the ground up, was to be my greatest achievement in business. I owned 1.5 million shares worth $33 million, but more important, I had created a highly successful business that employed hundreds of people, and provided a product that benefitted other businesses.

But, then, as can happen in business as well as in sports and in life, the bottom dropped out. In 1991, the market shifted, as corporations moved away from mainframe computers to personal computer networks. Knowledgeware was not the only company hit hard. IBM also slumped badly, as did many smaller companies that had not seen the massive shift into personal computers coming.

In October of 1991, we reported an unanticipated loss of $4.9 million for the first quarter. Knowledgeware's winning streak had come to a rather abrupt end. But neither the company, nor I, had failed. Over the next three years, I refused to be defeated. I worked to protect the investment of our stockholders and, over the long run, I did that. I kept Knowledgeware out of bankruptcy and, in 1994, sold it to Sterling Software, because it was a company that could leverage the technology we had developed. The shareholders who stayed with us have been rewarded handsomely: the stock that had dropped at one point to $3 a share is now six times that price.

I took some hits in the media; if you are in the game, you are bound to hear some boos from time to time. But at least you are in the game; the people doing the booing are only watching.

GETTING BACK IN THE GAME

I lost three Super Bowls in front of millions and millions of fans and the biggest television audiences in history. Did it hurt? Oh yeah. You don't know what losing is until you lose a Super Bowl. The winner's locker room is full of television reporters and team owners and champagne overflow. The loser's locker room is like the back room of a slaughterhouse—nothing but lifeless, bloodied meat hanging on a hook. You are lucky if the equipment manager talks to you, and then it's just to ask you to make sure you turn in your stuff. You are shunned by everybody else for weeks afterward. Your friends don't call because they don't want to tell you how much money they lost on you, and your enemies know they don't need to bother. I've always said losing in a Super Bowl didn't exactly help me figure out who my friends were, but it narrowed the field considerably.

But I never felt defeated after a Super Bowl loss. I was angry that we lost, sure, but I always felt that we could have won it with a little more time and a few more breaks. Within a few hours of each of those losses, I was ready to get back in the fight again. I certainly never questioned my worthiness to be in the game. The same was true with Knowledgeware—the only difference was, the clock didn't run out on me there. I got to play it out and walk away with a win in the end.

THE PHILOSOPHY OF FAILURE

Around the time that I sold Knowledgeware, I attended a function in Atlanta at which I was asked to introduce Hank Aaron, who is an old friend of mine and one of the greatest baseball players of all time. Since Hank and I have a close relationship, I thought I might open my introduction by teasing him a bit: "As you may know, Hank hit the most home runs of any player in history. More than Babe Ruth. More than Mickey Mantle. Hank hit *seven hundred and fifty-five* of them!," I told the crowd. "But what you may not know is that Hank Aaron also struck out more than anybody in the history of baseball."

I got a few cheap laughs out of that, but then Hank stepped up to the plate: "My friend Tarkenton threw more touchdown passes than anybody in the history of football, and many of those records stood for more than 20 years, but what you may not know is that he was also intercepted more than anybody in the history of football!"

Actually, Hank was being kind. Others have pointed out that even though I completed more passes for more yardage and more touchdowns than any quarterback before me, and even though I ran for 3,674 yards and 32 touchdowns in my 18 year career while only missing 8 out of 254 games, I never won "The Big One." I never got to wear the Super Bowl ring. And for many years at the Super Bowl, it was always noted that I had lost more than any other quarterback.

That is why I was particularly interested in Super Bowl XXVII in Atlanta in 1993. It was the Dallas Cowboys against the Buffalo Bills, and even though the game was held just three miles from my house in Atlanta, I watched it in my basement on my knees, praying. Why? I prayed for the Cowboys to beat the Bills, even though I am not a big Dallas fan, and even though I like Jim Kelly, because if Dallas beat Buffalo and if Jim Kelly stayed healthy and played the entire game, then Jim Kelly, bless him, would break my record for the most Super Bowl losses. My prayers were answered; Dallas won. Kelly lost, and that monkey was off my back. That was one record I had no desire to hold on to.

Yes, I lost three Super Bowls, dammit. But did that make me a loser as a professional football player? They didn't seem to think so at the Pro Football Hall of Fame, where I was inducted in 1986. I didn't think it made me a loser in life either, but after going through all the turmoil with Knowledgeware, I suddenly began to wonder. Was I a failure because I had failed to keep it going?

I had walked out of those three Super Bowl losses disappointed and angry with myself, but I had never doubted myself then, and I didn't doubt myself when things grew tough at Knowledgeware. You fight and you find solutions.

Talking with Hank Aaron that night put me in a reflective mood. It got me thinking through the nature of failure and just what makes a person a failure. I concluded that the only thing that can make you a failure is to accept that mantle, and to quit with it on your back. I am no quitter. Neither should you be.

We all experience failures and disappointments. We lose games. We strike out. We fail in business. We blow relationships. People hurt us by talking about us or abandoning us. Some even steal from us. Failures, losses, and defeats hurt us and anger us and cause us to question our own value and worthiness. That is all fine and good. It is part of the process of living. Being hurt and angry and reflective are not dead ends. Those emotions go away if you release them, and so does the sense of failure. It is not a fatal disease. In fact, it is highly treatable. The lesson I want to share here is that the only way you can become a "failure" is to accept failure as a finality. It is not a finality, however. It is simply one step, a difficult step, but just one step in the process of living.

Here are ways to handle failure that I've found in my experience and in my research on the topic.

WINNING THROUGH FAILURE
. . . .

Step one: Think of failure as part of the process of succeeding.

How many times have we heard this as children and adults, but never really accepted it? Yet it is an undeniable truth. Failure is a part of everything we do, from sports to personal relationships to business. It happens sooner or later to everyone. Nobody escapes it. Not Hank Aaron. Not Michael Jordan. Not Bill Gates. Not Ted

Turner. Not IBM. Certainly not me or you. Welcome to the Failure Club, the least-exclusive club in the universe!

Stephen Phillips went broke when his restaurant went bust, then he went on an eating binge that did not stop until he weighed 325 pounds. He finally stopped trying to eat his way out of failure, and instead worked his way out, founding The American Institute for Nutrition & Diet of Bayside, New York, and also Park Avenue Medical & Nutrition Clinic, where he and his physician partners treat more than 200 patients a week.

Phillips told *Success* magazine, "A Nobel prizewinner once proved that a cell changes or grows only after going through a period of vulnerability. It was called the 'Rock Bottom Theory.' It's only after you hit rock bottom that you achieve the prudence, confidence and adaptability needed to grow and succeed.' "

Behavioral studies have found that successful business executives have learned to perceive failure as merely a false start or a missed step on the road to success. Are they deluding themselves? Certainly there are people who have failed and never recovered but, for every one of them, there is someone who hit bottom, got back up, dusted off, and began climbing.

Those who remain defeated are generally those who hang on to failure. They go into hiding, they become embittered, they get tied up in drawn-out court battles. They refuse to let go of it, and it eats up their lives. Those who remain in the game have learned to take a hit from failure and bounce off it to look for the next victory. Steven Jobs was the cocky, messianic cofounder of Apple Computers. After leading the wave of personal computers and being hailed as a genius, he lost a power struggle for control of his own company. His startup NeXT met with only lukewarm success. Two failures, however, does not mean Jobs is out of the game. His Pixar digital studio was responsible for the animation processes of the hit movie *Toy Story*, and in late 1996 it was announced that Jobs was returning to lead Apple once again.

Step two: Don't run from failure.

I know it may sound strange coming from an old scrambler, but you can't run from failure, loss, or defeat, so don't waste your energy. When life blindsides you, and it will, acknowledge the hit just like I used to do when Mean Joe Green or one of those other monsters knocked me on my butt. "Nice shot, outhouse-breath. Keep it coming." Failure, like Mean Joe Green, doesn't go away just because you ignore it. It hangs around and, when you least expect it, nails you. I had a friend who got fired from his job and thought he was handling it fine. He went home and immediately applied for a new job and got it. But once he settled into that new job, he found himself making mistakes that he had never made before. He also found that he didn't have his usual creativity. He felt depressed and disoriented even though it was a better job than the one from which he had been fired.

What happened? He thought he had bounced back; but he had really been running from failure. He had never taken the time to acknowledge that he had experienced a failure, a loss, or a set-back. He had not dealt with the emotions that accompany being fired and, eventually, those feelings caught up with him on the new job.

Men in particular tend to deny their feelings of failure and loss, and that can be destructive. I'm not suggesting that you put on a signboard that says "I Failed!" and wear it around town. But you should find someone who cares about you, or even a professional counselor, and sit down and talk through what happened to you and how it made you feel.

Step three: Acknowledge your role and your responsibility for what happened.

This is not to say that you should take *all* the blame if you don't honestly feel you deserve it. It is important to step back, examine your actions, and to evaluate what role you played and what you might have done differently. There is generally far more long-term value in admitting to mistakes than in denying them. It is awful hard work to maintain an image of infallibility and, often, people prefer to deal with someone who does not pretend to be perfect.

If you know your history, compare the response President John

Kennedy had to his Bay of Pigs disaster to that of Richard Nixon's in the Watergate break-in. Kennedy acknowledged that he had made a mistake, that a major screw-up had resulted, and he accepted responsibility for it. Immediately after JFK 'fessed up, he had the highest rankings of his political career in public opinion polls. Nixon, on the other hand, dug in and tried to cover up the Watergate break-in as a two-bit burglary. He was forced to resign in scandal, and his public image was forever stained.

When you experience a failure, ask people whose judgment you respect to help you gain fresh perspective on what happened. Career psychologists say that you risk continued failure if you are not willing to see yourself from the perspective of others. You may think that you run your business with a firm but fair hand, but if you can't keep employees, you may need to assess your management style from their perspective. Lion tamer Graham Thomas Chipperfield, a star performer with Ringling Bros. and Barnum & Bailey circus, was mauled by one of his 500-pound lionesses. He doesn't blame her, he said, because he understands what happened from her point of view. She thinks of him as another lion, so when he went into the lion cage to break up a fight, she figured he wanted a piece of the action, so she took a piece of him. Graham said that bite taught him a lesson that may save his life down the road: *The lion tamer should keep in mind at all times how the lions are thinking.*

Step four: Claim control of your life.

Things can happen *to* you, but you control how you respond and how you let them impact your life. The technology shifted from mainframe computers to personal computers. Nothing I could do about that. It was nobody's fault. I could have laid down and cried while Knowledgeware experienced difficulties, but I didn't. I did the best I could to save the company and protect our investors and employees. Some people attacked me and defamed me, but I did my best to stay on the high road. Hard times and defeat will test your strength of character, without a doubt. By refusing to blame or cry about what happened *to* you, and instead focusing on what you are going to do to remedy the situation, and to deal with the things within your control, you maintain a positive position of strength.

Golfer Greg Norman, the Shark, has won tournaments all over the world and he has also lost some tournaments that it appeared he was going to win. He has blown leads in some very big tournaments, but he is still recognized as one of the greatest golfers because he handles the defeats as gracefully as the victories. Greg has incredible strength of character, which was tested back in 1986 when he was informed that because his financial advisors had made some bad investments, most of his savings had been lost. He was nearly flat broke. He later said that he went through a brief period of wondering "How could this happen to me?" before he woke up and realized "that the only person who could change my situation was me."

He acknowledged what had happened. He took responsibility for his role in it. And then he went out and focused on rebuilding his wealth by winning golf tournaments, which leads to the next step.

Step five: Turn the negative energy into a positive force.

Greg Norman used his strength of character to turn his hurt and anger into a tool to help him focus on bringing his golf game to a new level and, because of that, he won his first major tournament that year.

The negative events in your life do not have to affect you negatively. That energy, which is often substantial, can be turned into a positive force for change and growth.

Step six: Build up your reserves of positive energy.

I am not suggesting here that you plaster smily faces all over your coat and walk around saying "Have a nice day!" to everyone you see. I am advising you, however, to practice optimism. While self-help books and many philosophers long have preached an optimistic outlook as conducive to success, they often have met with skepticism and no little cynicism. Today, behavioral scientists increasingly are conceding that an optimistic approach to life does breed success, that there really *is* power in positive thinking.

A University of Kansas psychologist, C. R. Snyder, compared the academic achievements of freshmen students judged to have high levels of hopefulness with those of classmates judged to have low levels of it. He discovered that hopefulness was a better predictor of first-semester grades than were SAT scores, which are supposed to predict how students will fare in college. Snyder found that students with high hopes set higher standards, and then worked hard to live up to those standards.

"Optimism, like hope, means having strong expectations that, in general, things will turn out all right in life, despite setbacks and frustrations," writes Daniel Goleman in his highly regarded study on *emotional intelligence* in the book of the same name. "From the standpoint of emotional intelligence, optimism is an attitude that buffers people against falling into apathy, hopelessness, or depression in the face of tough going. And, as with hope, its near cousin, optimism pays dividends in life."

Goleman warns that optimism has to be grounded in reality, and that being overly optimistic can lead to disaster, but developing an optimistic approach to life, and business, can be extremely helpful when you hit hard times. How do you develop this attitude? Practice, practice, practice. I don't have much use, personally, for seminars or speakers who claim that if you just listen to them or their audio and video tapes that you will find instant success and the key to happiness. I do, however, find that reading inspirational books about business leaders, or listening to truly inspiring speakers, can help pump you up when you are in need of a boost. Of course, you can't just lay claim to having an optimistic viewpoint, you have to live it, too.

I have read all the motivational books and listened to the tapes, and although there are useful and inspiring messages in them, they have not affected me nearly as much as when I really embraced the idea that I had the choice to accept failure as a catalyst for change and improvement, rather than as fatal flaw, and then went out and lived it.

Step seven: Face failure again by finding a challenge.

Anne Busquet was general manager of the Optima Card unit at American Express in 1991 and well-regarded for her drive and marketing savvy. But she went down with the ship when five of her 2,000 employees were charged with hiding $24 million in losses on Optima Card accounts. She was held accountable, though not responsible, for the misreporting and thus lost her job with Optima. Her self-esteem was shattered, she told *Fortune* magazine, but Busquet accepted an offer to try and rescue one of American Express's smaller businesses, merchandise services. She nearly turned it down, knowing she might fail again. However, she felt if she met the challenge of restoring a troubled division, she might also restore her reputation and her self-confidence. It was the old get-back-on-the-horse-that-threw-you scenario and, after turning around the merchandise services business for AmEx, Busquet rides again as executive vice president for consumer-card marketing.

Taking on the next challenge can speed your recovery from failure. I know. Shortly after several damning articles about the problems at Knowledgeware appeared, I got a telephone call from the speakers' bureau that books my engagements. It seemed that an appearance before 700 business people in Cedar Rapids, Iowa, had been canceled even though it had been on my schedule for four months.

"They read a negative article about you, and said if you were really that sort of person, they couldn't have you appear before such an important meeting," the representative told me.

If that cancellation had come even a few weeks earlier, it would have devastated me. But I had dealt with the demons of failure by that time. Instead of throwing myself on the floor or punching the wall or threatening to sue for breach of contract, I asked for the telephone number of the individual who had originally requested that I speak to the group in Cedar Rapids.

When I reached the person, I told him that I understood his hesitancy after reading the article written by someone who had never met me or talked with me. I then told him my version of what had happened with Knowledgeware, and I said if he and his group were still interested, I would come and speak to them at no charge, and would make his meeting successful because I had a better story to tell now—one about the importance of dealing in a positive manner with failures and setbacks and loss.

"It's a big risk," he said. But he allowed me to come anyway. I gave them an hour-and-fifteen-minute speech. They gave me a standing ovation. In fact, one of their executives wrote to a national organization to which he belonged, and his recommendation was so strong that I was invited to be the keynote speaker at their annual convention the following year.

That is what can happen when you refuse to let a failure knock you out of the game. I think there is power in using failure as a catalyst for success. I don't own a patent on this formula. In fact, scientists have used it for years. Scientific experiments are nothing more than trials in which failure is used as a step in the process of success. Edison tried hundreds of different light bulbs, and each one that failed moved him one step closer to finding the one that illuminated the world. Looking back, I used the same trial-and-error method as a quarterback. If my receivers couldn't get open deep, I went to short passes. If short passes didn't work either, I went to the running game. Trial and error. Failure and success. They are partners in the process. It is a simple truth, but so often we forget it and allow defeat or failure to overwhelm us.

I was in Chicago speaking to a group of supermarket executives recently, and dealt with this topic in my speech. When I had finished, a woman came up, introduced herself, and said, "You really got to me today." This very bright and attractive woman said she had been fired five different times. Each time, she said, she had blamed those who fired her and she had let anger and hurt build up. Even with a troubled employment history, this woman had reached the level of vice president at her company, but she said I had helped her realize that she had never dealt adequately with her firings and the failure she felt. "If I hadn't heard you talk today, I probably would have been fired again," she said. "I think you have given me the tools to use those past failures to make myself better, and to make this company better too," she said.

Failure will drag you down if you let it; there is no doubt about it. Most of us readily accept that not everything is going to go our way all the time. We acknowledge that accidents happen. We know there will be days when we don't feel well. We even accept that death will come into our lives. Why, then, should failures overwhelm us and cause lasting damage? They won't if we learn to ride with them. That doesn't mean you have to enjoy failure anymore than you enjoy stubbing your toe or having a cold, but it does mean that you can learn to handle failure as a natural occurrence in life. We all need to be reminded that, quite often, failure leads to even greater success.

Let me tell you about my hot-blooded highly charged friend Sergio Zyman. Back in 1984, Sergio was the head of marketing for Coca-Cola USA in Atlanta. He had just headed up the extremely successful launch of Diet Coke, when he was named to lead a top secret project. His job was to protect and enhance the public image and sales of what is undoubtedly the world's most recognizable trademark. But although Coca-Cola is an extremely well-run company, it had been locked in a 20-year-war with its chief rival, Pepsi. It had been a two-horse race for market share, and there was concern among Coke's researchers that consumer's tastes were changing and that a change might be needed in the Coke formula. Coca-Cola was doing great but, even so, their taste tests and market research were telling them that they might do even better.

Time out for a brief public disclosure here. I am partial to Coca-Cola, not only because I live in Atlanta in the same neighborhood as most of its top executives, including Sergio, but also because I sit on the board of directors of Coca-Cola Enterprises, Coke's biggest distributor and a partially owned subsidiary. That said, I now want to address what most people regard to be the biggest blunder made by Coca-Cola in its long and proud history —and it was my friend Sergio's idea.

Concerned about declining market share and the results of its taste tests, Coca-Cola's chemists began to work to develop a slightly sweeter formula for their soft drink, while Sergio, a former Pepsi marketer, lobbied for Coke to make a bold and unprecedented move to take a dominant lead in Cola Wars. He campaigned to replace the 98-year-old Coca-Cola formula with the slightly sweeter version that had done well in the taste tests. He said by introducing this *New Coke* with great fanfare, Coca-Cola would be revitalized in the global market. You could argue that they didn't need to do anything, they were winning, but the great thing about this company is that they are willing to act in response to the market place.

Sergio convinced the conservative leadership of Coca-Cola to make this daring move. As you probably know, New Coke ignited nothing but universal outrage and a lot of snide jokes. Sergio's master plan became known as the most disastrous product launch since the Edsel. My proud friend did not let failure weigh heavily upon him. Not long after this, he left the Coca-Cola Company. He didn't crawl into a hole. He used his expertise by promptly setting up a marketing consulting business and began raking in the clients and the fees.

In the meantime, back at Coca-Cola corporate headquarters, strange and wondrous things were happening. With the over-whelming rejection of New Coke, it was swiftly deemed advisable not to try and force it down anyone's throat. Instead, within 79 days of rolling out the generally despised New Coke, the company had a fast-food dinner of crow, and then reintroduced to the world *Coke Classic*. This highly public "Oops!" reversal in strategy resulted in the most successful reintroduction, or introduction, of a product in the history of marketing. Over the next year, Coke experienced the biggest-ever one-year hike in its cola's sales. The CEO of Coca-Cola, Roberto Goizueta would later say, "If I could have a New Coke situation every decade I would. Absolutely."

Goizueta acknowledges that mistakes were made with the introduction of New Coke, but he is wise and he sees through the failure to the lessons that were learned. He gained a greater understanding of how deeply loyal his customers are, and he also came to understand the value of having daring and imaginative people like Sergio Zyman around.

In his seven years away from Coca-Cola, Sergio and a partner started a consulting business with offices in Sergio's basement. "One Zyman Plaza," as he called it, had a computer, a phone, and a fax machine, but it also had a very impressive clientele that included Microsoft, Miller Brewing, and even Coca-Cola.

In 1993, Goizueta became concerned that Coke's marketing

had become too narrowly focused on advertising, and he asked Zyman to come back and shake things up once again as head of global marketing. Sergio held out because he was making more money than Coke could pay him, and he was enjoying his freedom. But in the end, he went back, proving that he has no fear of failure. "The biggest risk I've ever taken is coming back to Coca-Cola," he said defiantly.

When a reporter for *Fortune* magazine dared to ask the CEO of Coke if someone had slipped something into his soft drink to make him bring Sergio back on board, Goizueta gave a reply that I hope all entrepreneurs will keep in mind:

"We become uncompetitive by not being tolerant of mistakes," Goizueta said. "The moment you let avoiding failure become your motivator, you're down the path of inactivity. You can stumble only if you're moving."

The one thing common to Ruth Brooks, Hank Aaron, Sergio and Coca-Cola, and me, and probably to you and all other people, is that we have experienced failure in our lives. Who do you know that has not experienced failure or disappointment at some point? Failure is a big part of life, it is a real-life experience, and I've come to learn failing is also a major part of succeeding.

I want you to understand that what you experience everyday is what all of us experience. Failure is no big deal; recognize it for what it is, react to it, be stronger from it, just as the Chicago Bulls grew stronger after being beaten and shoved around by the Detroit Pistons. Eventually, the Bulls grew so strong that they are now the dominant force in professional basketball. They were forged by fire, made stronger by failure. If they had given up, felt sorry for themselves, or gone into hiding, they would have been defeated by, instead of being made stronger, by their failures.

> Somewhere storekeepin' ends and neighbors begin.
>
> — RUTH BROOKS

THE BUSINESS
OF CREATING
VALUE

MY EARLIEST memories are of our modest neighborhood just six blocks from the capitol in Washington, D.C. There was a Safeway grocery store just down 8th Street, and I used to watch the neighborhood ladies struggling to carry their bags of groceries home. This was in 1945, and there were not many two-car families back then, especially not in our neighborhood. Money was hard to come by for everyone, but as I watched the ladies lugging their groceries home, I saw a way to help them and to help out my own family.

That is how I came to start my first entrepreneurial business. It was just me at first, me and my little wagon, hauling groceries home for the neighborhood ladies who would pay me a few pennies, a nickel at the most, for the service I provided. I took the money home and gave it to my parents without keeping a penny. Although I didn't profit at all, I got a lot of satisfaction out of both helping the women and contributing, in a small but palpable way, to my family's welfare. I saw how hard my father had worked for us and I wanted to emulate him and to help him.

Having a product or service that adds value to the lives of your customers or clients may be one of the most emotionally rewarding aspects of being a small-business entrepreneur. Whether you operate a neighborhood grocery, a medical practice, a beauty parlor, or an auto-repair shop, it is a satisfying thing to know that your labors add to the lives of who come to you.

Even if you don't go into business for that reason, eventually it dawns on you that bringing value is an important part of doing business. Think about it: Every customer or client pays you, hopefully, but the ones who make your day and send you home with a smile are those who tell you that they appreciate what you do, or that what you do has somehow made their lives better.

As a kid hauling groceries, I learned that if you provided a worthwhile service to your customers, the money generally took care of itself. As adults, we often lose sight of that basic truth. True, you have to charge the right price for your service or product; if you don't know that you won't be in business. But it is true also, that if your price is not in line with the value provided, the demand for your product or service will diminish quickly.

Two years ago, at the age of 54, I went through the very emotional and draining experience of working to save my software company. I emerged from that experience with a greater clarity of vision than I'd ever had in my adult life. It had been a tumultuous time.

It was, for me, a time of great reflection on my life, and also on what I wanted to do for the rest of it. I entered into a period of mental clarity. If this was a male midlife crisis, I recommend it to everyone. It seemed like I could see things, including myself, as they truly were. It was clearer to me than ever before that I had a choice to make as to the direction my life would take, and that dwelling on ill feelings was a waste of the time I have left on this planet.

I realized as never before that you are what you do in life, and I decided that I wanted to work harder at bringing value to others through my business experience. I decided that it would be better to build another business, but to change the way I *do* business. Rather than looking for a product or service that I could sell to create wealth for myself, I began looking for a way to build a business around a heightened desire to bring value to other people—the clients or the customers.

There always had been value for them in all my other businesses, of course. If there hadn't been something of value for them, they would not have wanted what I was selling. I have always prided myself on providing good customer service and responding to the needs of the market, but this new approach marked a subtle but important shift.

I have made a lot of money in business over the years, but this time around, I decided to let the money take care of itself. I have no interest in retiring, ever, so it had to be another business. I didn't have any idea of what it would be, but I knew what it wouldn't be—it wouldn't be focused on benefitting me.

Shortly after I refocused my life, the speakers' bureau I work for contacted me to do an engagement for MCI in Texas. In order to do it I had to change my schedule but I did it. Then the next day, the speakers' bureau called and said MCI had to cancel because the budget had been cut.

The old anger churned up, but I realized this was a test of whether I had really changed the focus of my life. I called the woman who had been in charge of the event and she was apologetic, but said she had been under the gun to cut costs and, after a polite conversation I said maybe we could work together some time.

After I hung up, I was still upset with myself for my initial reaction. So, I called her back and I offered to speak for free because I knew she was in a bind. She said she had never had this happen before, but she accepted my offer. She called me a few days later and said she had been telling people all over MCI about what had happened and, as a result, I was invited to speak at a major meeting of MCI for my full fee.

USING BAD FEELINGS TO GENERATE GOOD

• •

When you are feeling anger or hurt, it is a tremendous energy force, and you have to choose whether to use that energy in a negative fashion or to do something productive that creates value for others. By choosing the positive outlet, your life will change for the better.

The challenge of saving Knowledgeware forced me to take a good look at myself and, in a sense, to finally grow up and realize that the best way to live is to focus on creating value for other people. As an athlete, this was quite a transition for me. Athletes are put on pedestals in our society, and I had been up there a long time: through high school, college, and for my first 18 years as an adult. Athletes are given special status in school and in society in general. Scholarships, special tutors, their own dining halls, dormitories, and training facilities are the perks for student athletes, and professionals are pampered even more. To be spoiled like that can tend to make you a self-centered person. In my heart of hearts, I believe I've always been concerned about other people and their feelings but, to some extent, I probably fell prey to the "me-first" syndrome like most other athletes.

Today, my goal as a person and as an entrepreneur, is to focus on providing value to the lives of those around me. That means being more giving of my time and attention to my wife and children and grandchildren, and it also means building my business based on serving the needs of my customers and clients. Do I still intend to make money? Certainly. Just as Robert Woodruff, the founder of Coca-Cola, wanted everybody involved in his business, from the chemists to the bottlers to the deliverymen, to share in the profits, I want to earn my share while sharing the wealth. We all want to profit from our enterprises. We have to profit from them. But we also want the people we buy from and the people who buy from us to walk away with something of value to them; that is what makes the system work. If my supplier does not profit, then he or she will go out of business. I want my suppliers to make a fair profit but I also want them to help me drive a business.

Suppliers, customers—we are all in this together. We are all looking to create value for ourselves and for those with whom we do business. The emphasis should be on making a profit by adding value to the life or business of your customer. If a business only benefits the owner, what good is it? Every business has to benefit the consumer or client in a measurable way but, too often, that is not how people approach their businesses. And as a result, most businesses do not last. They may start out determined to serve the customer, but somewhere the vision is corrupted, or it narrows into self-service. That is when businesses fail, and it is also when the business owner stops enjoying it.

The market has a way of exacting its revenge for that sort of neglect. It may take a while but, sooner or later, the customer strikes back. American car buyers did it when Detroit grew arrogant and kept churning out highly profitable, but poor-quality automobiles. The Big Three automakers decided that they could dictate to the marketplace. They sold poorly designed cars that, in some cases, seemed built to fall apart within four years. The marketplace responded by buying better quality European and Japanese cars, and it threw the entire American auto industry into turmoil until Detroit finally turned itself around.

Look, on the other hand, at some companies that have succeeded by providing one form of value or another, and sometimes two forms. Dell Computer has emerged as a major player in the personal computer market. It has taken on more established players by providing customers with reliable products at competitive prices and delivering them to the customer efficiently.

As a college student in Austin, Texas, Michael Dell jumped into the market by focusing on the value of an efficient delivery system that cut computer dealers out of the distribution process. This allowed him to keep the price of the product down, and make it easier for the customer to buy the product. By selling directly to his customers and building to order rather than having a huge inventory, Dell created a value-driven business and, in less than ten years, his small business achieved revenues of $1.7 billion.

Home-improvement giant Home Depot is another value-driven

company that has moved into a dominant position by providing top-notch customer service. Its clerks are instructed to spend whatever time is required with customers to help them solve their home-repair problems. Home Depot employees are trained to make sure the customer gets the right product, regardless of price or profit. The strategy marks a return to the days of yesteryear when people could go to the neighborhood hardware store and actually find someone who understood their home-repair problems.

What these companies and others such as Wal-Mart, Federal Express, American Airlines, and Nordstrom's understand is that the important thing is not to make *a* sale. Instead, it is to make a *loyal customer,* who will come back again and again because of the value offered by the business, whether it is low price, excellent service, or a product or service of unsurpassed quality.

The challenge that a small-business entrepreneur faces is to decide what kind of value to concentrate on, and how to foster a value-oriented philosophy throughout the entire company. This is vital to insure consistency so that, when change occurs, the company and its employees will hold to their value-based philosophy. Sears, for example, lost its way when Wal-Mart and other competitors arrived on the scene. Sears tried all sorts of gambits that failed because it lost its focus on product reliability and customer service.

It seems to me that small-business entrepreneurs who focus on bringing value to their target market, and who communicate that focus to their employees from the top management all the way down, are the dominant companies today. One of the most popular books among corporate leaders in recent years is Steven Covey's *The Seven Habits of Highly Effective People,* which is, essentially, a guide to leading your life based on values such as honesty, integrity, self-awareness, and so on. Covey believes that a value orientation provides a more substantial basis for dealing with all that life throws at you. His philosophy has brought thousands and thousands of corporate clients to his door in recent years.

Take a walk through most bookstores these days, and you'll find that the many popular nonfiction books deal with bringing value to your life, your business, and your career. I think the entrepreneur has greater opportunity for this than anyone else, because, when you own your own business, you set the priorities for your life. I have met dozens of top corporate executives who tell me, in one way or another, that while they are successful in their careers and have made a lot of money, they are not happy with their lives. I had one who told me that he'd just been to his 22-year-old daughter's wedding and he'd felt like a stranger because he'd been away from her so much of the time as she was growing up.

I am here to tell you that it doesn't have to be that way. More and more people understand now that it is possible to be both in business, and a good person, which is something of a change over previous decades. In the 1960's, there was an antiestablishment, antibusiness attitude, as if business were a corrupting influence. This was, to a large degree, a result of the frustration and outrage over U.S. involvement in Vietnam, and the involvement of big business in providing weaponry and tools for that war. In the 1970's and 1980's, business itself became a battle zone, where no prisoners were taken. Wall Street, junk bonds, "greed is good"; there was very little emphasis placed on anything other than making money as quickly as possible and then getting out of town. I'm not saying that philosophy was shared by everyone in business, but that was the overall image of the business entrepreneur at the time. In such a cutthroat climate, many felt that the best career path was to get a job with a big, secure corporation and to spend your working life inside its protective embrace.

There was security in corporate life for many, but that came to an abrupt end in the late 1980's, as corporations began focusing more on the value of their stock than on the quality of life they could provide for their employees. This shift caused incredible turmoil and insecurity in the American job market, but it also helped launch a new wave of entrepreneurship. Now, to be an entrepreneur and a business owner is to be a freedom seeker, an adventurer, and a creator of jobs, wealth, and value in this country.

VALUE IS YOUR MOST IMPORTANT PRODUCT
. . . .

Bringing value to your customers or clients creates a focus for your business that has all sorts of positive repercussions. It subtly shifts emphasis from merely making money to improving the quality of life for you and those with whom you do business. It doesn't eliminate profit, but it shifts the focus to more of a mutually beneficial relationship between you and your customers or clients —a win-win situation. This is the approach I have tried to bring to the Small Business NETwork. In order to create as much value for its members as possible, I invited a small army of affinity partners to join me. At first, I had trouble getting some of the bigger companies interested but, as the concept for the network grew and began catching on, many of those who had turned me down initially asked to be a part of the network.

I don't think I have ever been involved in an entrepreneurial business that offered more opportunities for win-win relationships. I could have demanded a fee from my affinity partners to join the network, because once this network is up and going, we will probably have more than 10 million small businesses on our membership list. Small-business entrepreneurs are difficult to reach, so that huge pool of them is highly attractive to companies that market to small businesses. But instead of charging affinity partners to have access to the network, I asked them to provide something of value to the network members. Because of this, network members will receive more than $2,000 of free merchandise when they join. Hertz offers a discount on rental cars. Sir Speedy includes a discount coupon. The member wins, the affinity partner wins, and I win. This is a perfect example of how the value entrepreneur can benefit by putting the needs of others first.

It is far more difficult today than in our parents' time to separate our personal lives from our work lives. To keep pace with rapid change and the development of new products even those who work for someone else have more of an entrepreneurial lifestyle in which they never really get away from business. It follows them home on the telephone, or on the Internet, or on their notebook computers. If work is to be so much a part of our lives, then it seems vital that we work and live within the same guidelines and value system. I think small-business entrepreneurship that emphasizes the creation of mutually beneficial relationships between provider and customer is the best lifestyle today.

Is there a magic formula for operating a value-oriented business? No, but here are my suggestions for those who want a lifestyle that incorporates work and play, family and business, while making a contribution to the community and world around them.

THE VALUE ENTREPRENEUR

· · · · · · · · · · · · · · ·

1. Be obsessed with the customer's needs, not yours.

When Knowledgeware was just getting going, I went to Pacific Bell on a sales call to pitch our software to them. I was a bit intimidated since we only had five or six customers at that point, and Pacific Bell is a huge company. I didn't know that much about their operations and I didn't know their needs or how they could use our product to meet them. I decided it would be presumptuous and even foolish of me to try go in and say I had a product that would make their operations better or stronger, so I started my sales pitch differently. I thanked them for seeing me and I told them that I didn't know if my product and technology would be an asset to their company or not. I said, "Let me tell you what our product does. Let me show you how it is designed and how it works and then you can make a decision."

Immediately, I could see them relax. The whole atmosphere of the meeting changed because, suddenly, I wasn't trying to sell, I was only offering them the opportunity to judge for themselves as to whether my product was of value to them. The meeting went very well. They didn't tell me they wanted to buy anything that day, but as soon as I described our product and its capabilities, they began coming up with applications for their business. I didn't have to sell them, they sold themselves. A few weeks after the meeting, their vice president called me and said that they had excess money in their budget that had to be used by the end of the year. (I know, that's the sort of telephone call most entrepreneurs dream about.) They bought $350,000 in product, which at that point was our biggest sale ever. It was a huge deal for us. And, because of it, I changed forever the way I conduct sales meetings. From that point on, I stopped pitching my product to the potential customers. Instead, I offered them information and the opportunity to add value to their company. I believe that is the way to build a lifelong customer relationship. If you believe that your product can provide value, you don't have to sell anyone. All you have to do is try to serve their needs.

There is no denying that every entrepreneur needs to make money, but the value entrepreneur understands that the profits will come if he or she provides something of real value to the customers. If you can move self-interest aside and concentrate on how to serve the needs of your customers, I believe the rest of the pieces will fall into place.

Does that sound hopelessly optimistic or too simple? Perhaps, but the smart entrepreneur will find ways to make it work. Will people try to take advantage of you if they sense that you are willing to go out of your way to serve them? Perhaps, but there will always be predators circling. It is up to you to fend them off while luring those who constitute your customer base, and building from there.

2. Focus on building long-term relationships with customers based on adding value to their businesses.

You can wine and dine clients, take them to golf outings and island resorts but, in the end, your relationship with them will be depend on whether or not you and your business adds to the value of their business. If you do that, the relationship will grow deep roots.

Everybody has competition. Sooner or later, every product is duplicated or upgraded. In the end, our customer or client buys into service and reliability and trust. You may have a price advantage in the beginning, but eventually somebody is going to under-cut you somehow, either with a lower price or a better financing package or add-ons.

When I advise you to build relationships first and sell to them next, I am not setting you up to have a whole bunch of friends willing to testify on your behalf in bankruptcy court. You still have to make a profit, which means you sell your goods or services for more than it cost you to provide them. That is a given. What this rule refers to is the need to think long-term in building your customer base. A customer may be able to pay more for your goods or service later than she can now, so it may be wise to cut them a deal early on in order to win the customer long term. Sam Walton told me that the success of Wal-Mart was attributable to three things: quality, better value, and better service. He had such a commitment to his customers that when he opened his first store, he drove his pickup truck around town to shopping malls and other stores and asked people what he could do to win their business. He listened to what they told him and, from his first 8,000-square-foot country store, he built a business that now does over $100 billion in sales annually.

3. View every working day as a chance to build the character of your business.

I'll put it simply: Do the right thing. Every day, you will have to make decisions on which direction to go, whether you are making pricing decisions, offering discounts to good customers, or dealing with a dissatisfied customer or client. If you base your decisions on doing the right thing, the fair thing, the just thing, then the character and the reputation of your business will do more to attract loyal customers than any advertising or marketing campaign.

From the day you start your business, you will be provided with one opportunity after another to show strength of character, to do what is best for the customer or what is best for your bottom line, to enhance the overall quality of life in the community, or to further your individual goals as a businessperson. The decisions you make will ultimately determine the quality of your entrepreneurial lifestyle.

4. Don't pour money into your business, pour thought into it.

I recently attended a board meeting of Sterling Software in Atlanta, and someone there questioned why the company wasn't spending some of its $740 million in cash reserves on acquiring other companies. The founder of Sterling Software, Sam Wyly, replied that while they have been studying some acquisitions they were not in any hurry. "I have found that many of the worst decisions I have made in my lifetime as far as spending money occurred when I had a lot of money to spend. The best decisions I've made came when I had very little to spend," he said.

The business owner who pours money into advertising and marketing and other aspects of a business may realize certain benefits, but I've always found that my businesses do better when I pour thought into them rather than money. Early in my business-entrepreneur career, I didn't *have* money, so I was forced to operate that way. Now, I have the money, or at least access to it, but I don't need to spend it on advertising and marketing because I enjoy finding the most cost-efficient methods.

For small businesses, the best way to channel your marketing money is to direct-response advertising in some form; spend a little money to see if you get a direct response to measure whether it will pay off. In the television infomercial business we test the first weekend with $6,000 in expenditures. If we bring more than that back, we have reason to spend $12,000 or $24,000 or $50,000. We can afford to do that because we know for the expenditures we will get more back in product sales—with the direct response we know.

The other thing we can leverage is public relations, I have my own P.R. firm with Jeanine Addams called Tarkenton-Addams, and she has helped me reap hundreds of thousands of dollars in free publicity for my two new businesses by setting up television and newspaper and radio interviews—none of which have cost us a cent.

If you are tempted to keep pouring more and more into your business, hiring more employees, more managers, more equipment, more office space, ask yourself this question: Did money make this business successful, or did ideas make it successful?

5. Don't strive for perfection. It will only drive you crazy.

I have a friend who used to drive himself nuts because his garage was always a mess. He would spend an entire Saturday making it spotless, only to have his kids trash it by the weekend. Bicycles, balls, bats, jump ropes, books, sand, toys, tools, everywhere.

His kids were in early grade school, their neighborhood friends were all the same age, and they had no concept of cleaning up. It drove him crazy until he came to accept, and even enjoy it. How did he make this transformation? He thought about how fast his kids were growing, and that there would soon come a day when they would no longer be playing in the yard and garage with their friends. Instead, they would be gone off on their own lives as young adults.

He came to realize that some day he would have a spotless garage that no one messed up but, when that day came, his children would have grown up and left. With the messed-up garage came the pleasure of watching his children play and enjoy their youth. He taught himself to live with the messy garage because it was part of being a parent with children at home. He decided to focus for this brief time on the joy of watching his children play and grow. He took that opportunity while he had the choice.

Your small business is going to be a sloppy mess in the beginning. There will be continuous challenges in getting it started and keeping it going. There will always be litter in your path to a perfect business, so don't drive yourself crazy trying to make it spotless or perfect. It won't happen. An entrepreneur cannot expect perfect order, or predictability. I am not saying you should adjust and not deal with the problems; instead, understand that they are natural to the process and that problems and challenges are opportunities for growth and increased value.

I read recently where the two founders of Home Depot opened their first six stores and suddenly were swamped with problems and people telling them their concept was never going to work over the long term, but they just kept their heads down and kept working and solving problems one by one. They didn't try to make it perfect, they just made it work, and now Home Depot is working to the tune of $50 billion a year in sales. Problems and imperfections are part of the day-to-day operation of any business. They are not a sign of poor management; they are a sign that you are in the game.

6. Share your ideas.

I believe that all of us are smarter than any one of us. I think that if everybody in your company is thinking about ways to make it better and if they are encouraged to share their ideas with each other, your company will flourish. The more we talk and share ideas, the better our decisions become. That is my philosophy in business today just as it was during my football career. I was known as a great play caller but the truth is that my real talent was for gathering information from my teammates, so that I could make good decisions in the huddle.

I ran a very democratic huddle, and not only because I was generally the smallest guy out there. I respected the other players and listened to their suggestions. I knew I could make better decisions if I had the information I needed from the guys in the trenches doing all the work. I'd ask my great receiver Ahmad Rashad what he thought would work against the cornerbacks on him. I'd ask my offensive linemen what they thought would work. During the game my teammates were constantly running to me with suggestions and input. I tapped every source of expertise I could get: linemen, receivers, running backs. I even let the guy who picked up the jocks and socks in the locker room call a play once. It worked, too.

"Little Pete" Privette was the clubhouse man at Yankee Stadium for the New York Giants and the New York Yankees. He had been there since Babe Ruth and Lou Gehrig. His job was to pick up the equipment and dirty laundry after games and do general maintenance. I loved talking to him when I'd come in early on game days to prepare. Petey was a real student of the game. One morning before a practice for a big game with the Washington Redskins, he showed me a play that he had diagrammed on the chalk board. I was impressed. It made sense. I also realized that Petey had been paying attention all those years in the locker room. He had seen a lot of plays diagrammed by some great coaches. He had absorbed a lot of information.

I took his play and put it in our playbook and, without telling the guys where I'd got it, we practiced it a few times. I didn't really think I'd use it, but the Redskins were tough and I was going to need all the help I could get. Well, sure enough, as the game progressed, Washington manhandled us pretty thoroughly. Going into the fourth quarter, we were down by three touchdowns. Early in that final period, I managed to get two of those touchdowns back, bringing us within striking distance. Then, late in the quarter, we got a field goal so that another touchdown would put us ahead. With only a few minutes remaining, we got the ball back. Their defense jammed up the first couple of plays I called because they had seen them before. I had to try something different.

Then I remembered that I had a play nobody had seen before, including my teammates. In the huddle, I called Little Petey's play, a pass to Bob Tucker, and it worked. I threw it. Bob caught it, he scored, and we won. After the game, I told all the reporters that it was Petey's play that won it, and he became the hero of the game.

I can't stress enough how important I believe it is for the entrepreneur to be open to information from all sources by being accessible and receptive, even to those who may not first appear to be great sources of wisdom. I think you can win too by sharing ideas and plans and solutions with other small-business entrepreneurs.

This may seem like a radical concept at first glance. After all, this is the country in which we fend off nosey people by telling them to "mind your own business." Well, look around. Everybody is in everybody else's business. Your frequent flyer miles on the airlines get you discounts for car rentals, catalog purchases, and hotel rooms. When you buy an IBM, Toshiba, or Compaq computer, it comes loaded with free software from Microsoft, Corel, and America Online. What is all this sharing suddenly? Why is it no longer fashionable to simply mind your own business? Value.

IBM realizes that it adds value to their computers by including software from Microsoft, which in turn realizes the value of linking its high-quality product with IBM's. Both companies win, and the consumer does, too. It works for the giants of business, and it works for the small-business entrepreneur too. The concept of sharing also applies to sharing ideas for your business, networking with other people in business.

Even as major businesses cooperate in marketing and share ideas like never before, there remains a tendency among small-business entrepreneurs to be secretive and guarded about their plans and products. Certainly, you don't run to your primary competitor and give away the company store. Coke isn't going to hand its secret formula over to Pepsi. But I believe that you can create value for your business and for your customers by sharing your ideas and your concerns with other entrepreneurs. You know, you can only protect so much of your business through copyrights and trademarks, so why waste time and isolate yourself and narrow your potential for growth by being secretive and guarded? McDonald's can protect its golden arches and its Big Macs, but there is no way it can stop the Burger Kings and Hardees and Arby's from taking the fast-food concept and running with it.

I get so enthused about my ideas that I show them off like babies in a buggy. Look here! What do you think? I've never had an idea stolen out from under me because I've shared it like that, but I have had many ideas grow and improve by talking about them to other businesspeople and getting their feedback and input. If you are a small business starting up in a garage, you have to go outside your core business and talk to other entrepreneurs.

Carl and Carol Clover of Bloomington, Illinois, were just getting started with their new fitness club, a very tough and highly competitive business, when they went to a seminar on health-food products for health clubs. The Clovers took their floor plan for their club, which had yet to be built and, during breaks in the seminar, they showed it to other club owners who helped them refine their plans and avoid costly mistakes.

At the seminar, the Clovers interacted and shared ideas with more than a hundred other fitness club owners, including another young couple who had been in the business for a year and were doing very well. The Clovers learned what they needed to learn about health-food products at the seminar, but they learned far more from the other couple, who invited them to visit their health club in Indiana and to see what was working for them and what was not working for them. These two couples, two sets of small-business entrepreneurs, will both benefit from sharing ideas and solutions to their shared problems and concerns. What good would it have done either of them to guard their plans?

Small-business entrepreneurs have to communicate and network and share ideas and problems with each other. Believe me, the value that you add will greatly outweigh any problems it may cause. My philosophy is to share my ideas for businesses with anybody and everybody because, more often than not, I find that helps me develop and grow the idea and gives it greater value. In some cases, I've been told my ideas simply would not work, or that they were too narrowly focused, and I have been asked really good questions that opened up my thinking and created even greater opportunities. I think the same will happen for you. By sharing, rather than guarding, your ideas for entrepreneurial businesses, you will bring more value to them.

I enjoy life now more than ever before, because when I talk to people now, I am not so focused on what is in it for me or how it affects me; instead, I focus on them and their needs. This approach has opened my mind as a business entrepreneur, because business is all about bringing value to others so that they want your product or service. It is much easier to see opportunities to do that when the focus is on others.

Let me tell you about my friend Rich Guberti. About 12 years ago, I was standing in LaGuardia Airport outside New York City screaming into a telephone at the limousine service that had failed to pick me up. (This was before I became the kinder, gentler, small-business entrepreneur I am today.) As I was reading the limo service the riot act, a scraggly looking guy in a t-shirt hung up the telephone next to me and appeared to be listening. When I finished, Rich introduced himself. "I am not dressed properly right now because I'm off-duty and just picking up my own plane tickets, but I have a limousine service, Mr. Tarkenton, and if you need a ride into the city I'll give you one at no charge."

Rich was the right guy in the wrong clothes but at the right place at the right time. "Let's go," I told him, and we headed off to his limousine, so that I could get to my appointment on time. I jumped in the front seat with Rich, because, in spite of his appearance, he seemed like a sharp young businessman and, since he was doing me a favor, I wanted to talk to him. On the way into the city, we talked about his plans for his start-up limousine service and about his background. Unlike most limo-service operators, he didn't start out as a driver. He learned about limousines as a passenger. For five years, he was the road manager for the rock band Aerosmith, traveling all over the country with them. When the group had some major personnel changes and inner turmoil in the mid-1980's, Rich went looking for a more stable job. A friend owned a limousine and he invited Rich to join him in business, thinking that Rich could use his contacts in the entertainment industry to build up the clientele.

When he found me stranded at LaGuardia, Rich had just left the partnership because he wanted to make the business bigger and his partner wasn't interested in putting additional money into it. Rich already had added three cars, but he was in that difficult period that so many small-business enterpreneurs hit, that point at which you have attained some success but you have to make some big moves to ensure long-term growth. We talked about that and I encouraged him to go after what he wanted, which was to own the biggest limousine company in the nation. Today, when he speaks to business groups around the country, Rich often cites our talk that night, and the many we have had since, as key factors in the success of his Excel Limousine Service Inc., which operates over 50 vehicles, has licensing arrangements with other limousine services nationwide, and sales of more than $6 million annually.

Here is what Rich has to say about the value of sharing ideas for small business entrepreneurs:

"If Fran hadn't said a word on that first trip into New York City, I would have been happy because I was driving a guy I had watched play football for many years, but he talked to me about business—I hadn't realized how successful he had been in business—and he asked me questions and he was so positive and uplifting it motivated me to keep going. There are days when you are starting your business when you wonder why you are doing it, but Fran really charged me up. He turned me on to motivational materials and self-improvement and business books and told me to read management materials so that I could learn from professionals. From that point, I never looked back."

ALL OF MY HEROES ARE ENTREPRENEURS

Rich has become a devoted entrepreneur and I understand why. When you are an entrepreneur, you never go to work. You may be at the office, but it's never *work*. Instead, it's fun, it's exciting, it's challenging, it's your *life*.

One of the things that intrigued me about Ruth Brooks from the very first time I met her was the enthusiasm she has for her businesses. I like to tease her about the fact that she has been to Atlanta, which is less than two hours away, only once in her life. She has never been in an airplane. When I told her recently that she should get out and see more of the world, her response was "I can't think of anywhere I'd want to go where I would enjoy myself more than I do right here."

This is a woman who is up with the chickens, literally, at dawn, then in her restaurant cooking biscuits at 6 A.M. After the morning rush at the restaurant, she goes to work in her store until 8 or 9 P.M., then she goes and checks on her rental properties and the people in her trailer park. Yet, she'll tell you she doesn't really work much, and that she loves what she does because she is doing exactly what she wants with her life. The same is true of Charlie Poole, who got sick of going to meetings and headed for his favorite fishing spot to build a business.

These people are my heroes. They are all entrepreneurs. They are all in business for the love of it. And they all understand that the best thing about entrepreneurship is that it's not work. I hope that soon, you too will be part of the rapidly growing community of entrepreneurs. It beats working.

Good luck. And stay in touch.

For more information about the Fran Tarkenton Small Business NETwork, log on to www.ftsbn.com or call 1-888-FON-FRAN.

INDEX

ABOUT
THE AUTHORS

Football Hall of Fame member Fran Tarkenton played 18 seasons as an NFL quarterback and set four NFL career records after earning All America honors at the University of Georgia. Today, he is a successful entrepreneur who has run 12 businesses with annual revenues ranging from $1 million to $142 million. His latest ventures include the Fran Tarkenton Small Business NETwork, Tarkenton NETwork, and Tarkenton Net Ventures, an Internet and multimedia development company. He also serves as a consultant and speaker to Fortune 500 companies and businesses around the world. He serves on the board of directors of Coca-Cola Enterprises and Sterling software. Fran lives with his wife, Linda, in Atlanta, Georgia.

Wes Smith is a national correspondent for the *Chicago Tribune* and has authored or collaborated on 10 books. He lives with his wife, Sarah, and children Andrew and Jessica in Bloomington, Illinois.

Printed in the United States
By Bookmasters